DANCING ON THE HALF-BEAT

1942 – 1962

A Memoir

Noel Hodson

Copyright 2017 Noel Hodson

All rights reserved. This book is copyright material and must not be copied, reproduced, transferred, distributed, leased, licensed or publicly performed or used in any way except as specifically permitted by the author Noel Hodson. Any unauthorized distribution or use of this text may be a direct infringement of the author's rights, and those responsible may be liable in law accordingly.

For Art, Maya and Benjamin
A piece of your complex, rich family history.

Acknowledgments

I'd like to thank my wife, Pauline, for her tireless support and her agreement to be the main character in my life story. I must also thank all the characters in the book, the many friends from Heaton Moor and some from further afield, whose tales are the main-planks of the narrative. My brothers and sister deserve thanks and apologies for being rudely uncloaked in history – at least in my version of history.

Especial thanks to Lee Chadwick for his skilful and artful past and present photographs and for his permission to feature them here and to Carol Leader, a dear friend and Senior Jungian analyst who had the stamina to read and comment on the whole of the original, far longer angst-ridden text.

Finally, my thanks to Camille Mari, of Camille Solutions, Oxford, a very swift and decisive editor, computer expert, layout designer and cover designer; who has demonstrated extraordinary diplomacy making the final whole greater than the sum of its parts. - Noel Hodson

***

DANCING ON THE HALF-BEAT

1942 – 1962

Noel Hodson

**"Noel! Leave the class.
I can do no more for you.
You dance on the half-beat!"**
Miss Marjorie Barlow – Osborne Bentley School of Dance – 1958

Noel Hodson has worked on Green projects to reduce commuting and freight traffic; writing *Teleworking Explained, The Economics of Telework, The Transport Internet* and papers forecasting the future use of the Internet.

He has also written *The Haunting of a Favourite Son*, and two global warming novels, *Out of the Depths – London 2010*, and *AD2516-After Global Warming*.

27 March 2017

Contents

Contents	**6**
Introduction	**9**
Foreword	10
Part One – Childhood	**11**
1942 to 1952	**11**
Born - December 1942	**12**
Chapter 1 - Birch House	**14**
Chapter 2 - The Coronation	**19**
Chapter 3 - The Resident Ghost	**31**
Chapter 4 - Shooting at Shadows	**40**
Chapter 5 - Smog and Vertigo	**56**
Chapter 6 - The Eleven-Plus	**64**
Chapter 7 - Hares	**66**
Chapter 8 - Loathed & Liked	**70**
Chapter 9 - Guardian Angels	**79**
Chapter 10 - Medical Treatment	**86**
Chapter 11 - Gorsey-Bank	**98**
Chapter 12 - Lost Boys	**107**
Chapter 13 - Dr & Dr Sykes	**111**
Chapter 14 - The Scouts	**123**

Chapter 15 - Llandudno	128
Chapter 16 - Liliana and The Laurels	135
Chapter 17 - Jelly and Gin	151
Part Two – Teenage	154
1953 to 1962	154
Chapter 18 - Beauty and the Beast	155
Chapter 19 - Cherub	162
Chapter 20 - Marjorie Barlow	176
Chapter 21 - Fixed Wheel	187
Chapter 22 - Finishing School	193
Old Trafford	*198*
Chapter 23 - Blind Date	206
Chapter 24 - Gangs	212
Chapter 25 - Physical Education	217
Chapter 26 - Tank Corps	228
Chapter 27 - Big People	239
Chapter 28 - Party Time	254
Chapter 29 - Wrong footed by the Hun	260
Chapter 30 - Heaton Moor Rugby Club	271
Chapter 31 - Cleveland Road	289
Chapter 32 - Monte Carlo Rally	308
The Cat & Fiddle	*314*
Chapter 33 - Astral Travel	317

Chapter 34 - Drink & Be Merry 325

Chapter 35 - Cona Coffee Bar 328

Chapter 36 - And they all lived happily ever after 336

Afterword 337

Appendix 1- Stanley Mathews 339

Appendix 2 – Osborne Bentley School of Dance 339

Introduction

Dancing on the Half-Beat 1942 – 1962

This book is autobiographical and anecdotal, based on real people and real events, sprinkled with just a little creative imagination, which introduces readers to a typical northern family and the culture of the post-war decades. Britain, as they said, had "won the war but lost the peace". The nation was bombed, impoverished, tired, in mourning for its dead and wounded and mired in debt. The post-war depression lasted from 1945 to 1960 – but, as Churchill advised when in our Darkest Hours, when logic dictated that we were well and truly defeated:
"KBO – Keep Buggering On"

***

Foreword

Noel was born into a large Catholic family in 1942. His mother was a shy, timid and private woman, who told endless stories; stories which portrayed the world as she saw it to her captive audience of six children. Each child was assigned a role in the family which defined them forever, as they saw themselves through her eyes and identified with the stories she told.

Thus an intimacy was created, which depended entirely on the relationship with the story and not the people within it. The combination of a strong Catholic belief and vivid imagination, meant the stories had a magical quality, irresistible to young and impressionable minds. Stories that kept the children in thrall to an intelligent, but damaged and oft time paranoid mother.

Noel, the second child, arguably the most favoured and closest to his mother, follows in her footsteps, telling us through stories about a world long since gone. Some are very funny, some are sad, some are painful to read, but all give us an insight into the post war years, when children could roam freely through an environment where bomb sites were part of the landscape and grown-ups inhabited a completely separate world.

The stories span some twenty years. We catch glimpses of an increasingly prosperous family; we see Noel move from the symbiotic relationship with his mother into his father's sphere of fast cars, sport and work. He finds freedom within a peer group, teenagers empowered by the sixties revolution and meets the love of his life; the spell his mother cast those many years ago seems to be a thing of the past, but it is clear that spells are hard to break. It is Noel's determination, imagination and ability to create stories that is his real salvation; an inner world every bit as powerful as his mother's enchantment.

2017 - Pauline Hodson - Analytical Psychotherapist.

Part One – Childhood
1942 to 1952

Born - December 1942

Manchester Guardian on 7 December 1942

FROM OUR NAVAL CORRESPONDENT
A disclosure of the exact damage done to the United States Pacific Fleet by the treacherous Japanese attack at Pearl Harbour a year ago provides the world with an answer to the question asked so often last spring, "What is the American fleet doing?" It is now obvious that an entire battle squadron was rendered temporarily incapable of action by that attack and, although the long-term results of the treachery were slight, the immediate effect on the campaign in the Pacific was to give the Japanese that freedom of movement by sea which was essential to their plan of territorial conquest throughout Greater East Asia.

As Mother recalled the drama of my arrival, in one of her many story telling sessions, I was born (after our troop's humiliating retreat from Dunkirk), to war-torn, traumatised parents, Father (Edwin) and Mother (Winifred). Born in a small semi-detached house, in Audenshaw, Ashton, East Manchester. I emerged into utter darkness, in a small blacked-out room, in the small dark hours of a freezing December morning, as the second son of this young mother, impoverished and alone in the War, who, to her credit, consistently maintained that she disliked children. Unfortunately, no one believed her.

In the distance, German bombers hummed and boomed their sombre death songs, groping through the acrid, black clouds towards Salford Docks and the factories of Trafford Park on the west of Manchester. If they missed their targets the pilots blindly unloaded their lethal cargoes onto the little back-to-back brick houses of the poor, always on the poor, before gratefully turning for home. Thus, my new life, perhaps the rapidly returning soul of a recently killed combatant, began in the darkness of the World War Two blackout.

***

Chapter 1 - Birch House

Manchester Guardian 28 June 1946 - The introduction of bread and flour rationing from July 21 was announced by the Food Minister in the House of Commons yesterday. The ration will be on a varying scale for differing types of workers and children of different ages. For the ordinary adult it will be nine ounces of bread per day, part of which may be taken in flour or cakes. The Food Minister's announcement was described as "one of the gravest I have ever heard in time of peace" by Mr. Churchill, who demanded that figures of stocks and movements of cereals should be produced by the Government to justify "this extreme measure." 1946 - Bread rationing introduced. 1947 - Potato rationing introduced; 1948 - July 25: Flour & bread rationing ends; 1949 - March 15: Clothing rationing ends;

In 1949, in the winter's afternoon half-light, the four children, one destined to be haunted and all strangely disturbed, stared at their fingers seemingly glued to the inverted glass as the spirits moved it authoritatively from letter to letter of the alphabet, carefully drawn on twenty-six squares cut from a school exercise book and set in a wide circle. The demons of the Ouija board were spelling out the players' ultimate fates.

"And will Noel go to heaven or hell when he dies?" asked Mother of the attendant spirits, having saved me, her second and allegedly favourite son, till last.

Even at seven years old I guessed that Mother was not really communing with demons and ghosts, but how else to explain the uncanny, swirling energy of the glass and her pale-faced intensity and uncomfortable shift of fear when she learned from the magic tumbler that she herself was indeed, as she had always suspected, doomed to eternal torment in the burning fires of hell.

As the thin grey light faded from the Manchester sky and the spirits were forced to retire as they could no longer see the alphabet, we moved from the table under the large casement window to the flickering light of the fire, with her usual admonitions that the Ouija board was nothing but a silly game, which we should pay no attention to and that it was hugely dangerous to summon up the spirits that way.

"But are you really going to go to Hell when you die?"

The demons of the Ouija board spelled out the players' fates.

Of course she wasn't, it was a lot of nonsense. But her glittering pale blue eyes and tight-lipped mouth belied her words and we knew that she knew that she was indelibly marked by the demons for eternal damnation and torment.

Throughout the session, Father had sat by the fire, his back to the proceedings, sunk in melancholia borne with unacknowledged heroism, waving away Mother's jibes at his terror of all things ghostly, but leaving the room in fright at the repetition of the story of how his prematurely thinned hair had stood on end at a ghost film in their courting days before the war. He later returned from the silent and darkening reaches of the house as the winter cold penetrated the walls, chilling the Victorian tiles and seeping into the linoleum, to sit and gaze mournfully into the flames dancing from the coals.

It was, inevitably, my turn to re-fill the coal-scuttle. Richard, the eldest at nearly ten years old, had punched me on the arm with his hard sharp knuckle through to the painful bone, a persuasive argument, and Peter and Martin at five and four years old were still too small to carry a full bucket. Jeremy, the youngest, and our only sister Stephanie, both yet to be born, would never have to fetch the coal.

When summoned, the Ouija board demons obligingly predicted good and bad outcomes, but surprisingly for immortal entities from the other side, their prophecies were largely inaccurate. In fact, of the six children born to these able and ordinary-seeming parents, three were to be cursed by alcoholism, one of the three would die early and derelict from that liquid curse. One would become bankrupt and lose family and home to live in a lonely, penniless business fantasy. Three would make and lose quite comfortable fortunes. Two would be driven into

**Birch House
Ghosts & Ghouls**

psychotherapy, narrowly escaping breakdowns and insanity and they perhaps would discover redemption and the meaning of life.

Despite these unenviable destinies all the boys would marry beautiful and intelligent women and at times flew close to the sun of success on their wings of wax and feathers. We might blame the parents but to be fair, Mother, with her six unsuspecting offspring, always maintained she disliked children – but we chose not to believe her. Perhaps in retribution for being disbelieved, ignored or regularly impregnated, after she died Mother haunted one and perhaps all of her initially promising but ultimately self-destructive brood.

We blinked as Mother switched on the tall standard lamp by her armchair, dispelling the darkness in the morning-room but intensifying the blackness both outside and through the small stained glass window that let onto the hall. I picked up the bucket.

It was always a dilemma whether to clang and clank the rotund scuttle loudly to frighten away the demons or to try to keep it utterly silent, the better to listen out for them creeping up on me. The large door opened with a sucking sound from the draught proofing onto the icy, dark void of the hall. Heart pounding, I analysed the fearful threats as I closed the door behind me. The merest hint of light in that dark cavern came filtering through three small, arched, stained glass windows at the end of the hall, inscribed Morning, Noon and eternal, endless Night.

The inset black maws of the dining-room and lounge doorways, always bolted from the hall side, breathed ice on my left side, which shrank from the lost spirits eternally locked into those unused rooms, and shrank from the coffin-sized upright case of the silent grandfather clock, standing eerily erect on the damp Victorian tiles. I turned to my right with a shiver, urgently locking my gaze onto the patched light on the red baize, copper studded door at the end of the hall, to prevent my fickle sight from wandering involuntarily and unaccompanied up the wide front stairs to the dark haunted landings above and to the - horror piled upon horror - vast empty, empty at least of human presence, floor of unlit and unquiet Victorian attics brooding malevolently high above.

The upstairs needn't be faced until bedtime. I passed the vault of the main staircase and I made it to the relative safety of the baize door that also sucked open, stirring still icier air in the darkness. It let into a cramped back hall; which even for a brave youngster contained too many doors; each harbouring mournful and spiteful spirits that might seep out or pounce.

Real courage was now required. The open cellar door blocked the view of the back hall and pressed me close to the kitchen door, which contained its own mournful ghouls. I groped down the clammy bricks and snapped on the cellar light, which glimmered in the cobbled, whitewashed hall below.

The six hollow cellars were perhaps, at this time of night, slightly less terrifying than the five vacant attics high above. The cellars were closer to the kitchen, often occupied by others, while the attics were constantly remote from humankind. I doubted whether my screams could be heard from the attics. Once, during hide-and-seek, when Richard had locked me in the water cupboard at the top of the attic stairs, I had screamed unheeded for over two hours in that dark prison, while the huge and ancient galvanised water tank loomed crushingly over me with its black depths of liquid rushing in and siphoning out, stirring the bloated dead rats, or worse, that I would surely see – if I ever had the temerity to climb up and look into its sepulchral depths. The attics muffled sound but the cellars magnified and echoed it. Screams from below would be heard - I prayed.

Unlike the abandoned attics, two of the cellars had some practical function, which I speculated on as I descended the stone stairs. One sported Father's racing bicycle and cycle rollers, where he exercised diligently, staving-off his inevitable death. The other contained mounds of coke and coal, delivered in two-ton loads, forty bags at a time, via the chute from the driveway. The rest were empty. As I carefully selected and loaded the shiny black coals into the scuttle with my hands, a large piece at a time, the shadows stirred and murmured evilly behind me. If I were to be tricked into turning now, if I were to start with fear, I would almost certainly see the hand of a corpse pushing up through the coal, or the tall black-clad house-ghost, the shade of the grim Victorian butler from the main upstairs landing, standing close by and reaching for me with melancholy sadness.

Hodsons - in The Morning Room at Birch House, Mauldeth Rd. Heaton Mersey - Circa 1957

I bent over the scuttle, placing the coals with precise and deliberate movements, sweating with fear despite the icy cold, recounting the logical sequence of events which brought this coal from the mines to us, to keep us warm; the better to leave no room in my mind for those terrors.
The scuttle filled and, calling on my Guardian Angel for protection, I summoned up the courage to turn to face the ghouls – but they hid from me. Heaving the bucket and shying from the unlit sockets of open doorways, I struggled along the cobbled cellar hall, up the steps and into the back-hall, bolting the door on its inhabitants. I cheated by leaving on a ground floor light, wasting a penny an hour, and, hero of the moment, lurched up the hall to win the sanctuary of the well-lit morning-room – the only warm room in that vast groaning house.

The house ghost is usually a harmless and well-meaning creature. It is put up with as long as possible. It brings good luck to those who live with it. WILLIAM BUTLER YEATS ***

Chapter 2 - The Coronation

Atom-bomb-proof - "Manchester Guardian" is an underground telephone exchange in the centre of Manchester built in 1954. It is 112 feet (34m) below ground and cost £4 million to construct. The main tunnel, one thousand feet long and twenty-five feet wide (300m by 7m), lies below buildings in Back George Street, linking up to an anonymous and unmarked surface building containing the entrance lifts and ventilator shafts. There are also access shafts in the Rutherford telephone exchange in George Street. Duncan Campbell – Paladin Books.

After tea in the kitchen, a large winter's meal of Lancashire hot-pot, bread and butter and steamed syrup sponge with custard, at which golden haired little Martin, as usual, wept throughout without apparent cause; though we his brothers knew that Richard was secretly n'nn'errring at him across the table; and after Mother and Father had, hysterically as usual, warned Martin that they would have to take him to be locked up in a lunatic asylum if he didn't stop his incontinent weeping; a promise which strangely always failed to comfort him, as at four years old he had only a wavering, dim and negative understanding, cruelly reinforced by his three brothers, of life in a Loony Bin; we washed up in the scullery, using Lux Flakes instead of Daz, which was so bad for our hands, the condensation running down the newly enlarged 1950's black windows and white tiled walls; made a huge pot of tea, loaded the tray and carried it, with a plate of McVitie's Digestive biscuits, through to the morning-room, warmer than ever thanks to the new coals I had brought from the cellar, and we settled in for the night.

Neatly dressed as ever in white shirt, starched collar and cuffs, dark grey trousers, dark tie and polished black shoes, carefully posed for the sake of his observers, Father sat in his chair to one side and behind the television, to remain there until bedtime, watching his family watch the little black and white receiver for the hours it was on. Father, who had been a radar officer in the War, knew that the radiation from the screen could be harmful – so he sat behind the set out of the line of fire from the cathode-ray-tube; and watched his family slowly fry. Mother settled into her chair by the hearth, under the standard lamp with her Players cigarettes, which, despite later switching to Senior Service, another brand also inspired by naval colours and themes, ultimately killed her, turning her fingers, toes and chin black just before she died; and with Swan Vestas matches ready by her knitting, her book *The Lancashire Witches* backing the newspaper folded to the crossword and a blue Biro in her right hand. Three boys sat on the settee, and one sprawled on the carpet in a cool corner, grey flannel shorts crumpled round thighs and socks pulled up for warmth.

Mother negotiated bedtimes; Peter and Martin at seven o'clock, Richard and I could watch the fourth part of the *Quatermass Experiment*, a source of immense terror for me, and then, despite Richard's insincere protestations that being nearly three years older gave him demarcation rights over me; as he was secretly afraid of the journey to bed without me; he and I would go to bed.

Silence fell. It was six o'clock. Mother lit a cigarette, inhaled deeply and applied her Biro to the crossword.

"That won't do you any good you know, Mother", said father sadly, wagging his finger at the cigarette.

He got no acknowledgement and resumed his pretended relaxed posture for the benefit of whomsoever it was, who seemed to reside in the darkened upper corner of the room, who kept his every thought and movement under minute observation. The boys read books or gazed into the secrets of the fire.
"Mum" wheedled Peter slowly,
"Tell us about when Noel fell into the canal".

All eyes watched her expectantly. Mother gazed sphinx-like at Peter, giving no clues. She inhaled her cigarette for an eternity and slowly put down the Biro. Straightening her back and gazing unseeingly at her rapt audience, she began to speak, endlessly exhaling pale blue smoke from deep within, which seemed to take on the form of her words.

"Your Father ..." she began with mild criticism, making him shift uncomfortably,

"... was still away at the war when I was having Noel. It was in the blackout, and I was on my own. I had terrible nightmares when I was carrying Noel. Nightmares that I was being drowned."

She placed a hand high up on her breast and made gasping motions.

"I used to wake up gasping for air, dreaming that as I bent over the wash basin, with the mirror just in front of me, there; to wash my face, a man ..."
casting an accusing glance at Father who again shifted guiltily,

"... came up behind me and forced my head into the water; trying to drown me. And I couldn't breathe. It was awful. And I would wake up, in the pitch dark, because of the black-out, this would be in November; because your brother was born in December - without any help - I was entirely on my own when he was born, and it was about two o'clock in the morning - I thought I was going to die and the doctor wasn't brought until the next morning. Night after night after night, I had the same dream. Waking up gasping for air."

"What about Richard; wasn't he there?" said Peter looking at his ten-year-old eldest brother.

"Oh, Richard was only little" said Mother, glancing at Richard with what passed for a fond smile but one which any well advised Greek hero would do well to ward off with a highly polished shield.

"He would only be - let me see - he was born in August, Nineteen Forty and Noel was born in December, Forty-Two, so that's two years and September, October, November - three months, so Twenty-Seven months old. He was asleep most of the time. Though he was there", she confirmed.

Richard tightened his lips and stared unblinkingly at Mother, chewing his hollowed cheek.

"But the extraordinary thing was; that when Noel was born, after all these drowning dreams, he was born with a caul over his face". She traced a complete mask on her face as her audience's interest, as ever at this point, perceptibly increased.

"That means that whatever way Noel dies ..."
All eyes turned on me, speculating on the manner of my death;
"...he will never drown. Sailors collect babies' cauls to protect them from being drowned at sea, and as long as they have one, they will never be drowned. It's a good luck charm."

Her ex-Fleet Air Arm, seafaring husband, who had sailed the oceans in the war, gave no sign of affirming or denying this fact.

"That's probably what saved his life when Richard pushed him into the canal." She smiled warmly at Richard who bleakly denied the crime, but she brushed his feeble memory aside.

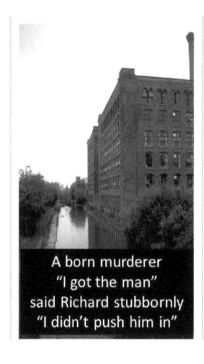

A born murderer
"I got the man"
said Richard stubbornly
"I didn't push him in"

"Noel was only about eighteen months; No, he was probably a month or two younger than that, because I was carrying Peter at the time; Peter was born just a few days after; and he was supposed to stay in the garden. He wasn't allowed out because he was too young. He was inside the front gate but Richard and your cousin Ursula and probably Bernard, who lived next door, not in the house attached to ours but on the other side, they came along and ..." She paused for emphasis and accusation.

"...they opened the gate. And took your brother, who was very little at the time, up Slate Lane past the factory and onto the waste ground by the canal."

I vaguely remembered the waste ground, on our side of the canal. It had a derelict small underground bomb shelter, overgrown heaps of builders' rubble and tall, tall cerise fireweeds. It was beyond the footbridge that arched over the canal at the end of the cotton mill opposite our house.

Mother sat even straighter, lit another cigarette and breathed in deeply while we waited with bated breath.

"Of course, it wasn't the only time Richard tried to kill him. There was the time when he unscrewed the handle of Noel's pram..."

Peter cut in hastily "What about the canal?"

"Well. If it hadn't been for that man who was crossing the bridge, Noel would have drowned because he was going down for the third time when the man got there and pulled him out of the water. Your Guardian Angel was taking care of you that day." She smiled tightly at me.

"I got the man," said Richard stubbornly. "I didn't push him in."

"Well when he fell in, he would have sunk to the bottom, once; and then again, but if you sink a third time, that would have been the end; he would have drowned. Just like in my dreams before he was born. Isn't that extraordinary? Those dreadful nightmares of a man, like your father, trying to drown me in the wash-basin, were like a prophecy. The caul he was born with protected him you see; and if that man hadn't been there, he would have drowned. And he didn't even leave me his name; wouldn't be thanked. If he hadn't come along at just that moment; another five minutes; and Noel would have been dead." She emphasised the last word with a heavy drop in tone.

"He just fell in." said Richard.
"I got the man".

Mother stared dispassionately at Richard, ignored his protestations and gathered in her audience again.

(When you're drowning, you don't say 'I would be incredibly pleased if someone would have the foresight to notice me drowning and come and help me,' you just scream. John Lennon)

"The funniest time was when Noel was much younger, still in his pram, and I used to go shopping across Ashton Old Road, which even in the war, was a terribly busy road. A very dangerous road. I'd put the shopping, of course you couldn't get much because of the rations, but I'd put the shopping in the tray under the pram. It had a sort of wire tray between the wheels. It was in the summer of 1943; Noel could only have been four or five months, and I left Richard with your Auntie Peggy, playing with Ursula. But unknown to me ..." her voice raised and softened with amusement and she looked fondly at Richard, her clever first born.

"...Unknown to me, Richard ... The pram had a shaped bone and silver handle which was held on with two wing nuts, well Richard had unscrewed the wing nuts so that they just stayed on. Right to the end of the thread, but just staying on, so you couldn't tell any difference. ... When I got to Ashton Old Road, it was as busy as ever and I had to go down a deep kerb to cross the road. The road had very deep kerbstones at that point. And as I dropped the pram down; Noel was lying down I think. I think he was asleep. As the pram dropped down the curb, the handle came off in my hands ..." She paused with an amused glance at Richard and a fond smile at me.
"...the pram ran off, without a handle, ran off across Ashton Old Road. Straight through the traffic. Straight across the road, leaving me

holding the handle at the side of the road. It was terrible. It was such a shock. The wing nuts were undone right up to the end of their threads. But just staying on. Richard must have done it while I was getting the shopping bag. And there was no way of telling. It was so clever."

"What happened?" said Martin, blue eyes wide with fascination and relating to this pram story, as he had a pram story of his own to be told.

"Well; if a lorry had hit him. Noel would have been dead. Flattened. It's a very dangerous road. But his Guardian Angel must have decided his time hadn't come and steered the pram right across the road, right to the other side. Without a handle. And it didn't even fall over."

"Trixie always slept in Noel's pram and usually kept him safe. She was a big cat and had lots of kittens – that we had to drown – but she was the terror of the neighbourhood. No dog was brave enough to tackle Trixie. They sometimes started to chase her, but she would suddenly turn on them, even the biggest Alsatians, and get her claws out – and they scarpered pretty fast. She loved Noel and protected him most of the time. But she wasn't around when his pram ran off across the road. That was his Guardian Angel" she added with certainty.

Mother smiled at us all, inviting us to join in her tacit thanks to my Guardian Angel. Richard tightened his lips even more and gnawed his cheek in silence; looking at nobody. The audience by their deep, concentrated silence demanded an encore.

"That's probably why Noel is terrified of water..." she continued obligingly.
" ...the canal was filthy. Dirty, dirty water full of rats and dead cats. People used to drown their kittens in the canal; and there was all sorts of rubbish in there. He's lucky he wasn't poisoned, never mind drowned. But what really frightened him..." she searched deep into an apparently painful memory..."

"...was the nuns."

"When Peter was being born. He was early you see and I wasn't well and there was nobody to look after the boys..."

Richard visits Slate Lane
(I think our home is on the right)

"Your sister Peggy was next door". Cut in Father to everyone's surprise. Mother silenced him with a glimmering icy stare. We all knew that Peggy was not mentioned, along with most other relatives who were taboo and could never be discussed. Father lapsed into silence.

"There was nobody to look after the boys, and so there was no alternative; they had to go to the orphanage for a few days."

This was a new twist to an old tale.
"Did I go to the orphanage?" queried Richard sharply.

"Yes; you both did. You had to. Just for a few days while I got over Peter. There was nothing else I could do. Your Father was still away at the war; one of Britain's horizontal heroes, even though the war was just about to end it was several months before he was de-mobbed."

Father looked fixedly at the observer in the shadowy top corner of the room, understanding the unspoken charge that he had somehow deliberately prolonged his stay abroad. The children waved this irrelevant interruption aside, silently insisting on the real story continuing.

"And the nuns did a very stupid thing to Noel so he had to be put to sleep for several days. I didn't know about it till later; but they weren't to know he had just nearly drowned and that he was frightened of water and they tried to bath him. Well of course he screamed and screamed and screamed; it took three of them to hold him down..." She looked at me with some pride.

"... But he kept screaming and so they called the doctor and he put him to sleep for a few days."

"I don't think you remember that, do you Noel?" she said doubtfully.

"How long was I there." said Richard purposefully; intrigued by this new information.

"Oh not very long..." answered Mother, beginning to glimmer dangerously.

"...Just until I got over Peter."

Nobody challenged her and she continued more evenly.

"Peter was born blue."

She paused for the statement to have its effect and smiled remotely and bleakly at Peter.

"...That's why he's not as bright as the rest of you. He had his oxygen cut-off you see. The cord was round his neck and we had to put him in the airing cupboard to keep him warm because he came so early."

"He was blue because he couldn't breathe. Babies are blue before they take their first breath, then they go all pink. They just change colour."

The family was silent while it considered all this information. *Why did she wrap a cord round his neck? Why could he breathe better in the airing cupboard? How did Richard and Noel get back from the orphanage? Was he blue with cold? Early; earlier than what? How less bright did less bright mean; he was undeniably not as clever as the other three?* No questions were put however. We each made and clung to our own private misunderstandings.

"Good heavens!" said Mother with finality.

"It's nearly half-past seven. Come on you two; up to bed. Take them up will you Noel and see they get into bed. Father; will you build up the fire and we'll have another cup of tea before the *Quatermass Experiment*."

Father, an ex-radar officer, sat behind the screen – safe from the killer radiation

My stomach contracted in horror at the thought of the terrifying serial, but it couldn't be missed. I put every hall and landing light on as I herded Peter, cheerfully unaware and little golden haired Martin, silent and terrified, up to their room; waiting impatiently at the bathroom door while they ineffectually scrubbed brushes across their teeth and turning a blind eye as they hurriedly put thick pyjamas on over their clothes, as it was too cold to contemplate changing. I ensured they took their shoes off, but, out of empathy, not their socks, saw them get under the piles of thick blankets and turned off their light, before hurrying with back-long glances into the attic stairwell and other dark and haunted regions, down the stairs to the parentally approved treat of watching the Quatermass monster absorb people into its ecological biomass, in the stone corridors of the crypt of Westminster Abbey.

A black and white TV broadcast that reached most of the population of Great Britain, and the largest empire the world had ever seen, was The Coronation of Queen Elizabeth II in 1953.

Not many families owned a television set, black and white with a twelve-inch screen, because kitchen and electrical goods had to be saved for – sometimes for years, and bought for cash. Buying on credit was a decadent American invention, feared and frowned on by all upright citizens; but the advent of television, supplied on weekly rentals and hire-purchase was the thin end of the wedge, heralding the decline of the British Empire and puritanical economic frugality. Those who did have the good fortune to own a TV, invited all their neighbours in for the day, to celebrate the accession of Our Noble Queen, and marvel at the pomp and circumstance and the uniquely drilled and disciplined British troops, "the greatest fighting forces in the world".

Mother of course knew as much about the protocols and participants as did the TV commentators, led by Richard Dimbleby who kept up his live commentary from early morning until the last post sounded.

"Isn't she absolutely beautiful and radiant. And she drove trucks during the War. They never left London, you know. All through the Blitz, they stayed in the middle of it all; in Buckingham Palace; even when the palace was bombed they stayed. But her sister though; she's a different cup of tea, that Margaret. A bit of a good time girl. She drinks gin, flirts and smokes all the time…"

"Ooo! Look at those fine men in their Busby's and redcoats. They wore red in the old days to hide the blood. Your grandfather – no your great-grandfather, my grandfather, fought in the Boer War – you know in South Africa. They got cut off and had no food, so they ate Rock-Rabbits. Do you know what rock-rabbit is? Rats. They ate rats, until the relief columns came…"

The excited build up to the event included all school children receiving model coaches or painted mugs, and packs of Coronation Coins – in shillings, pence, crowns (five-shillings), half-crowns (two & six), sixpences (a tanner), three-penny-bits (thru'pence), two shilling pieces, and farthings. The largess stopped short of scattering rust coloured ten-shilling notes (ten-bob) or green pound notes (a quid) and certainly the Treasury could not afford to give away large white five-pound notes (a fiver), which was as much as many men were paid for a week's work.

Coronation coins – issued to children

Explaining who was who in the magnificent long procession of open topped coaches back to the palace, in the rain, was a team of BBC presenters, including Noel Coward, led by Richard Dimbleby, who intoned with deep respect "And in this next coach, I think... Yes, I'm sure that large lady, that tall stately figure is the Queen of Tonga... the much loved Queen Salote. ...I think she is possibly the tallest monarch. I'm told that she is nearly six-feet-three-inches tall..."

"And who is that in the coach with her?" asked another commentator of Dimbleby's encyclopaedic knowledge; referring to a diminutive, shy little Malaysian man in uniform sitting nervously on the edge of his seat opposite to the giant queen.

"That's her lunch..." cut in the instant reply from Noel Coward; over live radio, TV and later newsreel transmissions.

There was a timeless shocked pause; a silence and collective intake of breath that paralysed the entire nation – and The Empire. From the depths of the deeply treasonable well of the inappropriate unintended insult to our honoured foreign guest, came the unmistakable, almost undetectable sound of shoulders quaking in the BBC box. None of them dared to try to speak, as that coach and others proceeded past the cameras – their occupants unidentified and anonymous, as muffled guffawing infiltrated the airwaves – until at last the heroic Richard Dimbleby magnificently suppressed his giggling – and rescued the dignity of The Coronation, The Procession, The Nation and the entire day. He continued:

"And here we see the Household Cavalry in their ceremonial uniforms, with those magnificent plumed helmets and their gleaming breastplates ..." etc, etc.

For which he was shortly after awarded with a knighthood.

Coronation day – 2nd June 1953

As the band of the Coldstream Guards played the National Anthem, we automatically stood to attention, in our Morning Room, as did the whole nation in the privacy of their homes – and men removed their hats.

***

Chapter 3 - The Resident Ghost

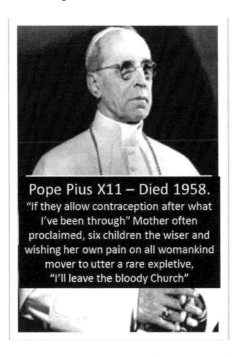

Pope Pius X11 – Died 1958.
"If they allow contraception after what I've been through" Mother often proclaimed, six children the wiser and wishing her own pain on all womankind mover to utter a rare expletive, "I'll leave the bloody Church"

Guardian – Korean War 1950-1953 – Author, John Hollands, fought in the war as a young second lieutenant in the Duke of Wellington's regiment, and says the conflict continues to be ignored despite the fact that 100,000 British service personnel were involved and more than 1,000 killed. Chinese and North Korean military losses are estimated at 1.5 million, and 37,000 US troops were killed – around one in 10 of the Americans sent to Korea. Add in civilian casualties and Hollands believes the war was responsible for the deaths of more than four million people.

That Quatermass night, back in 1951, lying in bed after the horror of the black and white TV serial, was like most other winter nights I could remember. Richard had braved the cold and changed quickly into his thick flannel striped pyjamas, folding his clothes neatly and laying them on the lino by his bed. I was 'nesh and, just as Peter and Martin had, I buttoned my pyjamas tightly over my grey flannel shirt, grey flannel shorts, grey V-necked jumper, snake belt and over my grey woollen socks with blue and red bands round the tops.

"They'll find out." said Richard threateningly.
"Only if you tell." I complained.

Richard didn't pursue this potential irritation and tease to its hysterical limits as he usually did. He; even he of no imagination, had clearly been rattled by Quatermass and prudently didn't alienate his only comfort in that large dark room. I burrowed under the heavy covers, squirming vigorously to warm the sunken hollow in the middle of my bed; the outer regions of the bed would never warm-up in that cold; and eventually made a narrow tunnel through the bedding and exposed my nose and mouth to the outside.

Unimaginative? Just before he died, Richard confided that he had only had one dream in his whole life, a recurring nightmare when he was an infant: "I was alone and frightened in a small igloo, on a vast grey plain, under a dark sky. The plain had no paths or borders. And I was alone."

As our parents never touched us, it was unlikely that my extra layers of clothes would be discovered, unless their suspicions were aroused by Richard. On a cold night such as this, only one of them would look in briefly, as ice thickened inside our window, on their rapid journey to their own immense bedroom and hence rapidly to their own individual double beds, one at each end of their thirty-foot long and ice cold boudoir. In winter, one of the most effective forms of contraception devised, as yet unimagined by the world's greatest authority on such methods, Pope Pious the Twelfth, who resided in the warmth of southern Italy and whose encyclicals we heard regularly on Sundays.

"If they allow contraception after what I've been through." Mother often proclaimed, six children the wiser and, wishing her own pain and fate on all womankind, moved to utter a rare expletive, "I'll leave the bloody Church".

Soon we heard them going through the ritual of taking the tray into the scullery, locking all the doors into the hall, ascending the stairs and switching off the money consuming lights behind them. Doing whatever adults did, one by one in the bathroom, which let onto the small back landing next to my bedroom door.

Our room had two doors, one near my bed, opening onto the back landing and the other by Richard's bed, letting onto the main front landing. Father, as ever, was last and he circumnavigated our bedroom, ignoring my door, went down three steps, up three steps onto the main landing and opened the door by Richard's bed on the far side of the room.
"You two lads asleep." he asked loudly and rhetorically.

Answer came there none and, assuming correctly that we were either asleep, which was unlikely, or feigning sleep, which was more likely and that we probably were not dead, he closed the door and pressed on to the front of the house. My illicit Arctic bed clothing went undetected.

As soon as the house was quiet, Richard asked me to tell him a story, which I obligingly did, spinning out a tale in the dark and cold air, of fairies and elves and summer meadows and wishes that come true for small boys. After a long-time I realised I had lost my audience.
"Hey Rick!" I whispered fiercely,
"Are you asleep?"
He was, and I was left awake and alone with the ghosts. I burrowed deeper into the bed and picked up the daydream which turned the bed into an indestructible, magic and powerful vehicle which carried me safely anywhere and into any adventure, without the slightest danger, as long as I stayed within it.

Later I fell asleep and woke at what I always imagined was midnight to hear the resident ghost, The Grim Butler, (who many years later was seen by several visitors to the house) making his lonely and heavy walk down the main landing to stop outside Richard's door across the room from me. From continual experience I had reconstructed his every movement. Six heavy steps down the narrow landing from the front of the house; pause outside Peter and Martin's door and then three heavy steps, where the landing broadened out, to the banister outside our door, where he stopped and looked down, sadly and lugubriously, over the main staircase into the darker hall below. He never went back from whence he came, but was never there in the morning.

I was frightened by this haunting, which occurred in precisely the same manner every night until I was sixteen and, despite many a silent resolve, I never, ever had the courage to cross our room, even when we had fitted carpets and central heating, and throw open the door to confront this persistent spectral intruder. I never saw this ghost and he never invaded our room. We tacitly respected each other's right not to know.

I fell asleep again to wake at some unfathomable time in a state of tension as Richard sat up wildly in bed, thrashed his arms around and muttered loudly, almost but not quite coherently, at something at the end of his bed. This was another familiar routine I was always too afraid to challenge. Fortunately, it wasn't as recurrent as the resident ghost. I once, when I was about twelve, shone a torch on Richard while he muttered. He turned wild, rolling, unseeing eyes in my direction, waved his arms to ward off invisible attackers and then, to my horror, started to climb out of bed and cross the room towards me. Never has a light been extinguished more rapidly; never has a bed of heavy covers been sealed from within with such terrific strength. Richard, clearly confused with no beacon to guide him, meandered round the end of my bed for a while before returning to his familiar, and therefore, to me reassuring, posture of sitting bolt upright in bed, gesticulating wildly with his eyes starting from his head and muttering. He never remembered those incidents. I never forgot them.

Ghostly butlers and other disturbing spirits were not allowed to interfere in my games and, in the winter, these were largely centred on our bleak, icy bedroom. The room was at least fifteen feet square, with two doors, one from each landing, with an extra bay for the tall window of eight-foot-wide by four-feet-deep and with alcoves on either side of the fireplace. It was sparsely furnished with two single beds, a wickerwork chair and a large, high wardrobe that stood across one of the alcoves, leaving a large dark space behind it. Richard had a chest of drawers with a mirror, in the window bay and I had a plain set of drawers in the other alcove. Next to my bed were built-in cupboards from floor to ceiling in two parts, the upper had six shelves, the lower had two – so Richard had the top section for his endless neat collections of stamps, stones, sweets in Lent, scout badges, and papers that he carefully padlocked and I had the lower area, that was unlocked. Little did Richard know that I had long ago learned to unscrew the hasp that he padlocked so religiously, affording me sight of and access to all his worldly goods, neatly assembled on his six exclusive shelves.

The walls were papered with a nondescript beige-pink colour with nearly invisible vertical lines running through it. Father had meticulously papered the walls with great effort and even greater precision and we were not allowed to make holes in it or stick glue on it – so there were no pictures, just acres of blank walls. The lighting exuded post-war depression. A single weak bulb, costing a penny an hour to run, with a plain mean shade, hung from the ceiling above Richard's dresser in the window bay. The floor was covered with beige and vaguely patterned lino, with pale reds, browns and cream waves that had neither rhyme nor reason to them. Under Richard's bed was a thin rug. The lino was subtly buckled so that if, as a seven-year-old would, you put your face on the floor and squinted with one eye, it became a tedious beige seascape with a slight swell across the entire surface.

Marbles of every colour, were my platoons of soldiers.

These dips and crests of waves in the lino were just right for marshalling armies of coloured marbles. I had hundreds of glass marbles that could be amassed in troops and columns by colour - deep reds, deep blues, greens, yellow, rainbow, white, non-coloured, - and by size from common or garden alleys up to highly prized giant dobbers. The collection also boasted some metal alleys that were most likely poached from engineering bearings. Most were purchased with my weekly pocket money, some were won in the school playground, but I was just as likely to lose them again, so the net accretion from gaming was probably zero.

Corralled with string and edges of exercise books these globular glass armies were sent on marches, set in battle and put back in barracks, across the lino battlefield that echoed with a hollow drumming as they thundered over its convoluted surfaces. For hours at a time, I, the Field Marshall, would kneel on the floor with the bitter cold biting into my knees; this being decades before children wore long jeans; and with the single dim bulb casting thin shadows across the theatre of war, as wave after wave of troops would cooperate or clash or interpenetrate, smash and kill each other as the night wore on and ice built up on the inside of the window. Eventually, beaten by the cold and becoming conscious of the threatening shadows behind the wardrobe and of unexplained creaks and groans from the walls and landings as the house contracted with the tumbling temperature, that might well augur a visitation of the Grim Butler, I would retreat downstairs to whichever room had people and heat.

It was some years before my nightly sensing of the Grim Butler outside our bedroom door received any reassuring third party confirmation. Mother and Father were out together, probably during Father's political period when he canvassed to become a town councillor and later to try to become a Member of Parliament.

They had recruited as our minders Leonard and Hilda Cowlishore. Len, a small, spare, wrinkly, polished, nut brown outdoor man, who did the garden on Saturday mornings and Hilda, solid, as wide as she was tall, and no nonsense, who came daily to clean. We, the four boys, were in bed. Peter and Martin were in their room above the morning-room, where the baby sitters were encamped with the fire and the television, and Richard and I were asleep in our room above the kitchen. Hilda heard an odd sound in the hall. She looked at Len and he had heard it too. It was a big dark house. In those post-war days no lights were left on needlessly and there was no heat except where they were sitting. Some light filtered from the morning-room into the hall through the small stained glass window entitled "Night" that depicted an owl, a tree and the moon. With the morning-room door wide, the hall was illuminated with the full light from inside that warm retreat that reflected along the hall and up the stairs. Responsible for four youngsters, the intrepid couple emerged and left the door wide open. They came together, unable to pin down the odd sound and unable to throw off the growing feeling of being watched.

Together they mounted the main stairs, gently lit by the light from the open door. The stairs were wide enough to allow them to climb together. Reluctantly they came up two or three steps; then another; then ever more reluctantly, another. They felt overlooked, and they in turn looked upwards. Clear of the hall ceiling they could see the main landing above where the bannister curved around and joined the wall by our bedroom door. He, though they immediately knew it was not a person of this world, was looking down at them. The dark figure, looming up into the darkness and directly over them, was the figure of a man. He wore black and his shoes were black and well shone. Len and Hilda started and stared, rooted to the spot. They turned to each other and as they did so they both felt somebody or something, rush down the stairs pushing between them, something that disappeared without trace or any sound on the tiled floor into the recesses of the long hall.

Discretion overcame their surrogate-parental feelings of duty and protection towards the four children asleep in the rooms above. Wordlessly they turned and fled back to the lighted room, shut the door and pushed a heavy sideboard up against it. That was how Mother and Father found them when they returned; locked in, barricaded and refusing to come out until they had identified the people in the hall as real, substantial, human and from Heaton Moor. Len and Hilda refused point blank to ever baby-sit again.

Before we had the back stairs removed and built over to make room for an extra bathroom, Richard got into the habit of running card schools at Birch House with five and up to ten teenagers taking over a room for an afternoon and into the evening, for as long as it took for Richard's luck to run for him instead of against him, and therefore until he won on the day. These marathon games of three-card brag, pontoon and five-card poker, wreathed in smoke and with copious amounts of tea consumed, required great stamina from the players. When allowed, by Richard, they took a break and headed for the lavatory on the back landing. It needs saying that Richard, single-minded as he was and displaying no imagination at all, never discussed ghosts, ghouls and things that went bump in the night. He never saw or heard anything amiss in Birch House or anywhere else. So he did not prime his pals with spooky tales of inexplicable phenomena. I was far too young, two or three years their junior, to enjoin them in any conversation or even to come to their notice other than to be patronised if the mood was good with a casual nod of recognition. This was the era of Teddy-Boy grunts and minimalist communication – for example the archetypal, infamous and oft' quoted exchange:

"Yer dancin'?"
"Whose askin'?"
"I'm askin'!"
"I'm dancin'!"

Really was considered enough polite conversation to last a whole evening and if the couple subsequently married, to perhaps economically last them a lifetime of silent understanding. So Richard's macho friends were unlikely to have heard of my Grim Butler in light conversation.

However, one late afternoon, with the light fading, when the huge house was empty other than the card school, David Hall and friend stretched themselves and got up from the kitchen table, walked into the back-hall and started up the back-stairs to the bathroom. The stairs were narrow and turned after a few steps at a half-landing, bringing David's eyes level with the upper landing, with light coming in from a window behind him and from three plain frosted-glass windows on the landing above. As David turned, he saw the caps of two shiny black shoes and above them, well pressed black trousers and as his eyes followed the bannisters and the scene upwards, he found he was staring into the face of a mournful apparition, a large man dressed in black, which gazed back down at him. His friend, one step behind saw it also, though not so clearly.

Neither needed any discussion of the pros and cons of the situation before deciding to run like hell. They yelped, jumped the few steps down into the back-hall, jumped the few feet into the kitchen, disturbing the sacred game, and cowered there for some time, refusing to look again on the face of the mysterious stranger who lurked on the darkening landing. Richard went alone to check. He saw nothing. He berated his cowardly friends, they refused to budge and even refused to go alone or together to the bathroom, as they had intended. So cross-legged, they left the house and abandoned the game. Richard, on his winning streak for the day, thought it just a ploy to quit the game. I knew better. I knew who it was they had met, though, thank the Lord, I never did see him myself.

Richard, King of the Card Games, was the most obviously stressed out of us children. He kept his own counsel and watched the world with slow blinking, pale blue eyes, sucking in his cheeks to gnaw at them thoughtfully.

His main fault from my perspective, as my eldest brother with whom I shared a room for over sixteen years, was that he teased and taunted me persistently and mercilessly, and the other younger children, but me in particular, for the whole of those sixteen years. He was not violent and appeared to have no emotions (although I knew subconsciously that I was the keeper of his feelings and emotions, that I felt them for him). He was only a little taller but thinner than me so that, despite his two years and four-months age advantage, I could with my square frame and by summoning up an extraordinary violence and rage, defeat him or at least scare him away when his cruel mockery eventually drove me to screaming pitch.

Screaming pitch was reached most days, sometimes two or three times a day; climbing to infamous crescendos of rage; such as the day he locked me out of the house and taunted me for hours from the various windows and doors; as I tried the six foot high kitchen sash window, with its huge panes of glass, he unwisely pressed his face against it from the inside and pulled out his tongue. Richard was lucky to escape totally unscathed as, incensed to the unusual point of really trying to damage him rather than pretending to attack him, my fist crashed through the glass, propelling deadly shards and lethal sheets of it into his taunting face; but then he was ever lucky.

***

Chapter 4 - Shooting at Shadows

S.L.A. Marshall *did a study on the firing rates of soldiers in World War II. He found that the ratio of rounds fired vs. hits was low; he also noted that few soldiers were aiming to hit their targets. - Wikipedia*

No ghost could lurk around Birch House for long without encountering Mother.

"I had used the bathroom and was sitting up in bed waiting for your father", she recounted one afternoon to the children, now enlarged to an audience of five by the addition of our sister Stephanie.
"It was about midnight. It was late for us to be going to bed but it was about midnight and I was having a read while your father was in the bathroom. The door was ajar about two feet" she measured with her hands apart like a proud fisherman,
"...and the landing light was off, of course."

We all accepted that the "of course" meant that nobody recklessly burned electric lights unnecessarily unless, as Mother said, 'they were Rich-as-Creases.' - I never could make any sense of that phrase and never questioned it, until a classics scholar corrected my spelling and explained who the wealthy Croesus was. So the landing, long and narrow as it approached the front of the house and narrowing even more to accommodate the attic stairs that touched down just by Mother's bedroom door, was in its accustomed state of darkness.

Some-body pushed between them, on the stairs.

"You know that my bed is by the door and I have a view down the landing as far as Peter and Martin's door?"
"And I happened to glance down the landing and saw your father coming up the landing from the bathroom – at least I thought I did. But oddly, he was wearing his suit."

We wondered at this, as the narrator meant us to while she drew carefully on her cigarette. *Why was he wearing his suit if he had been getting ready for bed in the bathroom?* Customarily, he emerged in his white shirt, collarless or with the collar attached just on the back stud and flapping stiffly as he walked, and with his cufflinks undone and his sleeves rolled back.

"Anyway; I thought nothing of it and I saw him go into Stephanie's room, and expected him to tuck her up quickly as usual and come into the bedroom. But he didn't come out!"

Stephanie, just four years old, was agog, her eyes fixed on Mother's. Mother exhaled her blue smoke.

"Well. I waited. And I waited. And he didn't come out. And I began to get worried. Perhaps he'd fainted or had a heart attack or something."

Stephanie now started to look alarmed, sensing that a heart attack was a very

serious matter, that she would rather not have her father have one in her bedroom at midnight – thank you very much. He could go and have his heart attacks somewhere else.

"And naturally, I was watching the landing all the time; waiting for him – but he didn't come out. So I called him – quietly so as not to wake the children. But there was no answer. So I called again; thinking he might have gone into the box-room to look for something. But I couldn't hear him and there was no answer. I couldn't think where he had got to."

Father came into the kitchen while she was telling the story, looking for his waistcoat, moving chairs as he commandeered the room, in a timely reminder of how robust and substantial he really was. The children could judge for themselves that he was not the sort of figure who could easily disappear – darkness or no darkness. Mother pressed on with the story.

"So I was just about to get out of bed and go and check if he was ill, or worse; because I was convinced he was still in Stephanie's room..."

Father, catching the drift of this tale of the supernatural, glanced anxiously and nervously in our direction and seeing all eyes weighing him up and down, he slipped rapidly out of the room.

"...but before I could put my book down I saw him," Mother paused for dramatic effect and the children rewarded her storyteller's art by becoming even more rapt and attentive,

"I saw him, in his shirt, carrying a towel, coming up the landing from the back of the house!"

We each silently considered the situation. Knowing every inch of the stage she had set we knew it was physically impossible for Father, in a dark suit, to have moved up the long narrow front landing towards

Edwin Hodson
1914-1980

Sportsman – cycling & swimming.

Lieutenant in The Fleet Air Arm 1939 - 45

Stockport Councillor.
Parliamentary Candidate.
FCCA Committee Chairman
Justice of the Peace.

Car racing & rally driver.
Leader of Triumph cars works rally team.
"The fastest man on ice" in the 1962 Monte Carlo Rally

Mother's lighted doorway and to turn left into Stephanie's bedroom and then a few minutes later, without having left that room and without retracing his steps down the landing, in full view of Mother for at least half the journey, to effect a Superman instant transformation of garb, to about face, and to bumble back up the passageway again with his seafaring gait.

"Who – I said to your Father – Who is that man in Stephanie's bedroom?"

Stephanie gripped her Teddy more tightly and drew closer into the circle around Mother's chair while Mother took another long slow pull on her Senior Service cigarette and held the smoke inside while the clock ticked away three tense seconds.

"We both rushed into her room, snapped on the light ..."

Turning on a light at midnight signified for us the level of the crisis that had occurred.

"... and there was nobody there. Just little Stephanie fast asleep in bed with her Dolly. Well; we looked under the bed, looked behind the curtains; looked everywhere – and there was nobody in the room. So we checked the box-room. Maybe the man had not gone into Stephanie's room – though I'd swear on the Holy Bible that he had – as I'd thought; maybe he had gone into the box-room."

I had for some years suspected that the Grim Butler emanated nightly from the unused box-room positioned over the front door between Mother's and Stephanie's door, so this possibility had also occurred to me during the narration.

"So we opened the box-room door – and both went in. And there was nobody there either."

Father, Jeremy, Mother, Stephanie.
Birch House 1956

When you have eliminated the impossible the explanation, however improbable, becomes obvious. It had to be a ghost. A ghost in a black suit. A tall man-sized ghost who stalked the landings and visited the children's rooms at midnight. This fact, testified to on the Holy Bible by Mother and implicitly evidenced by Father, as he never denied or indeed commented on the tale at all, did little or nothing to calm my already overheated nervous system or improved my ability to get a good night's sleep.

"By this time...." Mother concluded scornfully,

"...your father was really spooked and when I asked him to go and check the attics he was too frightened."

We all knew of Father's terror of things that go bump in the night and the very idea that anybody might be foolish enough to check the upper empty echoing floor of attics, where no lights worked, at midnight, for a wraith in a black suit who was at least as big as Father and was possibly homicidal in intent and, logically, who was dead, struck us as a pretty sane response – and we thought no worse of Father for it, whatever Mother would have us feel about his courage.

Father, still without his waistcoat but having donned a sturdy seaman's navy blue crew neck sweater, came back into the kitchen brandishing a three-o-three rifle with telescopic sights that could punch a hole in a brick wall a mile distant.

"Keep the children out of the cellars will you Dear, I'm going to have some target practice" he announced.

Mother was unimpressed by this show of manly skills and valour.

"Of course" she pressed on, collecting her audience again and keeping Father hovering, against his better judgement and his own volition, by the door,

"He's not just frightened of ghosts – he's terrified of real people in the dark as well. Despite having a whole cupboard full of guns in the bedroom."

Father demurred but his defence was poorly constructed and in any case he could never have deflected Mother's tidal wave of narration when she was in full flow. He swayed from foot to foot attempting to take a step back out of the door but he too was entrapped, a reluctant witness at his own trial and assassination. His feet stayed where they were. Mother, sure that she had pinned down all of her audience, had time to take a leisurely in-breath, drawn through the neat white tube of tobacco, transforming its grey tip into a bright glowing beacon for a few seconds. With the out-breath her words punctuated the blue smoke that curled up into the dusty sunbeams that glanced into the kitchen through the scullery door. Her voice carried a tone of mild, dismissive amusement.

"I was lying in bed going to sleep" she told us, "and your Father as usual was taking forever in the bathroom – what he does in there every night I'll never know but normal men can't spend that long getting ready for bed – and I heard a noise from downstairs. No!" she corrected herself, thus demonstrating her scrupulous attention to detail and to the truth, thereby adding credibility to the story, "your Father was in bed asleep – 'cause I had to wake him up. I heard a noise from the lounge – I heard the lounge window going up ..."

The lounge was a thirty-foot long room immediately under their bedroom that was never used and was therefore cold, damp and gloomy. It had a stout door into the hall that, like all the hall doors, was bolted with a large Victorian brass fitting on the hall side; whatever phantoms lurked in that large room were safely confined.
"...Edwin! – I whispered. Edwin! Wake-up! Wake-up! There's somebody breaking into the house. But of course he wouldn't wake up" she snorted derisively.

Mother, Stephanie & Brutus – 1952 (Sykes' house in background)

Mother's 'whisper' had to carry across the thirty-foot gap between their beds.

Father made another attempt to unglue one or the other of his feet and to step out of the kitchen and go and shoot bullets through the cellar walls. But he could not break the spell. He hovered in silent and silenced complaint by the open door.

"Edwin!! I almost had to shout. There's somebody breaking into the lounge window. Edwin – will you wake-up. I had to get out of bed, creep across the floor and shake him awake. There's a burglar in the lounge – I told him – he's come in by the front window."

"What about Bobby" I asked; "didn't he bark?"

Bobby was a skittish, snarling dog, who was difficult to love and the terror of all tradesmen who came to the house.

"Oh him. I'll tell you about him in a minute. Some guard dog he turned out to be. Anyway, I got your father up at last and he sat on the edge of his bed and listened – but the burglar had gone quiet. Probably all the noise I'd had to make to wake our horizontal hero, here" she nodded in Father's direction, eyebrows raised comically to indicate his level of mental retardation on awakening and the state of his general intelligence.

We all knew she should really have married her handsome German fiancé before the War, who had thick blond hair and was tall and alert, and we now understood, was of normal brain power and high in courage - compared to this bumbling balding Father who stood in the dock before us.

" ...'I can't hear anything' – he said. 'Go and look' I said. 'I'm positive I heard the lounge window being opened. There is somebody in the lounge. You might catch him if you hurry.' Well he stood up. Had to find his dressing gown. Find the key to the wardrobe. Unlock the box where he keeps that silly revolver that he shouldn't have in the house anyway. And he was pounding around like an elephant. It would have woken the dead, never mind alerted a burglar. He put on all the bedroom lights – he might as well have sent the man a telegram telling him he was coming. Then he had to get the ammunition from the top of the wardrobe and find his torch. And he was all the time talking at me – complaining that he couldn't hear anything and grumbling about being woken up. I could have arrested ten burglars in the time he took to get to the bedroom door."

None of us doubted it and we could pity the hapless intruders that Mother might accost. She needed no other weapons than her voice to render most men impotent and harmless.

"Then he was out onto the landing. Stamping about. Putting on all the lights as he went and shouting back to me that he couldn't hear a burglar in the lounge. Banging down the front stairs – the house was like a fairground by now, with so many lights and all the noise your father was making and then I heard him unlocking the lounge door."

She paused. We all leant forward for the dénouement, even Father, who gripped his rifle in soldierly fashion and stopped fidgeting with his feet.

"Then there was a long silence. And I was worried what had happened to him. But after a while I heard him locking the lounge door and coming back upstairs, switching off the lights. He came into the bedroom, with his damn silly gun and torch looking like the Territorial Army and do you know what he said to me? Do you know what he said?"

We didn't and we all shook our heads obediently as she drew renewed strength again from her Senior Service.

"He said, your Father said – 'You damn fool Mother. You'd gone and left that lounge window wide open.'"

Father shuffled miserably by the door, the powerful rifle, complete with telescopic sights, across his chest looking limp and ineffectual, still unable to escape and now at the unyielding focal point of six pairs of eyes that challenged him to stand up for himself like a man, to cross-examine his accuser, to question the evidence, to at least put in a plea of mitigation and for mercy. But he had no defence and could make no such plea. He stared helplessly at the ceiling.

"Was there a burglar?" asked Richard, ever the pragmatist, trying to extract the facts from this seething marital material that Richard found irrelevant to his life.

Mother snorted again "Of course there was a burglar. The next morning when we examined the window there were footprints, large footprints, in the flowerbed and on the windowsill and across the carpet. Then your father called the police. 'I had left the window open', indeed. What a stupid thing to say. 'I had left the window open'. He knows we never use the room. What does he think I would be doing opening the window in midwinter and leaving it wide open. I couldn't even lift the window. Have you seen the size of it. It's far too heavy for me to even think of opening. I don't know what was in his mind. I'd left the window open. 'Mother – you damn fool' – he said. 'You've gone and left the lounge window open all night.' He said."

"And that dog of yours" she suddenly turned on me.

I quailed and Bobby scuttled under the table out of the glare.

"'Did the dog bark Mrs Hodson?' asked the policeman. Did he heck bark. When I came down to the kitchen he was cowering; yes cowering" she insisted, poking me in the chest as the dog was considered to be mine – simply because I tried to defend it from the regular threats of being put-down every time it bit a postman, knocked a passer-by off his bike or attacked the grocer's boy.

"He was cowering…," she repeated with the merest hint of a sidelong glance at Father that we all caught and correctly interpreted,

"...right under the table and looked as if he'd been like that all night. Ears flat down and whimpering. Some brave guard dog he turned out to be – I don't think."

The renewed threat of extinction hung in the air over the spot where Bobby stood hidden by the table-top. Father at last wrenched himself free from the dock and stomped down into the cellar where, via a well-positioned hole in one of the walls he had made a shooting gallery the length of the house, and where he could slam bullet after bullet hard into the targets, logs and sandbags sixty feet away from his sniper's bed of sacking.

Mother was twenty-five when I was born in nineteen forty-two. She had married Father on the rebound, we learned when we quizzed her about a photograph of her at eighteen, very blonde and blue eyed and with, as she boasted, an eighteen-inch waist, on the arm of a handsome, equally blonde young man, with hair (Father had not a lot of hair due, he unconvincingly claimed, to wearing a tight skull cap to reduce drag in cycle races). The blond god was a German; A very handsome and intelligent German; taller than Father. But along came the War and the German beau was repatriated and the romance was over. It was never made clear to us where Father had arrived from, but he did, and the War, when so many young men may have died, injected a fatalistic feyness into relationships that hastened couples into marriages that they afterwards – when they realised they had both survived instead of being romantically nuked out of existence by enemy bombs or bullets, - had to get on with.

With divorce still a major social scandal and an option only for the rich, posh and educated classes - and with the Pope, God bless his Holiness, having recommended Coitus-Interruptus for a few decades and found it wanting, now selling the Rhythm Method for all he was worth as being the only contraceptive technique that would (A) prevent conception sometimes (B) make sex more exciting not to say stressful (C) teach couples how to read the calendar and take their own temperatures (D) guarantee condom-less sinners a well-deserved dose of clap when they consorted with prostitutes and (E) was a prerequisite for gaining your Crown in Heaven (if you really simply HAD to do it and couldn't get along, as higher beings did, with celibacy); the birth rate soared and the Baby Boom, including me, was established as a large proletariat lump working its way up the demographic tables for the next seventy years and causing any number of societal problems along the way.

Father, however, not Herman the German, won the hand of the fair maiden, and his coming home from the war provided another plausible theory for my social-phobia problem; My Oedipal Complex. Father joined up in the Fleet Air Arm before I was born and he came home after demob in nineteen forty-five, I suppose about September when I was nearly three years old. Mother recounted how I would not accept this man in our house and how hard she tried to reconcile us.

"One day" she related, "to my surprise, Father was sitting in the armchair with his legs stretched out onto the footstool and Noel was sitting on his legs, bouncing up and down. 'Do you like your Daddy, now Noel?' I asked him. 'No', he said grimly; 'I'm trying to break his legs.'"

As I've said, I was a robust and square child but not a leg breaker.

So Father came home. I, so the theory goes, hated him. He was far too large to attack or remove, so my rage became bottled up and emerged as an acute social fear. Or so the theory goes.

Father, to his great credit, could count at astonishing speed. In those far-off days, once upon a time, people counted their money in pounds, shillings and pence – and in halfpence, farthings, thru'-penny bits, half-crowns and guineas. A guinea was one pound and one shilling – and all professional people tendered their fees in guineas. There were four farthings in a penny, twelve pennies in a shilling and twenty shillings in a pound. Before Sir Clive Sinclair, pocket calculators were undreamed of. Clockwork adding machines were expensive office desktop items, sometimes driven by electric motors that tripled their weight. To add a column of figures, inevitably inscribed in an indestructible fifty-line ledger, with a dip-pen using real ink, required a good head for figures and a dab hand with the blotting paper.

Father was one of the few people who could add pounds, shillings and pence items, say a payroll list for two hundred people, entry by entry, creating a running total in his head, using five arithmetical bases, as his finger ran down the page. Most others, as I painfully learned to do, plodded down the pennies, carried forward to the shillings, plodded wearily down the right-hand shillings, then the left-hand teens in the shillings' column, carried forward to the pounds, toted down the single pounds' column, carried forward to the tens, then to the hundreds, then to the thousands and so on. After three years of intensive training average clerks could add up such a page in their heads, check it on the adding-machine, and if they had not lost concentration on the long,

long slow journey down the endless columns on the page – the two totals might sometimes agree. And all of heaven rejoiced.

Father, unknowingly or perhaps not so unconscious of what he was doing, may not have deterred burglars but he eventually drove the Grim Butler away; or we could say he released that sad spectre from its compulsion to repeat its nightly tour of the landing.

***

One Saturday morning when most of us were at home, the front doorbell rang and I went to see who it was. We rarely had social visits. In the front driveway was a limousine that I recognised, parked at an arrogant angle; caught in a moment of rare repose, as the posh car adverts said. The caller, to my surprise, was Eddie Rider – father of my close friend Peter-John – bronzed and groomed like a gentleman, and confidently in charge of the universe, as befitted the successful boss of an old established shop-fitters and owner of the, admittedly now diminished by the advent of new-fangled freezers, Manchester Ice

Works, which for decades had supplied the ice to hundreds of traders in Smithfield Market. "Uh! Hello…" I started to say, but was eclipsed and bypassed by Father stepping in front of me.

"Hello Eddie…" Father said as he held out his hand, in manly and equally confident manner.

"Good morning Eddie…" said Mr Rider, shaking hands and flashing a broad smile.

As far as I knew they hadn't met before and I felt I should act as host – but I wasn't needed as they practised their one-upmanship. My dad was Edwin. Peter-John's dad was Edward. Both were abbreviated to the chummy "Eddie"; and were also bound together by the comradeship of having fought in and survived the War. This never mentioned battle bond existed between most of our parent's generation, men and women who had faced death and lived, and seen dozens of friends and relatives slaughtered – as had also happened in their parents' generation in the Great War. It infiltrated all social and business transactions, injecting an unquestioned ethical base into our world, where "My word is my bond" still held true. In the War, disinformation, lying and mistrust had led to death and treachery. Cheats and cunningly worded contracts were not tolerated. Black-Market spivs were blackballed, and many imprisoned. No one talked of their war experiences. My Godfather, a quiet man, Charlie Derbyshire, had been incarcerated in a Japanese prison camp and though the film industry told the stories in Films such as Bridge Over the River Quai, the real participants rarely if ever spoke of the horrors they had witnessed. Father had volunteered for the highly dangerous North Atlantic ammunition convoys, running the U-Boat gauntlet where thousands of sailors drowned – but he never mentioned the sea battles he had been in.

"Now let's see what we can do" said Eddie Rider, stepping into our wide hallway, as Father, stood aside and waved him in. "We'll look around the house first – shall we".

Mother appeared from the back of the house, wiping her hands before shaking Eddie's. "Ah! Good morning to you, Winifred. It's an honour to be in your lovely home"

"Would you like a…"

"No, I won't have tea thank you. Show me the house and tell me what you want to do." He said, taking charge again.

It was a surprise to me and the rest of us that anything was to be done. Father just acted – without consultation, with anyone. But intrigued, we all trouped from room to room; each door thrown open by Mr Rider and the space reviewed and commandeered by his professional eye. Mother was paralysed into silence; "What if she hadn't dusted – and this flamboyant guest gossiped in the neighbourhood? "

We all went into the Morning Room, which had a ten-foot square heavy framed leaded window looking onto the back porch and garden. Eddie Rider quickly spotted the problem he'd obviously been asked to address. Above the big window was an area of flat roof, covered in solid Victorian lead sheets, which was accessible from Martin & Peter's equally large bedroom window. That roof had sprung some leaks in its one-hundred-year life. Not helped perhaps by being regularly used as a lofty fortress in our games, which we vigorously invaded or defended with ladders, sticks, stones, balls, soil, arrows and other missiles.

"Aha! Damp! This wall is running with water; isn't it Eddie?" said Eddie without fear of contradiction, and running his hand up and down our fairly new smart wallpaper – which didn't look damp to me. But builders know best. Then to Mother's horror, causing her to disappear to some hidden-shame-cupboard where she could await this handsome man's discovery that Mother had not, or might not have (in her panic she couldn't recall) made the beds – or ironed the sheets and pillow cases properly; thus consigning her to social isolation for life. "Let's go upstairs and look at that roof."

And we all, except Mother who hid, trouped up the main staircase in Eddie's wake.

Martin, now fifteen, had grown considerably. He no longer wept when teased by Richard, and, still blond with large blue-eyes, he was well on his way to winning body-building and weight lifting competitions. In fact, his six-feet-one-inches height and bulging muscles, dwarfed Richard's lean, whippet like, five feet ten and a quarter inches, which in turn was a quarter of an inch smaller than me; a fact that Richard hotly disputed all of his life. Peter, a year older than Martin, clocked in at six-feet high – and he was by far the most handsome of the first four brothers. It was evident in many families, that children born in the War were stunted compared to children born after the War. In our case, our youngest brother Jeremy, seven years younger than Martin, born after food and clothes Rations were scrapped, grew to be six feet four inches – and became a stuntman. Family photos of the males showed a distinct upward gradient from the oldest to the youngest.

Martin and Peter shared the bedroom above the Morning Room – where Martin kept his weight-lifter's barbells.

Eddie, short of stature but large bodied, immediately focused on the barbells and spare weights; all thoughts of leaking lead roofs forgotten. He appraised Martin with a professionally competitive survey.

"What's the weight on that bar? Young man"

"Oh! Its two hundred pounds" said Martin as modestly as he could muster, being too polite to this old man to let any hint of superior strength into his voice.

"Is that your top weight for a press?"

Martin was surprised that Eddie seemed to know the sport, but still managed to answer modestly, without showing off. "Er; yeah! I've just got up to snatching it from the floor and over my head". He said, with the very slightest challenge in his manner – not least because I, his weakling older brother was there, and Father was unconsciously flexing his Charles Atlas honed arms.

"I'll bet you, young man, a fiver, that I can lift it with one hand" said Eddie, smiling up into Martin's face.

We all, even Father, politely held our breath. We had all, secretly or publicly, tried to lift the barbell over our heads, with two hands – and show our superior strength to our upstart kid brother. And we had all failed. Eddie was very likeable, but small, maybe five feet six or seven, and a guest. We didn't want to see him embarrassed.

Martin didn't know how to handle the challenge and the bet from this man of business. So he said nothing. Eddie stayed in charge. "I can lift it from where it is – with one hand."

And without more ado, he walked across the room, bent his knees, grasped the bar in the centre with his right hand – and lifted it waist high – turned the bar over so that his hand was under it – and easily pressed it above his head – with one hand and one arm. Then he carefully lowered it by reversing the movements.

***

Birch House, when restored to good repair was a handsome example of early Victorian quality building. The front was particularly well designed and attractive with a wide front door approached up four generous steps, flanked by two wide bays that soared up three floors, four floors including the cellars, which terminated in neat leaded roofs under the high eves, roofs that we often played on, risking death or disablement. The frontage was an excellent example of the bricklayer's art, with friezes of smaller curved edged and coloured bricks emphasising subtle features. Father, in a sudden and unexpected frenzy of personal creativity, ripped off the entire front of the house, when I was about seventeen, and replaced it with a flat fronted, cream painted, pebble dashed monstrosity, replacing the grand and solid main door and its fine porch with a flat wrought iron and glass affair that drove sensitive architects to gouge out their own eyeballs.

He, Father, also added, alongside the thirty-foot lounge, locked, unneeded and unused up till then, except used occasionally, by me, to play the huge classical record collection left by the previous owners, he added a vast conservatory with a ballroom floor. As Father never danced, sang, whistled or listened to music and, as he never discussed any of his initiatives either before, during or after the event, we could only guess at his impenetrable inspiration for this astonishingly barbarous assault on a fine old house.

The house now boasted an entire floor of unused but freshly painted attics, six unused cellars, a largely unused and always locked dining room that doubled as Father's office and an unused, renovated thirty-foot lounge with a six-hundred square foot ballroom attached – also unused. We were nevertheless still forbidden from hanging or sticking anything on the interior walls, so as not to spoil the expensive redecoration.

In the process however, the box-room over the front door porch, the room that I had long suspected as being the lair and source of the Grim-Butler, had its front torn-off by the builders; pipes were run into it to feed a central heating radiator and it was for the first time in our occupation and probably for the first time in a hundred years, repainted. After the house settled down its vibrations were changed; and the Grim Butler never appeared again, nor did I ever hear his lugubrious footfalls traversing the landing to my bedroom door.

The story of the shades of Birch House does not quite end there however; we sold the house, not long after Father's modernisation, to the Conservative Party Agent for Manchester, Mr Lawson, who moved in with his large family. His wife met Mother some months after and recounted the haunting they were dealing with. On several occasions, they had felt a presence on the main stairs that pushed past them and fled down into the hall. They detected perfume emanating from and accompanying this visitation; and thought they felt the presence of a distressed woman, doomed to wander the landing, stairs and hall of that unquiet house.

***

Chapter 5 - Smog and Vertigo

Stephen Mosley - *School of Cultural Studies & Humanities, Leeds Metropolitan University.*
In 1950, the sight of sulphurous black smoke billowing out from industrial and domestic chimneys still dominated the skylines around Greater Manchester. Coal smoke was responsible for blackening urban architecture, blocking out sunlight, destroying vegetation and, not least of all, damaging people's health. It was closely associated with high levels of mortality from bronchitis and other respiratory diseases, particularly during the cold winter months when demand for domestic coal fires was at its peak. Manchester's ugliness, as J.B. Priestley put it, was 'so complete' that it was 'almost exhilarating.'

SMOG "You couldn't see your hand in front of your face"

The impenetrable winter smog that fell in 1950 in the dark early evenings was very exciting.

We had all managed to get home safely through the streets without being able to see our hands held up in front of our faces. Long woolly, double knitted scarves, in red and white bands, were inverted to make head hugging balaclavas at one end, with the other end wrapped several times and tightly around mouths and noses for warmth and air filters, the end being tucked into the neck of a tightly buttoned gabardine. Sound was deadened before it could travel even a few feet. Lampposts served as reliable landmarks in an otherwise featureless dark sea of cloud and chemicals. We could taste the bitter soot, from countless coal burning chimneys, in the wet cold soup as it clung to our clothes, making everything filthy and clammy to touch. The mile or so walk from school in that impenetrable darkness was hugely exciting - hand over hand along suddenly unfamiliar garden walls - navigating across streets that mysteriously seemed ten times wider than in daylight, with no landmarks nor even sounds to guide us to the safety of a pavement.

The school had disgorged a hundred and fifty or so, five to eleven-year-old children alone into that dark oily smog to make their way home as best they could. They were wrapped mostly in dark navy gabardines, swathed in those popular double wool scarves, most with blue hands and fingers but some boasting woollen or even fabulous fur backed gloves, with one or two deeply envied boys sporting leather gauntlets. Most wore black lace-up shoes, some crept stealthily like Red-Indians in white or black summer cotton plimsoles or "pumps"; or swaggered along in swashbuckling wellies with the white cotton interiors folded down to the ankles. At the school gates they dispersed into the gloom to go their separate ways, disappearing in seconds from each other and from the world. Little groups trailed together along silent and cloaked suburban roads, guessing at the direction. At each junction the groups divided and smaller parties groped along walls and pavements towards, they hoped, their homes, reassured briefly by a sudden lamppost looming by a recognisable wall before blindly creeping another fifty yards to where they hoped the next light might be found. The lampposts always surprised the fumbling travellers, leaping into view just six inches from their frozen noses, casting a feeble yellow or blue glow on the slowly stirring smog, but failing to illuminate the ground. Our breathing made the improvised woollen masks wet, but it was more comfortable to keep the warm poultice of the scarf hugging the mouth and nose than to pull it aside and suck in the cold, cloying blanket of filthy fog. No cars or buses threatened the slow crossing of streets. No anxious parents appeared out of the blackness, waving torches and proffering comfort and guidance. No one came and no one was expected. The children managed the journey alone and hugely enjoyed their small adventure.

I made it back to Birch House and crept around the garden in that pitch darkness for a time, enjoying the privacy and silence, before hunger and cold drove me into that brooding house.

At that time of year, it was dark by four-thirty and in that weather all honest people were in their homes by six. Even Father had made it back from Manchester, full of brief bluff comments, thrown out to his personal, private watchers in the high dark corners of the kitchen, which left no doubt as to his manly skills and courage, a foretaste of his amazing rallying and racing skills yet to come, in cleaving his way instinctively through the smog while lesser mortals abandoned their cars and fumbled their way along the miles of impossibly dark, muffled pavements.

The smog even seeped into the kitchen, making the light dimmer and casting an imperceptible shadow over the table. The coal fire warmed the room, adding its slow exhaust of smoke, carbon, tar and sulphur to the overburdened atmosphere, burning slowly and dully in the grate as the smog pressed down the chimney and choked the draught that the fire needed. By now Stephanie had been born, though she was too young to be up at the table for tea. The rest of us sat at the kitchen table, including Father, still happy with memories of our adventures outside, and we waited in unaccustomed quiet while Mother heaved and juggled with pans full of potatoes and piles of plates in the cold condensation of the scullery. The meal was sausages, fried eggs and mashed potatoes; a firm favourite, which ensured that not a scrap was left.

Martin wept only briefly and silently at this meal and was threatened only lightly by his parents with permanent incarceration in a lunatic asylum, as they couldn't understand what was wrong with the boy. Richard didn't find anything to taunt anybody about and Mother, having delivered her familiar self-pitying rebuke for not being offered any help and her "slaving over a hot gas stove" monologue that she often delivered at tea-time - sometimes accompanied by tears squeezed from a crumpled face, was mellow as she lit her apres-tea cigarette, sucked smoke deeply into her lungs and reached for The Peterloo Massacre, her newspaper and her biro.

"Mum", said Peter,
"Tell us about when Richard climbed on top of the houses."

The table held its breath while Mother silently considered this request. Taking an extra deep drag on her un-tipped Players cigarette and putting aside her book, paper and pen she composed her public self, swept her audience with a professional glance, waited for the moment, and then began.

"Well..." she said, the merest stream of blue smoke issuing from deep within as she spoke,

"...Richard was a proper devil. He was the scourge of the neighbourhood even before he was a year old."

Richard neither moved nor betrayed any expressions as he became the focus of the story; but we knew he was intrigued and this pleased us younger sons as it might maintain his pacific mood well into the evening. We were pleased that he was pleased, though a stranger could never have guessed it.

"Richard could walk before he was – no! He couldn't just walk, he could run. Really run. I've never known a baby who learned to walk and run that early. Before he was ten months old, he could run round the house like a little squirrel."

"How old was I when I could walk?" I asked, not liking these accolades being heaped upon Richard.
 I shouldn't have asked.

"Oh, you were much later than Richard. You were quite the opposite.

You never moved unless you absolutely had too. I always remember watching you and Richard in the garden with a ball. Richard ran after it, wherever it bounced. This way and that way; and Richard would be after it, like a whippet. But, Noel ..." she resumed addressing the whole audience,
"...Noel just sat and watched the ball. He sat and watched until it had absolutely stopped, then and only then would he go and get it. He took a long time to learn to walk."

"Richard though; he gave us some moments. The neighbours were forever coming round, just when I thought Richard was safe and asleep in his pram and they'd say 'Mrs Hodson, Mrs Hodson, we don't want to worry you but we're sure we've seen your Richard on the building site.' And I'd tell them not to be ridiculous. He wasn't even eighteen months old and I knew that he was fast asleep in his pram. But they'd be right. There he was - there were six half built houses in Slate Lane across the way from us, abandoned because of the War, - teetering along a fifteen-foot wall, which couldn't have been more than six inches wide, with his arms out like this, calm as you like, balancing fifteen feet up in the air." She paused for breath, the memory bringing back the fear of it.

Richard sat tensed and slightly forward, listening with feigned indifference but deeply pleased at his notoriety and unrivalled early physical development. He blinked his pale blue staring eyes, eyes like his mothers, slowly and sat even straighter in his neat thin way.

"Once..." she continued reflectively
"...when your father was still away at the War..."
A thousand innuendoes communicated themselves to this experienced audience who understood from that one subtly enunciated phrase, that he of no name, sometimes called Father, had volunteered for active service despite being in a reserved occupation as accountant at the Gas Board, only to escape his responsibilities to wife, home and children. Further, that he had somehow deliberately contrived to serve time on the incredibly dangerous Atlantic ammunition convoys and then, having wilfully survived the U-boats, be transferred to a horizontal position in a hammock, under the palm trees, in an entirely peaceful and luscious tropical island base in Ceylon, for the rest of the war. Further, that he returned only rarely to take leave at home, each time impregnated his loyal wife, ate the family's entire meagre food rations for a month in seventy-two hours and returned blithely to his hammock, unlimited food and warm sunshine in Ceylon.

This underlying message was not denied or affirmed by Father and we, the jury, believed what Mother cared us to believe. Mother continued.

"...Richard climbed out of his bedroom window onto the sill - it was only this wide" she held out her Players Cigarette packet with its rich colours and reliable looking bearded sailor, between thumb and finger, "...and he walked along it - he could only have been fifteen months old, no, he must have been nearly two; yes almost two - teetering along this narrow sill..." her audience was wide eyed with anticipation, raptly trying to reconcile Richard's feet with the size of the cigarette packet "...and I came into his room to see him through the glass; but I couldn't reach him, I didn't even dare to try. I might have knocked him off and killed him."

His brothers contemplated this potential premature death of the first born in silence, each with his own thoughts carefully concealed. She drew hard and long on her cigarette which burned fiercely and brightly while a third of an inch of the paper transformed to neat, light grey ash. She held the smoke deep inside, mouth tightly closed, moved the cigarette carefully away, sat up even straighter, and continued, her voice subtly deeper from the effects of the smoke.

"I could only hold my breath and hope. He edged along the sill; right to the end, twenty feet high; and I couldn't see how he would turn round and get back - I didn't know what to do."

This sentence was visibly punctuated by a controlled stream of thin blue smoke, issuing from the very foundations of her, then still healthy, lungs.

When she died, wishing she could have a cigarette beneath the token but ineffectual oxygen mask supplied by Stepping Hill Hospital staff, supplied in an uncomprehending imitation of what they imagined happened in real hospitals in such cases, her lungs were no longer able to carry enough oxygen into her bloodstream, which was in any case sluggish due to her enlarged and weakened heart, to prevent her fingers, toes and parts of her face from turning black beneath the skin. Peter may have been born blue and un-bright; she died black and friendless.

Notably, I, her alleged favourite son was the only one of six babies who was not breast-fed; a fact to which my relative sanity has often been ascribed by professional and amateur analysts, family and friends.

However; we left two-year-old Richard teetering on his window sill at twenty feet and must rescue him so that he can be around to fulfil his karma.

"He reached the end..." she still held out the indicative width of the cigarette packet, "...and stopped. I couldn't see how he was going to get back. I thought he was going to fall off. But he stepped out, with his little bootees; no, I think he was in his socks, and he stretched across to the next window sill, managed to get his foot on it - it was only a tiny semi-detached - and crossed over onto that sill. That window was open and he came back inside."

Richard's dead-pan face, so profitable to him later in life in games of poker and three card brag, reflected some satisfaction to those who could read his impassive features - and Mother looked over her audience, satisfied with her own performance; seeing her audience gazing with awe at her and at her wondrous son. A silent moment of family self-congratulation was broken by Father "hrrrumphing" up out of his chair and making wordlessly for the kitchen door, en-route, we surmised, to the lavatory.

This incredible tale of infant derring-do becomes less apocryphal in the context of Richard's later adventures. Birch House, had four bays running from cellar to roof level. One bay, at the side of the house with a small flat leaded roof, could be accessed through an attic window. It was fifty feet high, had no balustrade and only space for two brave and agile children. It was separated by protruding eaves, slate roof, gutters and downspouts from another bay, rising perpendicularly from the ground far below, which had no window behind it at roof level. This second, tiny flat roof was about five feet away. Richard once took me out of the window onto the minuscule lead covered plateau, poised himself on the outer edge of the raised lead, where he had about nine inches of space to avoid the eaves, and leapt across that precipitous chasm to the other roof. On landing he pounded his feet in rapid, tiny, dance like steps to brake his momentum and stop himself from going over the far edge. Once there, there was no window to escape into. The only way back was to reverse the jump. I clung onto the window frame, pressed against the wall on that vertiginous, dangerous platform, as Richard measured the distance, edged out to avoid the protrusions, and sprang over the stomach churning drop. His feet landed on the edges of the five-sided roof, jigged rapidly inwards and he grabbed the overhanging eaves.

Fort Clonque, Alderney.
Dangerous rocks to climb.

I was eight, he was ten. And I remember the adventure particularly well because he then persuaded me, against all my natural instincts and in defiance of my square, less agile frame, to do the same. I remember being trapped on the second roof with no way back but that deathly leap; heart pounding, stomach in knots, the light beginning to fade, Richard getting bored and starting to leave and my courage having fled. I am here to tell the story, so clearly I did at last made the return trip. I however knew the dangers, Richard appeared not to and I am sure this indifference to heights was not bravado but was natural to him, affirming Mother's stories of her agile infant; agile due to a lingering primate instinct perhaps.

Similarly, on a holiday in Alderney, we rented a flat in Fort Clonque, joined to the island by a causeway which was undersea at high tide. At the back of this isolated castle, the walls plunged 150 feet to the sea, surrounded by towers of jagged rock. Richard and I risked death to jump across heaving seas onto the base of the tallest needle – and climbed it to where it was level with the top of the fort. Just as he had led the way across the attics' platforms, Richard leapt from the jagged rock tower, across the precipitous, perilous gap, and grasped the edge of the wall – and heaved himself over to safety. Then it was my turn.

As I have reassured you before, gentle reader; I am writing this and so obviously survived – but very nearly didn't. With rising panic and vertigo, I flung myself off the pinnacle, seas crashing far below, slammed into the wall, arms stretched up; fingertips scrambling for the edge – and managed to get a hold. My trusty all-purpose school shoes, with breathing leather soles, scrabbled and found a niche in the wall – and I hauled myself up and over; collapsing on the inside battlements. Yet another near-death-experience.

I found peace away from Richard, away from the house, away from the family and away from people.

Sam inquired in a low voice, "You don't like heights?" Caleb shrugged his shoulders noncommittally and replied, "Maybe it isn't so much a fear of heights as it is a fear of plummeting to my death."
Author: Katie Lynn Johnson

Chapter 6 - The Eleven-Plus

When I was 11, I received a letter saying that I was to go to the local grammar school. When my sister was 11, she was told that she was to go to the local secondary modern. Our lives were to show a marked contrast from then on. – Independent Newspaper

It was of paramount importance in those days to pass the Eleven Plus examination.

Those who did pass went to Grammar Schools and from there, if they were very lucky and bright enough, could go on to University and join the top two-percent of the country. Fail the eleven plus and the child suffered the ignominy of attending a Secondary Modern that boasted metalwork for boys (as Britain needed engineers) and domestic science for girls (as the nation equally needed devoted housewives).

Having been top of a class of some fifty children for most terms over five years, I was rightly expected in 1953 to sail through the formal exam as my older, less able brother, Richard, had. It was to be conducted at another, larger school, recently built about a mile down the road from my own school.

I set off in good time that bright morning, new pencil case clutched in one hand, filled with sharpened pencils, ruler, rubber and all the tools needed for the job. I walked alone down Mauldeth Road, past the church and on towards the junction with Didsbury Road. As I made the unfamiliar turn to the right instead of to the left, as I did on a normal school day, I felt disembodied. My eyes stared blankly. The light was unnaturally bright and the fences and shrubs glowed with a luminous Technicolor. I couldn't quite remember what I was doing on this road, or why I was going to the rival, Protestant school. But I kept on and let my feet guide me in through the wrought iron gates, up the newly paved drive and into a large light hall where other children were gathering. Nobody spoke to me and I didn't try to initiate communication with anyone. I sat at a single desk in a vast space. Papers were put on the surface in front of me. I watched them carefully. They glowed bright as had the fences and shrubs. I read them but they made no sense. I made marks on the papers, but had no idea what the marks meant. I wrote things where writing seemed to be required, but I couldn't make sense of my own writing. Eventually all the children were sent home or back to their own schools.

My headmistress and schoolteachers were very surprised when it was learned that I had failed. Perhaps it was a marking error that my parents should insist was looked into. But, NO, said Mother. "We wouldn't want to put anybody to any trouble."

***

Chapter 7 - Hares

In 1947, the Hobhouse Committee recommended legislation for public access to open countryside. This led to the National Parks and Access to the Countryside Act 1949. Under this legislation, local authorities were required to survey open countryside, assess the level of access provided to walkers and to secure further access by means of agreements with landowners, by orders or by purchasing the land. In practice the legislation has secured very few improvements for walkers.- Ramblers Association
The freedom to roam, or everyman's right, is the general public's right to access certain public or privately owned land for recreation and exercise. The right is sometimes called the right of public access to the wilderness or the right to roam - Wikipedia

On a warm spring morning in 1949 I took our dog, Bobby, a black, unpredictable half breed border collie who snapped at callers, off his chain that slid along a fifty-yard wire running the whole length of the driveway of Birch House, from gate to garage, and we set out together. Maybe I had a sandwich and a cold drink with me. We turned right at the road and right again, down the path alongside the Lawless's house, past the bombed out house the "Laurels", now cleared of rubble and enticingly overgrown and fit only for imaginative children to occupy, past the acres of allotments and onto the farm land beyond. There were rabbits, or we thought there were rabbits, which was just as good. Bobby pelted after them, I ran after him under the wide sky. However blue and clear, there is always a touch of misty cloud in a Manchester sky that hints of the inevitable daily precipitation, however lightly it might fall, that drifts in across the Cheshire Plain, rises to cross the Pennines, cools and falls over the city. Today it would not rain, but nor would it get too hot to run and walk.

The rabbits and the trails took us to the right, along the farm track, by the large barn on lower Mauldeth Road where we holed up for a time in the copse of elderberry trees that filled the corner between barn and garden wall abutting the roadway. The flavour of the sap of those trees still evokes powerful memories. I broke off a straight elder stick to be my sturdy staff that looked the part but, with its soft spongy filling, could not do any real work. We moved off again, down the hill, and off to the right into the golf course, still empty at this early hour, where we ran and hid and lay down in dens and ran again. Bobby really found rabbits this time and a hare that he chased and I could see as it bounded high and fast, jigging over the clipped greens. Across the golf course, into the Shaw Road farm alongside where I took a turnip, or ears of wheat or whatever was growing then and ate it with my penknife, we pursued the hare and away now to our left, into unfamiliar territory, over fallow fields left to grow long delicate grasses and tall cerise fireweed. Between chases we rested in the long grasses that I tied together to make small conical, living houses for elves and dormice as we lay there. Up again and there was the hare – or its cousin, so we chased after it and it took us into the huge acreage of the Fairey Aviation recreation land abutting the Mc'Vitie biscuit factory, laid out in parts as football and hockey pitches but mostly just open fields, that let onto a border with Wellington Road as it streamed towards Levenshulme and Manchester city centre.

A boy and his dog don't want tarmac roads and harsh pavements, so we turned and wended our way north and west on a compass setting pointed towards the heart of Manchester but keeping always to the open fields and natural trees and avoiding all human contact. Hedges, fences and restricting signs had no meaning for us as we traversed the land and grounds of playing fields and schools and large houses and golf courses without let or hindrance, up through Mauldeth Home for Incurables, slowly re-crossing Shaw Road farm, skirting through Mauldeth Road's open spaces, park and allotments, through side streets and up to Didsbury Road and into the steeply sloping Leeman's Field. There we dug in for the duration, by the steep little stream that came cleanly out of the ground higher up near the St Winifred's school fence and down through a deep earth chasm to the acre of pond below. We built dams that day, of stones and sods – some of which held back the waters for minutes, before being overwhelmed and swept away. We closely observed and caught newts in the margins of the pond and, with the most rapid of reactions, caught sticklebacks with our hands; that we let go again as we lacked any container to carry them home in. In the gully, by the stream there was no wind and the warm spring sunlight imbued the scene with a dreamy somnolent comfort.

Eventually, driven by hunger, we wended our way home taking in the Library, the park, the open land behind the Bank, opposite the old protestant infant's school, in the crook of the Heaton Moor Road S bend, down Balmoral Lane, pausing only to clamber up two inviting oak trees, and back to Birch House and food - a perfect, silent day.

There was a time, for a time, that the Public Library fed me with books that filled my days. For day after day after day I went to the counter, handed in a book, watched them do the magic thing with the blue and buff tickets that lived in the cardboard cutaway inside the cover that made it mine for a few days and I came away with another volume of *Just William*, or *The Famous Five* or *King Arthur's Knights* and found a place, a private place, on a roof or in an attic where the sun fell in the window, or high up in a sycamore or hawthorn tree where I could dine on the soft new leaves, and read the new book from cover to cover, without pause. If bedtime intervened I smuggled the book into bed and took my torch to read it under the covers. However dim and feeble the light became I could read on and on, opening the heavy blankets every half hour to let in fresh air. What supreme satisfaction. Then I fell into arrears. I had exceeded the allotted time. I would be fined. I was now in an illegal state – not unlike being in mortal sin. So I did not dare go the Library again. After some months I lost the borrowed book and could no longer remember its title. The Library became a source of fear with the potential of arrest and incarceration. I became an outlaw. I skirted it apprehensively at a distance in case they recognised me. I missed the intensive reading experience.

But we had comics to read that fell through the door several times a week and were strongly competed for. *The Dandy* and *The Beano* and, as we grew older, these were supplemented by *The Hotspur*, *The Adventure* and occasionally by *The Eagle*. Households were either Eagle families or they were not Eagle families. Eagle families grew up to listen to Jazz. We were not an Eagle family, but the glossy comic did from time to time find its way into the house.

It was a first come first served system. Whoever saw the comic falling onto the mat had absolute rights to grab it, make off with it and read it fully and completely without argument or intervention. But to gain that unassailable privacy, most boys made for the lavatory, locked themselves in and fiercely defended their cubicle territory against bribes, threats and all out physical assault. Forty-five minutes of sitting on the lavatory, legs dangling, brought on crippling pins and needles that necessitated remedial action and could take three or four minutes to recover from, while hopping from one tingling leg to the other. Only-children, children reared alone, never had to develop such territorial rights and cannot in anyway understand why otherwise normal, sensible adults seem incapable of going to the toilet without a book, magazine or leaflet to read. They, the only-children, wrongly assume it has to do with bowel actions that are different from their own. That is an invalid assumption. I also followed and collected the *Adventures of Fudge and Speck*, two elves who were featured in a cartoon strip in the *Manchester Evening News*. I am yet to meet another living soul who remembers this magical pair. (n.b. – Lee Chadwick remembers them).

***

Chapter 8 - Loathed & Liked

The V1 is difficult to classify as a weapon as it was not a true rocket in that it did not leave the atmosphere, but it was also clearly not a plane. Perhaps it could best be described as a winged but pilot-less fuel propelled flying bomb. C N Trueman

"What's the earliest thing you can remember Richard?" asked Mother, courteously turning the course of her tales over to the audience for a moment.

Richard puckered his lips and bit at his cheek as he reluctantly reviewed the past ten years from his birth in 1940 to this day in 1950. "I remember us being in Aberdeen," he said at last.

"That's where your father trained for the Fleet Air Arm and we went with him for a few months. A wet and cold place. It's called the Granite City,"
Mother obligingly picked up on Richard's scant text.
"You were less than two. And that's where your brother was conceived." she added looking at me.

"What's conceived?" I asked.

"That's when a baby is first made. When it starts being made. When its soul comes down from Heaven. Then it takes nine months before it's born. What's the first thing you can remember?"

I searched hard through the obscuring clouds of her stories, books I had read, radio programmes and vivid imagination, trying as hard as possible to be objective in this search for real memories.

"I think I remember being on the little porch over the door and jumping onto the grass." I said uncertainly. "...And..." I hastily added before she could interject,

"...I remember being under the kitchen table when there was a Buzz Bomb coming over."

Mother picked up the bomb.

"We didn't get many of those but near the end of the War the Germans sent them as far as Manchester and they killed quite a lot of people. They were very big bombs so when they fell they'd destroy lots of houses. I remember that one and we did get under the table. There hadn't been enough time to get to the shelter and anyway, it was unlikely to come down near us. They used to cruise over towards Trafford Park with a sort of stuttering engine noise, not very loud but stuttering high in the sky. We'd listen and listen and if the engine cut-out you knew it was coming down not too far away. It'd be in nineteen forty-five, so you'd be ..." Mother gazed at the window as she went into calculation mode,

"...about two-and-a-quarter, about twenty-seven months old. Peter wouldn't be born yet. And you jumped off the porch earlier than that." she added quickly as the reconstruction fell into place.

"That was Richard – again. Oh he was a little devil."

Richard sat dead still, poker faced again until he learned whether this was to be another accusation of attempted fratricide or another celebration of his early motor skills.

"He took you into the little bedroom, which had a window above the porch, and persuaded you to climb out onto the porch. He didn't go with you. Just persuaded you to get out there. You were tiny – I mean young; very young. Not tiny as you were always a big baby. A bit overweight..."

I caught Richard secretly securing this confirmation of yet another fault he could tease me with, to and beyond screaming point, at some future date.

Mother pressed on, oblivious to this pre-torture data storage.

"...and he told you to jump off. Or he'd locked the window behind you, so you had to jump off. Anyway, your Aunty Peggy..."

We were all very surprised to hear an unmentionable relative cited without rancour – a rare unconscious off-guard moment allowing for the existence of Mother's sister, Margaret nicknamed Peggy, who lived next door in Slate Lane. We knew enough, slip or no slip, not to allude to the invisible aunt, uncloaked for a mere microsecond in eternity.

"...Peggy saw you do it. You were sitting on the porch above the door. She couldn't see any sign of Richard but we guessed how you came to be there. And you suddenly stood up and went to the edge... and jumped. Fortunately, you jumped on the side where the grass was – not onto the concrete, but you still came down with quite a thump."

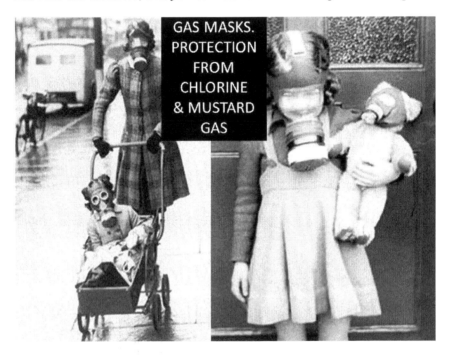

I could see Richard snigger through his poker face and I regretted that I had no way to steer Mother out of these fat-boy allusions that would be used against me over and over before their torment-value was fully spent. I insist that I was not fat. I was square and robust. Martin looked at Richard, then at me, with full comprehension of the complexities in his huge blue eyes. Peter, a year older than Martin, smiled evenly at us all, oblivious to the undercurrents.

"That was right in the middle of the War. Right in the middle of the blackout" mused Mother.

"Oh those were such bad times with your father away at the War and everything on ration." She meandered back into her memories, forgetting her audience for a time.

"It went dark at four o'clock – earlier if there was a smog – and it was too dangerous to be out in the dark. You really couldn't see anything and you couldn't show a light. If you wandered about you might easily fall into the canal – where everybody drowned their kittens. So we'd go indoors and listen to the radio and draw the blackout curtains. I only had Richard for company."

I demurred, unable to imagine a universe existing before or indeed without me. But Mother was fixed on a time, impossible and unbelievable though it might be, before I appeared on Earth.

"I'd put on the radio and listen to the news of the War; that was always awful, even when we were winning; then I'd listen to The Man In Black. Really frightening ghost stories – they were terribly good. And we'd listen to Sherlock Holmes and to the murder mysteries. And I'd read an Agatha Christie or something like that. Then I'd have to put out all the lights and get into bed in the black-out – with the planes coming over. I'd often have nightmares. And you'd never really know if you'd still be alive in the morning – though not many bombs fell on Ashton – it was mostly Ardwick and Gorton and places near the centre – slums mostly."
Mother lit a cigarette and drew the warm comforting fumes reflectively into her lungs – and stayed silent.

We stayed silent too; unused to such a break in the narrative.

"I played next door with Ursula and Cousin Bernard." Richard volunteered into the vacuum that Mother's reflections had created.

It was the wrong thing to offer. And Richard should have known better than to raise our cousins, the Mundens, from the list of banned memories. Not that Mother held any grudge against Ursula and Bernard, after all they were only children but they inevitably drew one's thoughts to Peggy, and from there possibly to Grandma Sauce – not that any of us had the courage to follow the trail that far, or, God Forbid, to make the link from Grandma Sauce to Uncle Bernard, Mother's half-brother, her vile, hateful, loathsome, younger, unmentionable, unthinkable, unclean, non-existent half-brother. Not only that but Mother had, without any quotable words or directives and for no discernible reasons, created the impression that she had lived and coped alone – entirely alone – throughout the War years. Having a sister living next door contradicted this construct and we all knew not to provide any evidence of our Aunt, Uncle or Cousins. Fortunately for Mother's version of history, the Mundens had migrated to Australia in the early fifties, taking their inconvenient evidence with them to the antipodes.

Two heresies had thus been committed by Richard in one brief statement.

Mother looked balefully at Richard who slammed down the hatch on his hermit-shell, put on his poker face and moved not one muscle, not a twitch or a blink, until Mother's attention was distracted away from him. Only then did he breathe normally again.

The key to the disturbed and fractured adult lives of the children may indeed lie in the effects of the War or the Wars, One and Two, or in the histories of Mother and Father, in their parents in turn and in their parents before them. The 'Begats', the ancestral line, may have been irredeemably polluted.

Father had a brother, Alban, and sister, Margaret, and a sickly mother, Kitty, whose husband walked out when Father was twelve, making him "The Man of the House". Grandmother, who had a degree in music from Edinburgh, lived to a ripe old age cared for by her dutiful daughter, who followed her mother swiftly to the grave once her life's work, of caring for her hypochondriac mother, ended.

Father had had no fathering. I met my absent Grandfather once only, when he was eighty and I was twenty or so. An upright, tall handsome gentleman who arrived by appointment at our Manchester office to see his son (after how many years I have no idea) bringing a large salmon wrapped in brown paper. Little or nothing was said; but we took the salmon home, reported the incident to Mother and ate it silently.

Mother loathed her mother-in-law, Kitty, and refused to have her in the house. The lifetime ban extended to the dutiful daughter, our Aunt Margaret, depriving us of almost all contact with our paternal grandmother and our only remaining aunt. So powerful was her veto that though I later cycled daily to my secondary school past grandmother's house, by Wythenshaw Park, it never occurred to me call. How could I have explained such a treasonable act to Mother? Even Father only visited when his mother was terminally ill.

Mother, surprisingly, had a mother, who she loathed with a venomous passion. Grandma Sauce or Neal (she had married twice) was old and bent, with a shin-bone, shaped by Rickets, like a banana. She had long and gappy teeth, national health rimless spectacles and grey unkempt hair. She was poor, living in a terraced house in Denton with a horse hair, leather covered settee with cigarette burn holes a bored child could poke its fingers in, and with her son Bernard, an alcoholic, chain smoking, building labourer who had flowered early as a World War Two pilot, and then faded rapidly into comfortless obscurity, bachelor-hood and beer. Mother loathed Bernard, her step-brother and our uncle, with an intensity greater than all the other people she loathed. But, unique amongst her pantheon of the loathed, she gave a reason for this which also neatly explained her terror of mice.

Francis Hodson, Kitty Merone, Alban, Margaret
Edwin & Winifred, cycling in Scotland.
Winifred, Anon, Peggy
Babies - Richard & Ursula

Uncle Bernard, - born of the second marriage after Mother's father, a stretcher bearer, had died young in 1914 in World War One - had crept up behind her and put a dead mouse down her dress. For this crime she expunged him from her world forever, spoke of him only in hatred and dared any of her children to acknowledge his merest existence.

Actually, I rather liked him. My earliest memory being of Uncle Bernard in blue uniform, with an RAF ginger moustache, looking heroic and confident, visiting us in Derby Road when I was five and doing (quite good) conjuring tricks in the sitting room one sunny winter's afternoon. I saw him again many years later. He was jovial, wrecked by physical labour and bad habits, but had working-class homely wisdom for young men and appeared unaware of the screaming vitriol Mother had poured on his very name for decades.

Mother also had a step-father, who died when I was about three. I was taken up dark, narrow steep stairs in a terraced Manchester house, turned right into a meagre bedroom and my step-grandfather lay there dying. I remember only the fearful atmosphere of that staircase and the tales Mother told of this "fine man", an ex-professional soldier who had married her family after her own father had died, and helped keep the corner-shop running to provide continuity and security. On dying, we were told, he frightened the respectful relatives gathered to usher his soul into the next world by sitting suddenly bolt upright and shouting loudly, minutes after they thought him dead. A claim to fame deeply admired by us fascinated boys.

Mother had an older sister, Peggy. Peggy had a large family, a harassed and ineffectual husband, Pat – short for Patrick; and she chewed her fingernails away completely, digital objects of great fascination for me, before emigrating to Australia in the wave of cheap passages and incentives in the early 1950's. Mother disliked Peggy a lot - but stopped short of loathing her.

Mother loathed a lot of other people and expressed her rage with vehemence and a powerful vocabulary. Where she gained her education, I find difficult to imagine. She went to Notre Dame Convent School until she was fourteen, and then trained as a comptometer operator (a mechanical desktop abacus of devilish complexity used, prior to computers, to calculate reams of invoices and other repetitive sums). With this barely adequate schooling she had vast stores of knowledge, sufficient to rapidly complete the *Mephisto* crosswords in the *Times* and other brain-teasers. She always read, mostly serious novels, histories and biographies; kept up to date with news and current affairs, displaying an effortless memory for names and events, read newspapers thoroughly and critically and went often to the theatre and cinema.

The combination of a wide vocabulary, passionate hatred of relatives and neighbours and her natural skill as a raconteur, made her attacks, carried out at home behind closed doors and out of earshot of the victim, completely devastating. We, her children, had to learn early in our lives not to give her any angle on our friends or their families, or risk a relentless, long campaign of character assassination until some other hapless, innocent object of hatred distracted her attention.

There were, on the other hand, many people she admired; Winston Churchill for one; Margaret Thatcher for another. She loved the Queen *"our dutiful Queen"*, fondly tolerated Princess Margaret despite the gin, cigarettes and fornication Mother assured us that that royal personage indulged in continuously; she liked Father's clients' Claude Hemmerdinger, Idris Owen and the Italian head chef at the celebrated Midland Hotel, who she admired for his fine head of hair which he kept healthy by running his food greased hands through it (seriously). She loved Alec Guinness, Margot Fonteyn, Rudolph Nureyev, Laurence Olivier, Tom Courtney, Morecambe and Wise, Kenneth Horne, Gilbert Harding, despised Wilfred Pickles as patronising (I here modify and soften her views). She liked President J F Kennedy, despite his whoring ways and his support for the black Irish murderers (I again modify her views). She liked Nixon for his nerve. Loved Bob Hope, Marilyn Monroe, Bing Crosby and Frank Sinatra (the truths she told us of Frank Sinatra you would not believe), she liked Macmillan, Alec Douglas-Home and Aneurin Bevan. She admired Clement Atlee, Lord Beaverbrook, Anthony Eden, Rommel (our noble enemy) and The Russians - because of their scorched earth victory over Hitler – and the brave Polish troops and airmen. The Russians and Poles remained our friends and allies ever after in Mother's data bank of strong views. She detested Harold Wilson and could shout him down when he was speaking on television, countering his statements before he even thought of them. She knew of Marcia and her affair with Harold before Harold did. She liked the McClaren Brothers our local grocers, Hilda Cowlishore our daily and her husband Leonard who did the garden on Saturday mornings.

She knew of and liked many celebrities, local people and some friends. She liked handsome men. She said she disliked children; but as she had six, we foolishly never believed her.

Father had no views. He never picked up a newspaper, let alone read one. He never listened to the radio, watched television, went to the cinema, theatre or ballet ("ooeee bare bot" he offered as archived Nijinsky on television leapt impossible distances through the air). I never saw him with a book, even text-books on accountancy his profession, or a magazine other than an occasional car magazine. He never entered into any discourse on any subject with anyone. He neutered all discussions by uttering platitudes and incredibly bad puns, taken from his non-existent "Bumper-Fun-Book". He never had conversations at home other than giving directives which brooked no argument. He knew of no politicians, no heroes, no famous people. He had no sense of history or curiosity of the future.

He was a competitor. As a teenager he had cycled in races and won. He had a box full of gold and silver winner's medals. London to Edinburgh, Lands End to John o' Groats; and he won at track racing using one very high geared cog and a fixed wheel. Later he swam competitively, and won. At forty-something he won a bet to swim five miles at the local pool. As he became wealthier from his solo-owned accountancy practice, he took up car rallying as a forty-year-old amateur and won sufficiently to be given a place on the Triumph works team in the Rome-Liege, Tulip and other major events. He was given the first engine for the TR4 sports car, engine number-one. He entered the gruelling three-day Monte Carlo rally many times as a private entrant and was once described in the press as the fastest man on ice. But he was also the only man to drive all the way to Monte Carlo, have a nap and return the next day because he had no social skills to enjoy the après-rally conventions.

He never entered team events, belonged to no clubs or societies and yet astonishingly stood for Parliament as a Tory candidate three or four times. And I swear he didn't even know the name of the Prime Minister. The fact that he failed to win a seat is the one shred of credibility the Tories still retain in my eyes. He was a local councillor and headed the finance committee on Stockport Council for a number of years, but there is no evidence that he ever spoke there.

He was modestly successful in business - until he started to compete with his eldest son Richard in financial speculation and lost all that he had so hard won. But that is another story.

***

Chapter 9 - Guardian Angels

A Guardian Angel is a heavenly spirit assigned by God to watch over each of us during our lives. The doctrine of angels is part of the Church's tradition. The role of the guardian angel is both to guide us to good thoughts, works and words, and to preserve us from evil. – Catholic On-line

RC Sex ...no reason, however grave, may be put forward by which anything intrinsically against nature may become conformable to nature and morally good. Since, therefore, the conjugal act is destined primarily by nature for the begetting of children, those who in exercising it, deliberately frustrating its natural power and purpose, sin against nature and commit a deed which is disgraceful and intrinsically vicious. - Pope Pius XI, Casti Connubii, December 31, 1930, Section 4, Paragraph 4.
Our Predecessor, Pius XI, of happy memory, in his Encyclical Casti Connubii of December 31, 1930, once again solemnly proclaimed the fundamental law of the conjugal act and conjugal relations: That every attempt of either husband or wife in the performance of the conjugal act or in the development of its natural consequences which aims at depriving it of its inherent force and hinders the procreation of a new life is immoral; and that no 'indication' or need can convert an act which is intrinsically immoral into a moral and lawful one ... This precept is in force today, as it was in the past, and so it will be in the future also, and always, because it is not a simple human whim, but the expression of a natural and divine law. - Pope Pius XII, Acta Apostilicae Sedis, XLIII (1951), page 843.

My nightmares of Mother started, if it had not been a timeless and continuous process, a few weeks after she died in the summer of nineteen eighty-three. Mother had always been fascinated by the history of local witches, reading extensively and often about Lancashire witches. When I first saw her lying in hospital; in the deadly dual green ward at Stepping Hill Hospital, of which the immortal phrase must surely have been written "Abandon Hope all ye who Enter Here" and where Death is regularly invited to staff case discussion groups as senior consultant; I did not know she was as ill as she was - but I noted with fear how witch-like she had become.

Mother's hair was iron grey and often favourably compared in terms of its tensile strength and durability to best industrial quality wire wool. As an older woman, despite carrying her smoke raddled lungs on raised vulture like shoulders where they might catch an iota or a few atoms more air, she retained her straight back and proud bearing and her iron hair was tamed and scraped close to her head, held there by her iron will.

As I entered the dark green women's ward on that hot summer's morning, desperately seeking a nurse or doctor to guide me to the right bed to avoid engaging with the old, the infirm, the incontinent, the damaged, the sad, the befuddled and the insane, my anxious gaze fell to its fascinated horror on the first bed on the right. Its occupant, an old woman, had kicked off the lower covers, leaving her entirely naked and exposed to my sinful, lapsed Catholic sight. I looked away. I searched more desperately for a nurse, a sister, a medic. None were to be seen. I looked again at the raddled bed and its shamed, neglected, lewd occupant - face loosely covered by a plastic mask and tube. Grey hair splayed out, tangled and knotted over the thin National Health pillows. It was Mother.

In our house, in our religion, in our lives, we did not have sex. Sex had no place in our lives, in our language, in our thoughts or in our hands – or deeds. I know for a positive fact – and believe with every vestige of my being, with every fibre of my body - which I hasten to assure you I know little of - that Mother never could have had sex. Particularly not with Father. The thought is impossible, blasphemous and treasonable. Six children she brought into the World – and every one a virgin birth. Notre Dame Convent School would have been proud of her. There is an apocryphal tale, told by Mother to Stephanie, that at the age of fourteen the nuns ejected her from school for "pirouetting before the plumbers" undoubtedly a Mortal Sin which killed her immortal soul. But I can be certain that Mother never indulged in "carnal knowledge". With this clear and incontrovertible fact in mind, everything that might be reported to the contrary is a damn lie. A Protestant lie! A Black Protestant lie!

Along with the Spirits, Demons, Ghosts, Witches, Monsters and the Ghouls who invaded our minds continuously and who leapt unbidden and unannounced from dark shadows to terrify us, our heads – no, not just our heads but our very substances - were also occupied by Fairies, Pixies, Elves, Gnomes, Goblins, Leprechauns and Guardian Angels. The Angels were by far the worst.

Ostensibly the Guardian Angels, sent from Heaven to care for each of us, and assigned for life, were something of a comfort.

When the Grim Butler, as our resident house-ghost came to be known after terrifying Richard's teenage visitors one late winter afternoon, plodded menacingly and lugubriously along the dark and lonely landing and paused for eternity outside my bedroom door, a swift conjuring up of my personalised, model forty-two Guardian Angel, brandishing a shining sword of light, years before Alec Guinness in Star Wars got one, would see the bugger off. A grim butler, particularly if he was a depressed Victorian shade of a grim butler, was no contestant for an energetic Guardian Angel with a shining sword. Mother also assured us time after time, that my Guardian Angel had oft' times saved my life. I had apparently had, and may even yet have, a hyperactive heavenly messenger who dashed around pulling me out of canals, steering my runaway pram through heavy traffic on Ashton Old Road, alerting doctors to potentially fatal diseases in the nick of time and stopping my racing feet on a sixpence as I was about to fling myself, all unknowing, under a passing car. Angels were damn useful at times.

Noel – aged 6, At Fort Clonque, aged 14
Aged 15, aged 22.

But, I suspect it was or is my Guardian Angel who reported all my transgressions back to St Peter at his gate and the Communion of Saints in Heaven. All my sins, mortal and venial were broadcast to the Heavenly Host, by, who else, my very own Angel – a Fifth Columnist planted in my brain.

So, how to escape the inevitable fate at the hands of the be-clawed and perverted demons with whips and pitchforks who gleefully wait the arrival in the Fires of Hell of this fornicating, flesh obsessed eleven-year-old (I assume some of you may have started at around that age – as I might have done if I had not listened to my conscience and been frightened to death of Sister Anthony). Fortunately, there is a way. The Catholic Church is a religion of hope and forgiveness (and love but that's a bit of an ambiguous word, open to misinterpretation, so its avoided by sensible Stockport Catholics), so an eleven-year-old – or younger sinners of pure evil down to seven years of age – can and must go to Church, wait in a queue in a pew, and then go into a little room and tell a man behind a cotton screen just what Universally shattering evil act, or God forbid, ACTS, they have been performing. He (and God forbid it should be a woman behind the screen and behind the dog collar) will instantly and always forgive me, you or him; whichever of us did it – on the spot. Saved in an instant from eternal death and pain and suffering and torment for spilling your seed upon the ground – and I guess that lets out girls – but I don't think about those things.

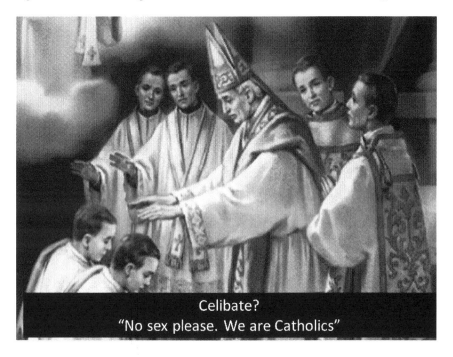

Celibate?
"No sex please. We are Catholics"

So – Guardian Angels are almost always great news up to the age of puberty, when the unclean realise they have secret desires, which they are not allowed to think about, let alone act on, and every time they do – Bingo, the thought police have got them dead to rights. This is how I know, proof-positive, that Mother reproduced only by way of the miraculous mechanism of Virgin Birth. Mother knew that my

Guardian Angel had saved my life on numerous occasions. She knew when my Guardian Angel made a move; Ipso Facto, she knew my Guardian Angel on a person-to-person basis. I never made that kind of contact. Humans who hobnob with Angels are clearly pure – and Catholic Sex is evil and dirty – so there it is; Mother did not indulge in sex. Most Catholics don't; and nor would you if your every thought word and deed was being relayed back to base from inside your head.

The Catholic thought-police are not only activated by smutty, sexual stirrings. In brainwashing techniques, the hierarchy are second to none and leave nothing to chance. A child who might, just might forget about these resident characters just long enough to indulge in pre-or post-pubertal sexual fantasising is reminded of the Thought-Police's presence weekly and sometimes daily by dietary restrictions such as fasting before Holy Communion and not eating meat on Fridays and giving up fattening crisps and sweets for the whole of Lent. Whenever a Catholic thinks of food or sex, guilt kicks in fast to repress their unnatural urges, and to make them sweaty and spotty.

With such daily education as we received about such deeply ingrained animal urges and with such persistent education about evil thoughts words and deeds - there was no sex in our house, thank you very much.

So seeing Mother in disarray and almost naked on that Stepping Hill Hospital bed in a common ward full of dying old women, was a shock to my Catholic soul.

We never touched in our house. Once, aged seven, when I had been in great pain with a mastoid behind my left ear and had been sitting on the kitchen floor weeping on and off, clutching the warm stove for some comfort, and had been there, on and off, moaning for three days, Father made a move to comfort me. A move that, thank God - or my ever-vigilant Guardian Angel - was never consummated. This man, my alleged Father, stood over me and leaned down as if to lay his hand on my shoulder. I instantly stopped crying and froze into silence. All sound, movement and autonomic processes ceased as I clung in rigid paralysis to the side of the kitchen stove. Eternity yawned over the moment; the terrible possibility that he may actually touch suspended the Universe for a long, long instant. Then, to both of our deepest relief, he withdrew, and I breathed again and took up my whining with pain where I had left off, as if nothing had happened.

To touch Mother or Father, other than being slapped at by Father in a rare moment of rage, when he was driving, was a libidinous, blasphemous, flesh crawling concept. It was just not done. To touch a brother or our sister was only ever done in anger or in the rough and tumble of teeth grinding siblings trying to dispose of each other under the guise of innocent childish play.

A Jewish girl from the South, the beautiful Ruth, visited Pauline and me in our first year of marriage. On leaving she moved to kiss me as I held the door. I instinctively ducked away in terror. Such contact meant only one thing for a well trained Catholic - and I could hardly indulge in a quick knee trembler in my own hallway, by the open door with my new wife watching - however attracted to the beautiful Ruth I might have been. My wife, though a Black Protestant, fitted well into this world-view of the sins of the flesh. She had also received her sex education only from illicit delving into medical encyclopaedia's. She also had a Father who never, ever touched her and a Mother who rarely did. She also knew that masturbation, self-abuse, made you mad, blind and deaf.

Those of you who, as lower mortals, have spent their lives wracked by constant self-abuse, torn between the agony of guilt and the ecstasy of delayed multiple orgasms, may yet convince yourselves that you have escaped the consequences of your vile pleasures - but time will tell; and God, who has nothing more important to do in the Universe than to poke around in the heads of, acutely observe and simultaneously admonish and record the inner thoughts of sexually mature individuals from one of the more prolific branches of the great apes, while they indulge in natural and unnatural acts (being the only vertebrate mammal capable of unnatural sexual acts and of doing naughty things with their erogenous zones), will strike you down, on Judgement Day, as your life and all its intimate details, including every single visit to the lavatory, which some undoubtedly enjoy more than God ever intended them to, are replayed to the Heavenly Hosts, in colour and with perfect surround-sound, including your parents, teachers and next door neighbours. How do you feel about that - you secret fornicators!

God is clearly very concerned with your private parts; with the large and small holes which give access to your insides; with any nerve endings capable of pleasurable stimulation. You may note the mating habits of butterflies and dragon-flies and dogs and cats and rabbits, and you may smile with unconcerned indulgence. Not so the Catholic God who made the entire Universe. He (sorry girls, but it is definitely a He) takes time out from making Suns and Moons and Stars and Galaxies which live twelve billion years and He minutely records every stray touch, every little spurt of precious bodily fluid, every sinful stimulation – and, informed by your Guardian Angel, He stores up his eternal revenge. He is something of a sadistic sexually obsessed psychotic maniac.

In my Catholic world we did not touch, other than to punish. And nobody had sex. Or even knew what it was; least of all, Sister Anthony, Father Burnley and Mother.

***

Chapter 10 - Medical Treatment

On 5 July 1948, Sylvia Beckingham was admitted to hospital in Manchester to be treated for a liver condition. Doubtless this was a big event in her life; but it was an even bigger event in British history. Sylvia, 13, was the first patient to be treated on the NHS. - Independent Newspaper

Once on a foggy morning, when I was about eight years old, I walked abroad with my faithful black dog Bobby. The area still had working farms and miles of open land and we were soon lost in the mists on an unfamiliar expanse of untended fields. The mists thickened and I realised I was disorientated and a long way from home. I pushed on to find a landmark and at last saw a farm gate ahead and a tall man standing by the gate with his back to me. "Excuse me Sir" I started as I neared the gate, "can you direct me to..." As I spoke the man turned - And, horror of horrors, he had no face!! Terrified, I screamed and I ran. I ran on and on gasping for breath, caring little where I was going, to escape that terrible apparition. Exhaustion at last slowed me and I noticed my surroundings again. The mist thinned from time to time and to my joy I saw a church I recognised. As I scrambled through the old graveyard, the mists closed in again but I knew there was a lane on the other side of the church wall - and, to my joy a stagecoach was waiting in the lane, with a seated coachman protected from the mists by a tri-corn hat and large collared cape. Still in deep shock and on my last legs I hurried to the wall. "Help, help", I cried - "I've just seen a man with No Face!" - "Like MINE?" he mocked mournfully, as he turned his blank visage towards me.

I was leaning by the radio on that sunny Sunday lunchtime as Mother prepared the Sunday roast, listening intently so as not to miss any of the jokes on the Kenneth Horne Show. We never sued the BBC or Mr. Horne for not issuing a health warning for any overly imaginative, under-tens who might not find the story amusing. I didn't. As the punch line "Like Mine" was delivered, I literally screamed, collapsed and screamed and screamed and screamed. Eventually, after an hour or so, they called Dr Fay who came up from Didsbury Road and injected something or other that made me sleep for two days. Then I was perfect again. For a time.

It was, according to Mother, the intervention of my hyperactive Guardian Angel and not of the rather terse and forbidding Dr Fay that saved me from an unusual and painful death from Mastoids. The unsmiling, overworked Dr Fay was most remembered by us for stitching my knee on the kitchen table after I had fallen onto a tree root while running hard at Alderley Edge, on a day trip with the Delaneys. Lawrence Delaney was my best friend at primary school.

They had brought me back home in their car, all the way from Alderley, with my leg gashed open to the kneecap, the skin folded in and under itself making a thick wad of displaced flesh over the white bone, and Mother summoned Dr Fay from his Sunday lunch, who without discussion or warning took out his curved needles and cat-gut, gathered several adults to hold me down yelling on the kitchen table and sewed up the wound with three substantial stitches that he tied firmly across the kneecap. For weeks after I limped twice a week the two miles to his surgery on Didsbury Road, sat for the statutory two hours with the infectious and the dying of the district in the doctor's waiting room, and was injected fiercely in the thigh with penicillin and stomped stiff-legged home again, until the wound was deemed germ free. "Crescent scar on the left knee," is the one identifying mark noted on my passport that will undoubtedly still be recognisable when the rest of me has decayed. I'm sure I can still detect Dr Fay's signature faintly inscribed in the scar tissue.

"Did the dry Dr. Fay, I now wonder, have a macabre sense of humour in decorating his waiting room for the halt, lame, wounded, hacking, spitting huddled masses with such a skeletal tale of bleak despair?"

In fact, the mastoid pre-dated the long-suffering Dr Fay; who I also remember for a short-case pendulum clock, loud and solemnly ticking that hung in his brown-on-dark-brown waiting room, next to the long Victorian print with reds and pale blues illustrating Tom Pearce, Tom Pearce, Lend me your Grey Mare, where all the players and the poor mare end as skeletons, haunting the moors in the final scene. Did the dry Doctor Fay, I now wonder, have a macabre sense of humour in decorating his waiting room for the halt, the lame, the wounded, the hacking, the spitting, and the spluttering huddled masses, with such a skeletal tale of bleak despair.

The mastoid, miraculously as ever, announced its sinister presence when I was just six.

School dinners, provided by Stockport Town Council in huge aluminium vacuum flasks just to ensure an advantageous early start into Alzheimer's, at St. Winifred's Primary were, apart from being inedible and stinking strangely, served in a large neglected conservatory, dripping with condensation, at patterned oilcloth covered trestle tables. As a course was finished children were detailed off to help the truculent Dinner Ladies clear the tables. When the dank atmosphere and sullen Northern inertia even defeated these combined forces, one or more teachers leapt briskly into the fray and whisked and wiped energetically to keep things moving. It was the homely and kindly Mrs Jarvis who taught the seven year olds, who standing over our table with a pile of used plates and utensils, dropped a knife that clunked hard behind my right ear as it fell to the damp concrete floor.

That afternoon I was sent home early crying with pain. I trudged the mile or so of streets in gentle rain, legs chaffed and reddened by the rim of my wet grey flannel shorts, a consequence of having thrown away my raincoat, and eventually arrived during Mother's afternoon rest, her time for sitting by the fire, under the standard-lamp in the Morning Room reading, knitting, sewing or whatever she was inclined to do after housework and before making the main meal of the day, our Tea.

In pain, I found some small comfort sitting on the cold tiles by the old metal-framed kitchen fire and pressing my ear against its warm extremities. The newly loaded clothes rack high above dripped in interesting ways, occasionally hissing and spitting when they struck the coals. But despite the warmth and the unpredictable droplets, I wept continuously. After three days Mother had had enough. We caught the number nine bus to the doctor's surgery on Wellington Road, where we were still registered from our previous address in Derby Road, Heaton Moor before we had moved in an upwardly mobile direction to Birch House, in tree lined Mauldeth Road, in the more refined if shabbier and overgrown district of Heaton Mersey.

The doctor acted immediately and I was whisked by ambulance, silver, shiny bell ringing gloriously and satisfactorily, to Stockport Infirmary where they decided the mastoid was too advanced to operate on. I understood with some glee and fascination that the offending mastoid was a mass of concealed pus and infection eating its way along the mastoid bone, above the ear, and eventually into the brain where it would kill me. But as an immortal six-year-old this medical intelligence did not frighten but only intrigued me.

It's important to understand here that Stepping Hill Hospital, Stockport, whose main entrance is still flanked by two undertakers' offices (this is still the literal truth) and where newly trained abattoir attendants are suddenly and uniquely recognised as fine medical surgeons and set to work on the patients; where Mother died in disgraceful conditions; was quite a different place from Stockport Infirmary, the white, late Victorian building opposite Stockport Town Hall, set on the hill climbing up out of Mersey Square in the direction of Buxton. Even though both medical establishments were on the same roadway and separated by only a few miles, they were distinguished by the latter having been a place of resuscitation and repair and the former, Stepping Hill, being an ante-room to medical incompetence at its worst and an unpleasant and unnecessary death.

My Guardian Angel, as Mother told it, was definitely taking care of me. Not only did it steer the ambulance away from Stepping Hill, but it took me to the Infirmary. The Infirmary doctors knew what they did not know and sent to London for a specialist surgeon. All free in 1948 on the new National Health. The specialist decided not to operate and to try the wonder drug, Penicillin that had saved so many wounded during the war. The good news was there was to be no operation, two pieces of bad news followed. First and foremost, to my mind, there were no empty beds in the children's wards - only cots. I suffered the huge indignity at six of being confined in a large cot. Second, the penicillin dosage was massive. I suffered an injection for each year of my age, six, in the buttocks, every few hours, for several days. In those days, parents were not allowed to stay and visits were strongly discouraged so I faced, or rather backed into, this ordeal alone.

I dimly remember only a high, long room in pale green, with my cot last in a row of beds. Other children were dotted around, some playing on the floor on the far side. The pain of the continual injections has receded leaving a residual phobia about needles. But I know even now that it hurt a lot.

Penicillin, that miracle of modern science, accidentally discovered by Fleming, developed in Oxford, and mass-produced in America; together with my Guardian Angel navigating the ambulance, and of course dropping a knife on my mastoid bone, saved me from certain death. And another great tale was added to Mother's repertoire of family mythology.

My mastoid was not Mrs Jarvis's fault. Even if it had been we would never have sued. Teachers were held in high regard and all parents in those good old days deferred to the teacher's better judgement and unquestionable good motives.

Saint Winifred's RC school was housed in a dilapidated but still proud Georgian style mansion with fat fluted pillars at the main entrance and had once all been painted white. It stood a hundred yards back from Didsbury Road at the end of what had become a large, flat, earthen school playground. The Gate-House was now a tuck shop where we could spend our pocket money and our sweets-coupons. The house stood right on the western edge of Heaton moor, with views across the Cheshire Plain almost to Liverpool, by a steep slope that had been terraced and planted lower down with rhododendrons, now neglected and leggy. Children were not allowed down the slope, so the land below was a mysterious forbidden place. Looking back to the road, on the left of the playground was the floor and yard of a large stable block - bombed it was rumoured - backed by a six-foot high brick wall. Behind the wall was the long driveway to another large house, hidden half way down the hill. This had been converted to a convent to which the grand-dame Sister Anthony, our unchallengeable Headmistress and the young and humourless Sister Angela, who taught the nine years old, repaired to of an evening after school. The parish congregation processed in the beautiful, steep convent grounds once a year when a girl was chosen to crown the statue of the Virgin Mary in May. All the children were dressed in white and the May Queen was photographed for the local paper.

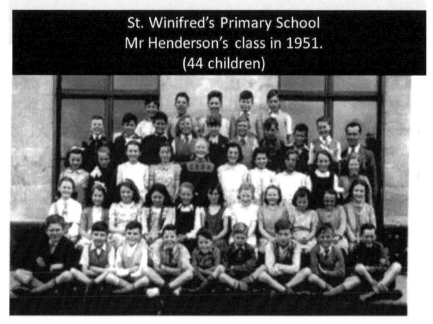

One year our young sister Stephanie was so honoured and was duly photographed for the local paper, attracting the attentions of a heavy breather who phoned us several times a day for two weeks until, one evening Father, ever a practical man, answered the phone, ascertained it was the heavy-breather, and fired a starter's pistol an inch from and directly into the solid black Bakelite mouthpiece. We surmised it had

had the desired effect of blowing the caller's ear drum out of his head – as he never called again.

On the right of the wide playground at Saint Winifred's and about fifty yards nearer the road and on a rise stood a tall, gaunt Victorian mansion, where the parish priest Father Burnley and his acolytes lurked behind closed doors and net curtains. It fell to me one day to hit a cricket ball through the priests' kitchen window showering, it was clerically alleged, a salad lunch with broken glass, causing a fuss for several days as I was identified, quizzed, reported to my apologetic parents, no doubt terrified they might lose a star from their crowns in heaven, and obliged to write a Note of Apology. I guess that Father paid for the window.

Infant and schooldays illnesses aside, I had no real pain until I was ten or eleven. Particularly in the winter, after or even during a meal, a searing pain gripped me in the solar-plexus and gnawed away at my innards for hours on end. Two treatments helped – the first being to sit with my back to the hot Aga stove in the kitchen and let the heat seep comfortingly into my middle and the second, when I was in bed or ready for bed, was to don my dark-brown, scratchy dressing gown and use the silk bi-coloured twisted cord as a tourniquet, tightening it more and more to squeeze the pain out of my centre to some other place. Often, I employed both remedies together, particularly late at night when the pain woke me up. I crept downstairs into the kitchen, clad in my ticking dressing gown, sipped a cup of hot milk, sat against the Aga stove and twisted the cord while rocking back and forth and moaning quietly. Mother, who knew almost everything, diagnosed indigestion and I took to keeping a constant supply of *Horlicks Tablets* and *Rennies* that I could suck in emergencies such as at school or in the cinema. Twenty-five years later the recurring attacks of indigestion turned out to be duodenal ulcers and were cured, thanks to the decisive intervention of our wonderful friend, excellent surgeon and my life saviour Anthony, who cut me open and sewed me up again in a meticulously straight line, having bamboozled me into medical examinations, kidnapped me from my vital office work, introduced me to a miraculous surgeon, Mr King at St. Stephens in Fulham, who performed a now extinct, intricate 'Highly Selective Vagotomy" operation, who is single-handedly to blame for my now rotund and well-padded waistline, and having personally assisted the fabled Mr King in the operation. Thank you, Anthony, for changing my life from one of continual pain and diet to one of painless, normal enjoyment of food and drink. Surely one of the archangels must have borne that blessed name.

The constant pain of the ulcers prevented me from drinking any beer, that may well have saved me from my brothers' curse of alcoholism and it changed my square and robust frame into that of a gaunt Giacometti-like stick insect. Most days I could manage the pain by diverting my mind away from it and containing it in a holding area until I got home, was alone and could rock and moan in private. Readers who are lapsed Catholics, as am I, may have good grounds to interpret these decades of acute pain as a just punishment for the sensual sins of youth and for having the temerity to question the Church's condemnation of Galileo who heretically claimed that Kepler was right and Aristotle was wrong and that the Earth did indeed travel round the Sun, not the other way about, as The Church then passionately believed; and believed up to Nineteen-Seventy.

Mother's comprehensive and catholic understanding of medical conditions was only a tad less than her grasp of history and politics.
"Noel..." she informed her mesmerised audience one winter's eve, "...was cross-eyed when he was born."

The brothers looked at me and stared piercingly into my eyes to detect the slightest signs of orbital drift. Even Father, not wishing to have to admit to having sired a defective or a freak, spared a non-committal glance in my direction to assure himself that, while he did not need to or indeed dared not doubt or challenge Mother's powers of memory and observation; whatever skink-eyed problem I might have been born with he had indubitably cured, on his return from the War in nineteen forty-five, by promptly and determinedly forcing the change over from a left-handed to a right-handed son. Though of relatively little importance in the general sense, if you had to have a second son, an embarrassed and largely mute second son at that, he may as well be properly orientated to his right, and not be a suspect left-hander with all the weaknesses and strangeness that could imply. He duly reassured himself and promptly lost interest. Not so the first-born.

"Yeah..." said Richard with deep relish, peering ever more closely at my startled and now scarlet and defended face,
"...he is a bit cross-eyed, isn't he?" Richard poked an authoritative digit at my eye and invited the others to join him in minute scrutiny of my increasingly alarmed features.

"I'm not cross-eyed." I protested loudly.

"You are you know." said Richard, warming to his theme.

"You can't see it yourself but when you're not thinking about it, that eye….." he again made to prod me harshly in my right eye and I ducked instinctively.

"…that eye doesn't move like the other one – it sort of sticks and makes you look like this…." He glared with one eye at his nose while contriving to keep the other pale blue orb of gristle peering at me mockingly.

"…It's not fully cross-eyed…." He persisted, now bringing both his eyes to glare madly at the bridge of his nose.

"…like that, but he's definitely not straight. You'll probably get worse as you get older; won't he Mum?" asked Richard rhetorically, seeking to add parental weight to his prognosis.

I jumped up and stared into the mirror above the radio on the sideboard.

"I'm not cross-eyed am I Mum." I protested, also seeking leave to appeal to the highest court. Mother looked through me, not recognising the rising panic and the urgency of this issue.

"You can't see it in the mirror…" Richard assured me.

" …'cause then you look straight ahead at it. It's when you're not thinking about it that it goes crooked" he added narrowly, feigning deep concern.

"I'll bet you see double sometimes don't you."

"No I don't." I protested angrily, my mind racing to recall any double vision. Lying in bed, the window did sometimes recede from me, as if I were looking down the wrong end of a telescope. This thought became evidence to unsettle my certainty that my eyes always worked properly.

"But you are a bit cross-eyed anyway." Richard pressed on.

"You'll have to wear glasses or an eye-patch to cover it up, or you'll frighten people; looking like that. It'll get worse and worse and worse, and you might go blind."

"I'm not cross-eyed." I yelled at him.

"Shut-up! I'm not cross-eyed."

"You are a bit." Richard assured me allowing one of his eyes to slide off the parallel by way of further demonstration.

"It's not too bad." he added in a conciliatory tone,

"Probably one of those really thick lenses like looking through the bottom of a bottle will fix it when you get glasses."

"I don't need glasses." I screamed at him wildly. "Shut your Gob."

"It's just a bit out of line. That eye now. Isn't it Peter?" asked Richard of the four-year-old, who was innocently and immediately drawn in to the taunting and who followed Richard's accusing finger with a serious contemplation of my face.

"I dunno" proffered Peter honestly, "It might be a bit slanted."

"There you are. You can't see it yourself. And it's not really bad. Just a bit sliding. It's alright really. It'll be alright but just a bit cross-eyed." Richard consoled me, keeping just out of range of my clenched fist.

"I'm not cross-eyed." I screamed at him lunging for the heavy iron poker that stood in the grate.
"I'm not cross-eyed. Shut up. Shut up." I had the poker in my grasp as Richard, anticipating every move, raced to the door and held it slightly ajar, his face registering nothing but a blank kind of curiosity as he wound the spring one notch tighter.

He said no more. He just stood in the doorway and slid one eye out of position and pointed at my face. The stage was now set. I was fully primed. He was in a defendable position and so the game, a game that was deadly in intent, was played out.
"I'm not cross-eyed." I screamed at him hurling the hefty poker with manic strength and astonishing accuracy at his mean head as it sneered at me from atop his narrow shoulders. Richard, inevitably, as it had to be, ducked behind the door, pulling it closed. The poker; one of my better shots; struck the door 'bang' at the gap where he had that split second disappeared, missing his one remaining finger by a fraction, and biting a sizeable chunk of wood off the edge near the doorknob before clattering and bouncing on the tiles.

"What the hell is going on?" roared Father; jerked out of his endless reverie as I followed up the throw with my own screaming body and slammed it against the door, trying to claw it open to get at Richard and tear his face off. But we had contrived the set and the rules very precisely and my rage was spent in a futile tug of war at the handle of the now shut door, with Richard resisting with all his strength on the other side. Father wrestled me away from the door, wrenched it open and dragged Richard back into the kitchen, the merest hint of a smirk playing over his thin features. Father picked up the poker, replaced it by the fire and began to lose interest.

"I'm not cross-eyed. Am I Mum?" I sobbed, sweating and pink with post-rage blood pressure.

"Well you were when you were born" she continued evenly, seemingly oblivious to the near death experience of her eldest and to my immense rage and distress.

"I took you to the clinic in Ashton. And they said that I should bring you back when you were three and they'd fit you with glasses – you know those awful national health glasses with pink wire frames; and blank out one of the eye-pieces..."

I was deeply aware of Richard almost visibly grinning as she told the story but we were all getting too engrossed for me to react.

"...You weren't really cross-eyed. They said. You had a lazy eye. One of your eyes didn't move as fast as the other one – it didn't work properly. Well I wasn't going to have a child with those horrible glasses with sticking plaster over them – like a slum child, like a street urchin from Ardwick or Gorton. But they said there was nothing else to do. But I took you home..." She said ruminatively, lost in her own deep memories of this important incident,
"...and I found a Doctor." She continued with a determination of purpose quite foreign in her.

"He was a very good Doctor." She assured us and herself, with such strength of expression that we knew beyond doubt just how useless, stupid and incompetent they were at the Ashton clinic; inexcusably incompetent, despite the War that poured all the nation's resources into the armed forces.

"I didn't want a baby with a squint."

I could hear Richard's mouth split into a mean smile behind my back.

"And I asked him about what They..." she almost spat the word,
"...had said at the clinic. Well he said that he could fix it. So he put drops in your eye..."
Mother turned her gaze on me but was still seeing her precious baby in the hands of the last capable doctor in Britain.
"...Not the bad eye, but the good eye. He made you blind in your good eye and forced the lazy eye to start working properly – and it worked. It took just a few weeks. I took you back three or four times and each

time he put the drops in your eye – the right eye was the lazy one, so he put them in the left eye; in the eye that was working. And within a month or two you lost your squint."

Mother concluded with deep self-satisfaction at the initiative that she, while Father was away, had taken to save her child from a terrible affliction and fate; a rare and valuable initiative taken by her – the lioness protecting her cub.

"And it was all free – even before the National Health" she added by way of historical footnote.

"Otherwise you would have grown up having to wear glasses and with a squint – because I very much doubt that the treatment they recommended at the clinic would have done anything at all. By the time you were three, it'd be far too late. They didn't know what they were talking about. Stupid people. 'Bring him back when he's three and we'll give him glasses.' Ignorant lot. And they were supposed to be trained professionals. A fat lot they knew."

***

Chapter 11 - Gorsey-Bank

The river has been cleaned up over the past 25 years by The Mersey Basin Campaign, which was set up after the river was condemned in the 1980s by a government minister. The then secretary of state for the environment, Michael Heseltine, visited the area and said the river was "an affront to the standards a civilised society should demand of its environment". BBC News

Aged five in 1948 I was initiated into the strange primary school community of Saint Winifred's comprising a couple of hundred children flanked by a house of celibate priests on one side and a convent of celibate nuns on the other. Being products of the War Bulge or Baby Boom our classes were fifty strong, teachers were little trained and resources over-stretched. In the first class, taught by Miss Halissey, a mild lady in her mid-twenties with red hair and a pale face, I fell in love with Alison. We never spoke, but I loved her neat silent demeanour, her grave little face, well-brushed brown hair and her pretty black dress with a white lacy collar. She left in the second or third term, still without us exchanging a word, and she disappeared. I never even knew her surname. My best friend was the good natured, powerfully built Lawrence Delaney who lived in a modern semi in Hawthorn Grove close to the north end of the clay-pits. I was also, pre-ulcers, a strong boy, and good at school-work. I was always full of ideas of games to play and things to do so, with my brains and Lawrence's boldness, we had a small following, rivalled by a similar group led by a thin, instinctively suspicious boy who lived in Heaton Norris; down the hill towards Mersey Square, where I had never yet ventured.

Two years later aged seven I was emboldened sufficiently to tag along with Richard and three other intrepid older boys when they ventured down into Heaton Norris and beyond into the dangerous territory of the violent local gang, known as the 'Gorsey-Bankers'.

On a deceptively mild and life enhancing spring afternoon, we turned right out of the school gates along Didsbury Road on our assortment of bikes, mine was small, as befitted a small boy, and was hand painted, by me, in silver paint – a veritable silver chariot that could take me anywhere on earth. We rode past Leeman's Field with its steep sledging hill, ponies, stream and pond and turned right into the passageway opposite the forbidding frontage of Barnes Home – rumoured to be a Borstal reform school for errant boys - by the eerie bombed house where I had once been stuck in the rubble blocked cellar, at the top of the hill above Stockport. The passageway was long and narrow, dark and hemmed in by tall spindly hawthorn hedges that we zoomed between in a headlong flight down towards the evil waters of the River Mersey. The steeply descending passage seemed endless as we bounced over its pitted asphalt surface but eventually it flattened out to a no-man's land in a nearly derelict farm, flanked by the stinking River Mersey, by dilapidated mills and, ahead of us, our terrifying destination, by The Bridge.

...by the stinking River Mersey, by dilapidated mills and, ahead of us, our terrifying destination, The Bridge.

The Bridge stood on huge oval brick piers, erected for eternity by the Victorians. Its galvanised iron shuttered sides started twenty feet above the river and climbed another thirty feet into the turbid sky. It spanned the polluted, filthy river at a long shallow angle pointing north-west, as if it cared nothing for the oily turbulent waters below and could afford to stretch endlessly over them, striding from pier to pier, staring straight and fixedly into the far distance. Where it eventually pressed its giant elbows on the far bank was the land of the infamously violent Gorsey-Bankers.

With the bikes huddled together for safety against a yellowing grassy mound we approached the brick pier on foot in awed silence. The pier, though immense, was obviously scalable. Bricks and stones had been smoothed over many years by many feet and hands, marking the eight foot climb up to a menacing thirty-foot-high black slot where the iron sheets slid themselves into the pier. The pier's foundations stood half on the thin sandy earth and half in the shallow scummy waters. We scrambled up to a stone ledge, inched along it and suddenly disappeared from sight into the dark echoing innards of that monumental structure. Incised and paint scrawled initials and gang symbols shouted that this was not our place we were left in no doubt that we were trespassing. This was Gorsey-Banker territory.

It was whispered that the gang's most recent apocryphal crime was to have attacked a girl, stripped her, tied her to a pole and floated her in the river. The pole rolled and the unfortunate victim was drowned. Or, perhaps worse, the filthy waters had poisoned her beyond recovery. These were mean and desperate vandals, to be avoided at perhaps the cost of your life.

Inside the vast structure, metal beams and spars criss-crossed in an intricate and brain defying pattern. The shade was deep and gloomy and the bridge was far, far wider than it seemed from outside. It stretched forward a long, long way, its far end hidden in deepening gloom. The immediate view on either side was stopped by solid sheets of iron cladding that climbed up and up into the intricate and ever darker patterns above. It was impossible to gauge the height over our heads. We gathered in a nervous whispering cluster, hovering between the earthed solid brick pier at our backs and the suspended bewildering fretwork of ageing metal ahead. One of the older boys launched out into space, his front foot stepping into a square bucket-like structure that gathered the ends of five or six angle irons. He drew his other foot forward and stood in the bucket. We saw that the buckets recurred in an endless procession, each suspended above the swirling, black, chemical foam fifteen feet below. Here was a cumbersome highway on which the brave and fool-hardy could with time and concentration cross the dead waters. The sound of the river was magnified over and over by the hollow tin drum of the bridge but despite the noise we kept our voices to a whisper. None could tell who might be listening, nor how close they might be in that industrial iron web. We followed the leader. Each step a full stretch to place a foot carefully and at an awkward angle into the next bucket then a pause to draw the back foot forward – clinging hard to the supports and shuddering whenever we glanced down at the oily liquid.

Without warning, the immense shock from the nerve shattering noise of a speeding train thundering across above us was intensified by it wrenching us from our furious attention on the perilous path we trod. Reeling and terrified we stared wildly at our thin line of friends, all grasping pocked iron bars and braces that trembled and vibrated as the skull banging noise filled the bridge, shook our bones and made the water below dance in minute standing waves. The noise roared on and on, seemingly without any prospect of ending. How long could any train be? We dared not let go to cover our ears – we simply had to endure. The storm passed at last and receded into the distance, the vast bridge booming its lugubrious song long after the train's passage, as the steel rails conducted its drumming signature from afar.

As the bridge stopped shaking, so did we. And we laughed, little short breaths of relief, as knowledge of the cause sank in. Our line was now well spread out; the boldest leading and me, the youngest, trailing behind with two or three boxes between each explorer. We could now see the whole surface of the river and the far bank. The far bank was shiny black with coal dust and absorbed oil. A cinder footpath flanked the river then gave way to a wide weedy flat plateau, defiled with industrial waste and derelict brick sheds that seemed to never have had a purpose. Beyond this depressing margin, grim terraces of Victorian brick houses huddled with their backs to us in surly ranks; every small blue slate roof punctuated by a thin brick chimney. From the chimneys smoke from coal-fires rose reluctantly into the habitually dank air.

Even today, with the sun announcing that Spring would surely come again, even here, the air over the blackened brick walls barely had the energy to conduct the blue smoke upwards and away. The terraces were quiet. Washing could be seen hanging in tight little backyards, but no people bustled about their daily business. The serried rows of dwellings half-heartedly acknowledged the existence and direction of the river at their backs but they couldn't maintain their forlorn interest in that sullen, natural phenomenon. After a sad gap of fifty yards of derelict land, as the bank came to meet the far end of the bridge, a mill of some sort, clearly working and sporting new aluminium smoke stacks at various junctures, poured an endless stream of something fluid - a bubbling poisonous grey white - into the already overburdened sewer that was the River Mersey.

We, children of the Second World War, born into the new but mean peace that followed, hung silently in our metal baskets, our leader about half-way along the span, over this broad sewer and silently, and we hoped secretly, observed the minutiae of a neglected, severely impoverished, slum area. All was quiet.

Things happened suddenly around this brooding bridge; and, as suddenly as the train had assaulted us, as if from nowhere, a gang came running fast along the cinder track. This was no gang of children like us. This was a gang of pinched-faced youths in hand-me-down jackets and patched trousers, some as tall as six feet, wearing adult caps and braces. They were running towards their end of the bridge – and as they ran they pointed at our suspended paralysed forms and shouted harsh imprecations. The Gorsey-Bankers had us in their sights and we were frozen in fear, frozen to the unsympathetic innards of their glowering and bafflingly geometric bridge.

"Run Noel! Run – it's the Gorsey-Bankers" somebody yelled at me; which was an improbable imperative, as running was not remotely possible through those shin cracking girders.

I was the last in and had to be the first out. I was small with short legs. Each box was about a yard from the last and a false step could have seen me dangling by one hand high above the almost certainly lethal river. But the choice was small. It was either cracked shins, plunging into the river, or capture by the infamous Gorsey-Bankers. The risk of cracked shins or of drowning had it by a mile and - as the Gorsey-Bankers swarmed effortlessly, hardly breaking stride, towards us through the struts, and their threats echoed again and again off the iron cladding – I did the impossible and almost ran from box to box, pressed ever closer by my terrified friends. Their feet were clumping down into a box almost before mine had left, snagging my heels time after time, threatening to lose my shoes and pitch me into the leering waters. After an eternity of scrambling through iron lattices, above the river, the immense brick pier was suddenly beneath my feet and my four friends arrived simultaneously at the narrow exit that we vanished through like insubstantial wraiths. The Gorsey-Bankers were astonishingly and frighteningly already two thirds of the way across the bridge as we leapt and fell down the pier onto the ground and pelted to our bikes. As the first ugly, gangly youth emerged from the slot and leapt to the ground – we were pedalling furiously, far enough away for even the fastest runner to give up hope of pursuit. Their threats and bitter scorn leant wings to our feet and power to our trembling thighs as we tackled the steep rise up the narrow footpath back to the civilised realms of Heaton Moor and Heaton Mersey.

I never went back to that spot and even after that bleak central town area was cleared of slums in the more prosperous sixties – unconscious memories always guided me away from that grim river valley that lurked in poisonous mist just a few miles from home.

One good thing about our childhoods was the freedom to go out to play without adult supervision, or even their knowledge. From the age of five I could leave the house and wander far and wide, alone or with pals, and go wherever we cared to. One early playground, near Derby Road, which I was sometimes allowed by the seven and eight year olds to sample with them, was a large empty closed-up house standing well back in its own grounds from the main Heaton Moor Road. The house had outbuildings, a fine garage with rooms above, a boiler house, several brick gardening sheds and glasshouses. It was an enticing arena for our imaginative games – made more exciting by No Trespassing notices at the fine wide gates; which guaranteed that we had the place to ourselves. I wasn't there when the local policeman caught my brother and friends inside the house – having made just a small entrance hatch through a rear door.

The arrest of those delinquent trespassing children (not saintly me of course) turned into a major case, deeply embarrassing to Father who was standing in the Stockport Council elections – and to Mother who was deeply shy, especially of duly designated authorities. There were letters and summonses and hearing dates discussed. In those days, rascally kids could be sent to Boarstal, children's prisons, to be beaten and starved and locked away for decades, we thought; so it was a worrying time. There existed such a hostile child prison at the edge of Heaton Moor, Barnes' Home, which behind dark green twenty-foot-high hedges and fences, had a sinister fifty-yards dark frontage and opaque windows, like a grim Dickensian mill from the days of The Poor House. "Abandon Hope All Ye Who Enter Here". No one was ever seen or heard in the grounds, at the windows, or entering or leaving.

In the event, Richard and the other criminals were washed, brushed, made to stand straight and in great fear were taken by car into central Stockport, to the Police Headquarters …and there reprimanded by the Chief Constable in person.

That changed their criminal tendencies and curbed their incurable curiosity – for a while.

But bombed out houses, in ruins, with shrubs and trees growing through the rubble, were fair game for our games.

Another large house, set back from another main road, was such a bombed ruin, which we commandeered for a time. It stood, or had stood, off Didsbury Road, opposite the forbidding mass of Barnes Home, on the corner of the narrow long pathway that wound down to Gorsey Bank. The bomb had left the back wall and some chimney breasts partially intact and had caved in the rest of the building, crushing it into the cellars. In ten or twelve years, the persistent Manchester rains had nurtured new growth from every space between the bricks and timbers. The boundary hedges, fences and walls had deteriorated leaving access for determined boys to wriggle through – and to disappear into the ruin. Inside, aged seven and alone, one day I found a deep fissure that took me down into a cellar, which was only part filled with fallen debris. A little light percolated from above, but there was nothing to see except an empty stone flagged floor and brick dust. I started out, scrambling upwards. Some bricks shifted; not far, but enough to narrow the passage and stop my climb. I tried to pull and push the bricks back to where they had come from – but the many tons above held them firm. I was trapped and claustrophobia crept into my nervous system. The word "entombed", plucked from a book about pyramids, echoed around my mind and chilled my soul. Astute readers will have already realised that as I am writing this story – I must have escaped and lived to tell the tale. Was my bike, leaning against the outer fence, recognised by a rescuer, who investigated and found my rubble filled narrow burrow? No, it didn't happen like that. In desperation I squirmed and huffed and puffed and scrabbled and skinned my hands and knees; and got stuck several more times on the way up that short tunnel. Fearing for my life, I eventually clambered out at ground level into the daylight – mounted my trusty steed and cycled home. And I kept the incident to myself, so as not to risk any hysterical lectures from Mother, or

---

NEW BOMBS AND OLD

One atomic bomb equals 20,000 tons of the type hitherto used in war. From 1939 to the end of the European War R.A.F. Bomber Command, as distinct from the U.S.A.A.F., dropped these tonnages on German towns :

Berlin	40,485
Essen	36,400
Cologne	32,000
Dortmund	21,000
Düsseldorf	17,750
Bochum	10,800
Münster	3,800

In all European theatres of war from 1939 the R.A.F. dropped 988,307 tons—the equivalent of about fifty of the new bombs. In London from September, 1940, to July, 1941, the Germans dropped 7,500 tons.

restrictions on my freedom.

Manchester had entire communities of flattened streets of homes and factories. Districts, such as Ardwick, near the centre of the city, with row after row of "Coronation Street" terraced Victorian homes, had been flattened by bombs originally intended for Salford Docks and the surrounding factories. For us, visiting Grandma in Denton or taking the bus into Piccadilly, the huge areas of bomb-sites were part of the normal landscape. We thought little of the people who had lived there, whose homes had been destroyed, and unquestioningly assumed they had made it to the Air Raid Shelters, which had been hastily built in most streets from sandbags, earth, bricks and curved semi-circular sections of corrugated iron.

Birch House had a reinforced bomb-proof cellar, under the Butler's Pantry, on the north-east corner, by the outside steps. It was windowless, with steel beams inserted into the ceiling and down the walls. We took it over for a while as our private den, illuminated by candles and furnished with old boxes – and wondered that if the four-storey mass of bricks, slates and timbers fell onto our sanctuary, filling

Many bomb sites were familiar & favourite playgrounds.

the outside stairwell, would we be able to dig our way out? Almost certainly not, was the answer. The trapped family would have had to rely on the neighbours, the Home Guard and the rescue services, with their dogs and shovels, to find and extricate us. Would the huge galvanised iron water tank in the attics, or the lead plumbing, burst in the bomb blast and flood down to drown us in that pitch-black room?

This was more than idle childish fantasising. The Laurels, a house built, but no longer standing, behind the next-door-but-one row of houses, a mansion in three or four walled acres, had suffered a direct hit and been flattened – leaving only two high stable walls and piles of rubble – now overgrown with shrubs, mounds of blackberry and young trees. Had they, we speculated more in fear than excitement, got out alive? Or had the bomb fallen without warning from a homeward bound Blitzkrieg pilot dumping his cargo?

Families had corrugated-iron & earth Anderson Shelters to sleep in – safe from bombs.

***

Page **107**

Chapter 12 - Lost Boys

From the Manchester Guardian archive, 27 August 1947: Indian Independence - proposal to Pakistan. According to the best neutral sources not fewer than 10,000 Moslems have lost their lives in the Amritsar district alone during August. Three battalions with tank support have been actively engaged in breaking up Sikh raiding parties – in one affray they killed 61 men – but now their main task is the protection of refugees. The Sikhs have displayed the same ruthlessness and brutality as in the Jullundur district. Out of one Moslem village of 350 people which fought off a large Sikh mob for six hours only 40 survived. Women and children have been beaten to death and tortures have been inflicted. Lady Mountbatten left to-day by air for Jullundur and Amritsar to tour the refugee camps and hospitals of the East Punjab. She is accompanied by the India Health Minister, Mrs. Kaur. Both are expected to return to-morrow.

Another carefully exhaled stream of almost invisible blue smoke spiralled upwards in the reflected evening sunlight that glanced low through the triptych, leaded, casement window that looked from the Morning Room out onto the back door and to the garden beyond. Mother held court again, her four sons enthralled and listening intently.

"...and Noel was just going down for the third time when a man came over the bridge, ran along the bank and just managed to reach down and pluck him out of the canal. The water was filthy... He saved his life. And he wouldn't even leave his name. I never knew who he was. But he must have been a stranger..." she mused, "...otherwise somebody would have heard and the story would be all over the district."

"And I didn't even know that Noel was out of the garden. The gate was supposed to be kept shut but Richard..."
Here Richard flinched, preparatory to again denying his guilt, but instead he gave the merest of shrugs and let the moment pass.

"...and your cousin Ursula. Who lived next door and was the same age as Richard. They took Noel out of the gate and onto the waste ground by the canal. If he hadn't been drowned he might have been lost forever."
She paused professionally just long enough for the drama of that statement to have its effect. Then she snapped up her audience again at exactly the right moment, before they could think or fidget.

"We did lose Noel once, for a whole day. And we almost lost Martin." Mother announced. And having opened the next chapter she took a well-timed and deserved draw on her cigarette, inhaled the sustaining gasses deep into her being then continued at her leisure.

"We had left Richard and Noel in the garden. It was only a tiny garden. The house was a little pre-war semi. You know, with one of those asphalted straight little porches over the front door held up with two metal poles. Just a tiny garden. Certainly nowhere a child could get lost. But I came out to get Noel for his lunch. And he'd gone."

Her outward breath expended on that sentence and the blue smoke was entirely gone. Mother moved her hand a few practised inches and neatly decapitated the ash from her cigarette into a large glass ashtray, before lifting the glowing white tube back to her mouth for another airy infusion of the magic blue fumes. The ash glowed hot and its grey residue raced a quarter inch nearer her thin lips.

"Well we searched everywhere. And I couldn't find him. The gate was shut and your Aunty Peggy hadn't seen him. I called and called. And Richard said he didn't know where he was. He was only about one-and-a-half. It was during the war, early spring and your Father wasn't there. And it was before Peter was born – so he must have been about one and a quarter and Richard would be nearly three. Three that next August. Well we looked everywhere. We searched the air-raid shelter on the waste ground. Though how he could have got out of the gate was beyond me. And of course one of the first place I looked was the canal." Her panic, though strongly controlled, communicated itself to the listening boys and their pulses raced in unconscious communion with this young mother searching for her toddler, coping alone during that dreadful war, with two young children, the Black-Out, air-raids and poverty.

"And we searched across the little bridge by the Mill. But he couldn't really have gone over there without being seen. And we checked in Peggy's house; and again in our house. Upstairs and downstairs; we searched almost the whole afternoon. But we didn't find him."

The four boys were spellbound; eyes still and wide; faces grave and taut. *Where could that overly solid child have got to? Where is he hiding?*

She issued another nearly invisible stream of blue haze and continued.

"It was nearly dark when we thought of looking in the coal house. Because it was bolted on the outside. So it was impossible for Noel to be in there. But when you've tried everywhere else, you start doubting your own mind. Anyway, we opened it. And there he was – sitting in the dark on the coke, quiet as a mouse. Not a sound."

His three brothers rounded on Noel, not critically but certainly quizzically. *Why hadn't he shouted or cried or something?*

Mother obliged with the official rationale.

"Of course it was Richard. Richard had pushed him in the coal hole and locked him in." She smiled fondly at the memory.

"The little devil. And he never said a word. All those hours we were searching and Richard never said where he was. Not a word."

Behind Richard's impassive, thin and composed features the acutely sensitised younger brothers detected a pleased smirk. It became a confirmed smirk as Richard did not rise to deny the accusation.

"But when we lost Martin. That had nothing to do with Richard. We had all been outside and it was going dark and we went in for tea. Your father was there so it must have been nineteen-forty-six. We were all sitting at the table having our tea, and it was dark outside and the fire was lit for the night. So we drew the curtains and were getting the room warm and it started raining. Lashing down. Pattering on the windows. And we finished our tea and I was clearing the table and I suddenly said 'Oh my God. Where's the baby?'

'Where's the baby' I said; 'Oh my heaven. Where is he?' Then I suddenly remembered." and she laughed guiltily to herself at the memory.

"I had put him out after lunch in the pram. He was still out there. In the rain and the dark. All on his own. So we rushed outside and there he was. Martin was a beautiful baby with white blonde, curly hair and huge, huge big blue eyes..."

Richard sniggered and cast a teasing glance at Martin who turned down his mouth while his eyes filled silently with tears and started to overflow. Richard gave a rare wide grin at the smallest boy and the tears poured forth – all in silence and all so familiar as to be completely ignored.

"He was sitting up in the dark. The pram top was up, keeping some of the rain off. And he was just sitting there, staring with his big blue eyes at the rain. And not a sound. He must have been starving but he didn't say anything and I had just forgotten all about him. He was so good, he didn't even cry. And we all forgot he was out there all alone. He'd been there for hours and hours."

All eyes turned on Martin, still beautiful with blonde curly hair, dimples and huge blue eyes, now brimming over with tears. Richard had a little upturn on one side of his mouth and his eyes glinted with amusement. He pointed a hidden cruel meaningful finger at Martin, triggering yet more mournful tears. Mother looked at and through her weeping youngest, her gaze drifting off to the window and the dark beyond. The fire burned high and reflected in the black glass.

"Close the curtains will you Noel" she cajoled. "It's getting dark. And your father will be home soon."

***

Chapter 13 - Dr & Dr Sykes

John Bolby - After the war, he was Deputy Director of the Tavistock Clinic, and from 1950, Mental Health Consultant to the World Health Organization. Because of his previous work with maladapted and delinquent children, he became interested in the development of children and began work at the Child Guidance Clinic in London, which was also known as the East London Child Guidance Clinic. Located in Islington, it was founded by the Jewish Health Organisation in 1927 and was the first children's psychiatric facility in the UK and possibly Europe. His interest was probably increased by a variety of wartime events involving separation of young children from familiar people. These included the rescue of Jewish children by the Kindertransport arrangements, the evacuation of children from London to keep them safe from air raids, and the use of group nurseries to allow mothers of young children to contribute to the war effort. Bowlby was interested from the beginning of his career in the problem of separation, the wartime work of Anna Freud and Dorothy Burlingham on evacuees, and the work of René Spitz with orphans. By the late 1950s, he had accumulated a body of observational and theoretical work to indicate the fundamental importance for human development of attachment from birth.

Bowlby was interested in finding out the patterns of family interaction involved in both healthy and pathological development. He focused on how attachment difficulties were transmitted from one generation to the next. In his development of attachment theory, he proposed the idea that attachment behaviour was an evolutionary survival strategy for protecting the infant from predators. Mary Ainsworth, a student of Bowlby's, further extended and tested his ideas. She played the primary role in suggesting that several attachment styles existed. - Wikipedia

"NNNNNnnnnnnnnn......Aaaaaghhhh !! I'll kill you, I'll kill you, I'll kill you!!"

My strangled incoherent screams yet again shattered the morning calm and reverberated from Victorian home to Victorian home in that quiet arboreal neighbourhood as I, aged eight, pursued ten year old Richard the Tormentor, Richard the Teaser, Richard the Mocker, Richard the Sociopathic Taunter, around the back lawn.

I swung the eight foot clothes prop, with all the furious energy of a madman, in a vicious arc that endowed the notched tip with a velocity of about two hundred miles an hour, that almost but not quite connected with the back of Richard's narrow, infuriating, nasty, rat coloured head. He, as ever, ran silently and as fast as a weasel. I, as ever, chased him with shouts, screams and imprecations that woke the dead – and that disturbed and invaded the neighbours' territory.

It was not by chance or lack of skill on my part that Richard, quick though he was, constantly, almost daily, escaped decapitation by clothes prop, being hoist and choked with a well thrown lariat or being pierced by home-made spears or kitchen knives, or being mortally scalded with boiling water or branded across his sneering face with a red-hot poker snatched from the fire. On the contrary, from behind my very real and morally and ethically excusable uncontrollable rage, that could in seconds pump me up from a docile, self-absorbed, squarish younger brother fit only for victimisation, to an Incredible Hulk capable of terrifying and of putting to flight whole gangs of tormenting youths, sat an inner man who, peeking between the bars of the cage of lunatic screams and barbaric actions, could finesse the swing of an eight foot pole or the descent of an iron bar to within fractions of an inch to just miss crushing that hateful, fleeing skull. The effort of being monstrous but non-destructive was however unending and exhausting.

Daily and for much of the day, the house and garden echoed to the screams of children, boy children, in rage, dispute or despair. Soil fights were a speciality; the soil in the flower beds after tilling being just right to clump into hand sized greying nodules that could be hurled with a reasonable certainty of being stone-less, like summer snowballs, at a brother, and on contact the soil not only delivered a satisfying thwack to an unprotected ear but, even more satisfyingly, broke into a million pieces and fall down the neck of the target victim. From time to time, when he was there, Father, in white starched collar and sober tie as ever, suddenly appeared at the back door, roused from his melancholy self-contemplation or disturbed from working on the accounts of a client in the front room, and he added to the mayhem and chaos by bellowing at his squabbling offspring to desist, be quiet and go away. Such interventions first trebled the noise and chaos and then calmed the area - for about ten minutes.

Rarely and always dangerously, Richard and I could be found working in close, concentrated co-operation; with me, the younger, only too pleased to have his undivided attention in an apparent truce. Such as the time we played *William Tell*.

I, aged seven, naturally had the apple balanced on my head. Richard, by happy happenstance, did not own a longbow, or a crossbow. But we agreed that the potato peeler would do just as well. The connection was that we also used the implement to peel apples. The target was an apple, a nice juicy green English cooking apple, so impaling it with a potato or apple peeler had sufficient elements of logic for us.

It was mid-afternoon and Mother was reliably settled in her chair in the Morning Room with her book, tapestry-by-numbers and cigarettes. The house was quiet. The stage chosen for the drama was the width of the kitchen. I was positioned with my back to the tall post of the high mantelpiece, next to the stove and the fireplace. The mantelpiece protruded some twelve inches above my head and was overshadowed by the empty clothes rack, set above the range and held up with a stout cord tied to a hook on the north wall. Richard stood opposite me as far back as he could get, almost into the scullery as I stood obediently very, very still, balancing the apple on my mercifully thick hair. The peeler was black, about six inches long, half of it a handle bound in black cord and the other half, the business end, an angle iron blade with a slot for the peelings and a sharp point to gouge out black-eyes, worms and rotten patches. The kitchen was fifteen feet wide and Richard stood in a little from the wall to allow room for his arm to swing, about twelve feet from me. As ever, we wore the ubiquitous grey short trousers; grey flannel shirts, mine open and crumpled at the neck, Richard's neatly closed with a school tie precisely positioned; grey v-necked sweaters with a twin colour band at the neck, mine with that "lived-in" or even slept-in look and Richard's seemingly freshly ironed; grey socks with a coloured band, mine crumpled down, Richard's neatly and straight up to knee with his elasticised tabs holding the socks in place; and black shoes with leather soles that soaked up water, were forever wearing thin and having to be repaired or cast aside. My shoes showed a rugged character and displayed the history of their recent journeys and sporting activities while Richard's were clean and new looking.

"Can you hit it Rick?" it suddenly occurred to me to ask.

"Can you hit it?" the question suddenly struck me as he hefted the knife and tested its balance in one hand and then the other. My skull moved as my jaw opened to let me speak – and the apple fell off. Richard paced impatiently across the room and plonked the apple back in place.

"Shut up and keep still." He ordered with ferocious concentration as he backed away from me, staring snakelike at my forehead.

"Now stay just like that," he murmured as he took his right arm back behind his head and rebalanced the knife on the palm of his hand.

We both knew it was vitally important that the knife flew point first which was difficult to guarantee with anything but a professional throwing knife whose blade is heavier than the handle. This peeler might turn over in flight and strike the apple, the apple standing on my head, with the rounded wooden end of the handle making a dull thud, instead of satisfactorily piercing the apple and burying its blade cleanly up to the haft as it was supposed to. Another problem to be avoided was the knife spinning on its centre of gravity and turning over and over on its journey across the kitchen making it difficult, not impossible but extremely difficult, to ensure that as it neared the apple, and my head, the sharp tip would be coming around at the precise moment required to plunge the point into the unoffending apple; or my head.

"Are you sure you can hit it?" I hissed at him, ventriloquist like without moving my lips to avoid unseating the apple again - intelligently, if selfishly becoming slightly concerned for my own safety.

"Shut up and keep still," he hissed back at me; his right arm waving backwards and forwards in a most professional and fluid looking movement.

I breathed in deeply, managing not to move my shoulders and therefore my head and keeping the apple in place. Richard stared through me with even greater concentration and with a beautiful whip action he brought his arm through over his shoulder, aligned his hand, palm down, with the target, the target on my head, extended three fingers to guide the blade as it fled his hand and he flung the projectile across the room. It flew point first. It showed not the slightest tendency to spin. It flew flat and true to the line of his shoulder, arm and hand. It came very fast and hard. The apple feared for its life. But it was spared. The knife struck me in the head, in the hairline, a remarkable eighth of an inch below the apple, very nearly a direct hit, and just an inch above my right-eye, that had in any case been established as a possibly defective eye, so not that valuable an asset to lose, and it buried its sharp tip into my skull with a perceptible "boi'ng" sound and sat there quivering with pent up disappointment.

"Aahhhgh!" I yelled; firstly because it hurt – and secondly as it was somewhat shocking to find, and be able to see with hardly an upward glance, a potato peeler sticking out of my head, above one eyebrow, and thirdly, the vibrations made my teeth rattle in harmony.

"Hushhhhhh! – you're alright. Husssshhh!" whispered Richard, wrenching the guilty weapon from its bony setting and realising, with the advantage of his greater age and presumed greater wisdom that this minor adventure, this little accident, was just the sort of piffling incident to tip Mother into a hysterical, overly-imaginative tirade in which she would endlessly and vocally and loudly speculate on what might have happened if the outcome of this scientifically conducted experiment had been marginally different. And we all wanted to avoid that at almost any price.

Most boys had a Scout Knife on their belts.

"It's OK." Richard reassured us both.

"It's in your hair. You can hardly even see it." He whipped into the scullery, dropped the forensic evidence into a draw and ran back with a tea towel soaked in cold water that he pressed onto the hirsute wound, banging my head back onto the cast iron post.

"Tell them you bumped your head." he confided, already rewriting history.

And I did. Though the potato peeler scar was easily identifiable, a leading white gap that seemed in an odd place to start a parting for my hair, for at least the next two decades.

A seven-inch knife through the foot was not so easy to pass-off however.

They were referred to as Scout Knives, to lend them a spurious maturity and aura of safety, and no self-respecting boy could grow up not owning at least one. Richard had a triple set. The knives had leather bound handles, the leather so tight onto the metal haft that they seemed more like carved wood than leather. They were housed in leather sheaths and held safely and of course responsibly by a leather loop with a heavy-duty press-stud. The steel blades, rounded on one edge and sharpened on the other, with lethal points, could be any length from three to ten inches. Richard had a long knife with a sheath that sported two shorter knives accommodated on the outside. I, appropriately, had a single sheath with a medium length knife – outshone by Richard's array of weaponry.

The favourite competition with such knives was The Splits.

Two boys (girls hardly ever played this entertaining, intelligent and skilful game) stood on grass facing each other about three feet apart. At the start their feet were together. The first boy threw his knife close by the opponent's foot – it had to be within a hand-span of the foot or the throw didn't count. The knife had to stick firmly in the ground, not limply fall over. The opponent similarly threw back the knife and moved his foot to cover the gash left in the turf. As the game proceeded the players' legs spread further and further apart. It was forbidden to put a hand on the ground to steady oneself. Wobbling at full leg stretch not only moved the target – a hands-breadth outside the well extended foot – far away from the thrower and onto a line of sight across the players' shins, it also created a desperate imperative to balance as the next throw was made. The loser was the first to fall over. Occasionally, particularly in a knockout tournament, with reputations at stake and old scores to settle, a great fuss was made by parents, or school teachers, or even by the offended boy himself if he were a wimp, over a simple, usually quite clean, paediatric and podiatric wound as, in the tension of the competition, a mistake was made and a youthful appendage, shoe, sock, flesh, blood and even bone, was pierced and perhaps briefly and painfully staked into the turf. Such errors of judgement were however extremely rare. With a good sized lawn, much of it in bright sunlight, and with a strong compact texture that welcomed and held strongly hefted knives, we often hosted the tournaments, witnessing a few distraught children limping off home with a bleeding foot, or two, composing unlikely explanations that might stave off the unjust, as it was the other boy's knife that did the damage, but certain confiscation and impounding of his own sheath knife.

Our house was large, being twenty-four rooms, including the cellars, of substantial Victorian brickwork on four floors standing in one-third of an acre of garden, boasting a wide double garage, a crumbling fifty-foot greenhouse and three or four brick outhouses, including an old boiler house that had once heated the greenhouse. But if our home was large, the house next door was huge.

Coincidentally, or would it be through Universal synchronistic planning at a psychic and spiritual level beyond our analyses, on one side of Birch House, container for our highly dysfunctional, knife wielding, screaming family, lived Doctor and Doctor Sykes. Not medical doctors but, would you believe, child psychiatrists; and not just one child psychiatrist but two of them – probably representing in those just-pull-yourself-together days, a goodly percentage of all the child psychiatrists in the country.

Dr Sykes & Dr Sykes, both child psychiatrists, lived in the huge house next door

Dr & Dr Sykes' immense house

Their immense house stood in two or three acres and had turrets with French style conical roofs. They were partly protected from us by the ramparts of a fifteen-foot high brick wall that started at the Sykes's conservatory and marched majestically along our driveway to our handsome garage. Their land went behind our garage and our greenhouse in an "L" shape with a cobbled stable yard and buildings backing onto our outhouses that let through more high walls onto a large lawn with herbaceous borders and then through fences and hedges into a grand vegetable garden surrounded by huge beech trees. Behind their land was a special school for retarded children, set in large grounds, and behind that was a farm, whose working acres capped the hill on which Heaton Mersey stood and continued down the slope for a mile to the large council house estate below in Burnage, just across the Manchester/Stockport border.

I say partly protected because of course at a young age we could climb the fifteen-foot wall and run along its concave top to access our slated garage roof, ascend that roof up a lead gully to the weather vane (was the vane ours or theirs?) and from that height, command a view of most of the Sykes's land.

When, as an adult, I first went into therapy to tackle my crippling, speech disabling, socially excluding, chronic embarrassment, before Mother died and her ghost drove me and accompanied me into the consulting room of a sage Zurich Jungian; my first therapist, Barbara Wadsworth, took me back to memories stimulated by painful or meaningful physical feelings and at the end of these very effective "Engram" sessions, she told me to close my eyes and restore my equilibrium by imagining myself in a safe and pleasant place. That place, in fact the only safe place my mind could conjure, was the broad, shallow lead gully on the blue slate roof of that garage on a cool spring day with the weak sunshine soaking into the slates and warming my back as I lay, invisible to brothers, sister, parents, priests, nuns, teachers, scoutmasters and all earthly visitors, and gazed at the scudding clouds and the blue sky that becomes black and limitless as your gaze penetrates its local colouring and travels on to the infinity of space.

The Sykes's also had a full sized, log built Summer House on their side lawn, with cricket, tennis and croquet equipment stored in a large window-seat chest. Their main protection from our natural inclinations to invade, pillage and destroy came, however, from their alien strangeness.

We were a Northern Catholic family struggling to repair and heat a large house that had been sold cheaply in the late nineteen-forties depression to us by Mr and Mrs Green, retired Radio Three presenters who left us a legacy of wonderful, marvellous vinyl records, in bound leather volumes, of all the great symphonies and operas; that after introducing me to Benjamino Gigli and the classic composers, made great throwing disks – and the lutes and mandolins they left made really good boats, after we failed to get any music from them.

We were real people. The Sykes's did not speak with a northern accent. They spoke like people on the BBC. They did not shout and scream; they conducted themselves quietly around the house and grounds. The odds were Ten to One that they had been to university. They almost certainly wore open-toed sandals in the summer. They rode bicycles – not racing bikes like Father's, but sit-up-and-beg bicycles with heavy, grumbling Sturmey-Archer gears and wicker baskets. They gardened. They kept goats and rabbits and allowed us to feed them. Hugh, who was my age, refrained, for no discernible reason, from beating up his little brother Martin, two or three years younger and a really easy target. If he accidentally poked Martin in the eye and Martin cried; Hugh would hug him. This was very, very odd. Several of them wore glasses and were, we would have conjectured, probably physically deficient in other ways as well. When we played with them in their garden, Mrs. Sykes, tall, thin and very English, appeared at eleven o'clock with a tray of home-made cakes and orange juice. This strange and welcome ritual we learned was called "elevenses". Hugh and Martin played musical instruments – odder and odder. They had a much older brother who was away most of the time. It transpired that he went to boarding school. Was that a punishment for some unforgivable crime, we wondered. When the older brother came home he went on some days to the top room of the conical tower, opened the windows and played a piano; playing classical music that drifted over our garden. Mother said he played well, and that he was quite good and that she wished one of us would one day play like that. Of course we didn't; 'cause learning music was only for pansies and cissies. When Hugh was eleven or twelve, he disappeared. And I never knew where he had gone. All very peculiar.

So with all their alien ways, the Sykes's escaped our direct attentions by bemusing and distracting us from our natural inclinations. Not so the Lawless'es.

On the other side of Birch House was a Victorian house, slightly later and smaller than ours but with a long narrow garden that marched purposefully back as far as the end of the Sykes's land. Two-thirds was devoted to vegetables set in military ranks and protected on the far, lane side by a high, new chain-link fence held erect by white tall concrete posts. Beyond the fence was the lane that went to the farm, across that lane was a fine but dilapidated wall that surrounded The Laurels; a large, large garden of a mansion, bombed in the war, most of the rubble gone and the garden returned to nature. The Laurels backed onto acres of allotments that in turn backed onto Fylde Lodge Girls School playing fields, which linked by an exciting dark path to the Clay Pits and beyond those dangerous and enticing pools, gully's and borders, down the hill to Didsbury and Manchester. All this gave us an infinite amount of open space and fields to play in.

But the Lawless'es had the double misfortune of the father being a Headmaster and of the only child, Gerald, being a plump wimp – separated from us only by a seven-foot privet hedge.

We had six or seven cooking apple trees and a thirty-foot pear tree. We also had four or five tennis racquets. It is an indisputable fact of artillery warfare that four eight-year-old boys, invited and trained for the purpose and furnished with old tennis racquets and an endless supply of windfalls, can sky twenty apples a minute to a height of seventy-two feet and on a narrow tangent bring them thumping down to smash onto the perfectly honed lawn of the next-door neighbours. With good preparation, in five minutes, one hundred fruity missiles can be thus delivered. Boring holes in the larger apples made them whistle like war-time shells as they climbed into the blue yonder then dropped from the skies to thud and splat on the unsuspecting enemy territory.

Even more lethal than apples weighing up to two pounds falling seventy feet onto one's head, though we were immensely careful not to pierce anyone's skulls but merely to worry them with narrow misses, were our cord-arrows.

Always an inventive child I discovered that taking eighteen inches of woven, not spun, cord, tying a stout knot at one end, notching the cord around the knot just below the feathers of an arrow, the heavier the better, holding the arrow tip and cord between finger and thumb, with the cord running tight up the arrow from the feather-band, then hurling the missile with a practised flick and with a whip action from the cord, made a long distance weapon of devastating and lethal accuracy. Forget your aboriginal spear throwing sticks with their feeble reach; forget your English and Red Indian bowmen piercing armour and slaying cowboys and Blue Jackets, forget even the primitive crossbow, capable of driving an iron bolt through solid oak. My cord-arrow beat the lot of them. We could hurl an arrow hundreds of yards, right across the Lawless'es garden, across the lane, over the tall, tall elm trees and into the open centre of the grounds of The Laurels. Just occasionally, with the greatest of care, and having first made sure the people were indoors, we elevated our aim onto the narrowest trajectory, checked the wind for drift and launched an arrow, or two or three, several hundred feet into the air and watched it plummet at bullet speed down into the Lawless'es previously pristine lawn. From where, of course, we had to trespass to recover it – as arrows, homemade or bought, didn't come cheap in those days.

These cord arrows could outdistance arrows shot from my professional Slazenger bow by miles.

Beleaguered as they were by screaming children, bellowing Father, soil bombs, whistling mortar-apples (and pears in season), lethal cord-arrows, innocently shot but aggravating footballs and cricket balls and the occasional insulting graffiti along their front wall; 'Up with the Law and Down with the Lawless', our neighbours were not, as you might expect, reduced to the status of victims. They had a secret weapon. Mr Lawless, the closet headmaster, was surprisingly fit.

After several seasons of blitzkrieg and bombardment, with little or no discernible satisfactory reaction other than seeing him clearing the lawn of mashed apples; four or five of us were quietly conducting the war by casually lobbing deadly missiles from the junction of the lane by The Laurels, safely close to the old post we always used to swarm up and over The Laurels' wall and even safer in the knowledge that he was in his closed up garage, behind his own high brick wall, when to our consternation Mr Lawless suddenly appeared on the top of his wall, in an SAS Commando straddle and leapt like a pouncing tiger down into the lane. We did not scatter; we knew our territory well and we had our escape route. Faster than the average Headmaster can think, we scampered up the pole, over the wall and raced for the hidden paths between the dense foliage in The Laurels. But to our horror, and tacit admiration though now was not the time to stand and applaud, Mr Lawless vaulted the wall like an Olympic champion, soaring over the top with one hand gripping the pole, feet neatly together and out at an angle of sixty-degrees, landing lightly and effortlessly on the balls of his just proven and demonstrably most agile feet - and he came after us with an alarming purposefulness. Then we scattered like a shoal of fish; and even a superman like Lawless can only pursue one rapidly moving small boy at a time.

It wasn't me he caught. It was probably one of the Keegan's, another large Catholic family, mostly boys, who lived a few houses down the road with a back gate onto the lane. But he must have used techniques of duress learned at the Headmaster's Training HQ and under cruel and unusual torture the captive cracked, resulting in gross parental interference, recriminations, confiscations and graffiti cleaning. What saved them from further persecution at our hands however was Mr Lawless's inarguable, indisputable athleticism. Who would ever have dreamed that a Headmaster could leap like a gazelle and hunt like a hungry leopard; better left alone. So he bought himself, and his overweight son, a reprieve.

Even when a year or so later on winter evenings in the dark, we took to the exciting game of creeping illicitly through private gardens and escaping any irate householders who detected our rustling and our clambering up their fences, we left the Active Headmaster's house well alone. I wonder if he missed us.

Opposite our gateway, across the road, was Mrs Challenor's house, a black and white half-timbered affair hidden behind high, evergreen laurels and rhododendrons. She was an elderly, impeccably groomed widow who we treated with all the respect due to her age and the grief we imagined she must still bear; Mrs. Challenor was never bothered by us, thus demonstrating our inherent chivalry.

Across the road, catty cornerwise to Birch House and on the corner of Balmoral Lane lived another only child, Willy White, in a modern house with a long, fenced garden that stretched the full length of the lane. Balmoral Lane led up to Heaton Moor Road with its shops, cinema and buses. On the other side from the White's, the lane was bordered by iron railings and allotments. Oak and hawthorn grew in long narrow patches in the lane and it was investigating the climbing and den building properties of these trees that first brought us into contact with the, by our frugal standards, overfed, over-indulged Willy. But he had his own friends who we did not know, presumably ferried in by his father who managed The Jaguar Car dealers in Manchester, and they had a fully fenced garden to protect them from tykes such as us. With no common border and no means of sighting them in their heavily screened territory – an uneasy peace pertained between us, though both sides recognised that we were natural enemies. My den in the lane, up in one of the smaller oak trees, remained a favourite and undetected reclining spot for some years. I established a similar lair in a small leafy beech tree, by the front wall of Birch House, which overhung the pavement below, from where I could silently mark the comings and goings of adults and children.

The White's eventually sold their large house having split the one-hundred yards long back garden for the building of another equally large house at the far end of Balmoral Lane, and Dr Arthur Berwitz, a GP, bought it and moved in to Mauldeth Road with his wife and their son Andrew.

***

Chapter 14 - The Scouts

BBC – 4th July1954: Housewives celebrate end of rationing
Fourteen years of food rationing in Britain ended at midnight when restrictions
on the sale and purchase of meat and bacon were lifted. Members of the London
Housewives' Association held a special ceremony in London's Trafalgar Square
to mark Derationing Day. The Minister of Fuel and Power, Geoffrey Lloyd,
burned a large replica of a ration book at an open meeting in his constituency.
But the Minister of Food, Major Gwilym Lloyd-George, told a meeting at
Bebington in Cheshire he would keep his as a souvenir and praised all those
traders and organisations that had co-operated with the rationing system. For the
first time since the war began in 1939 London's Smithfield Market opened at
midnight instead of 0600 and meat sellers were doing a roaring trade.

Though I had numbers of dens, in Balmoral Lane, in the Laurels and
as far away as the farm hedges, my favourite den, my place of retreat,
remained the shallow gully on the garage roof. It was from there in
1953 that I made good my escape when the scoutmaster from
Levenshulme Scout Troop called to speak with my parents, to convince
me to continue attending. Richard had joined the troop and was rapidly
progressing to Queen Scout status, with badges festooning both sleeves
of his uniform, so although it was five or six bicycle miles away I was
persuaded, despite my chronic shyness, to tag along, and so I joined the
Curlew Patrol and learned to make dampers, twisted onto peeled green
sticks (green so that the sticks don't burn) and cooked over a fire I had
lit with one match, and to tie knots and to sing scout songs.
What drove me away was the Gang Show. I could sing – in private. I
could speak – in private. But suffering as I had all my conscious life
from excruciating embarrassment, the thing most certain to make me
take for the hills was doing either or both of those on a public stage. I
was a brave child. I asked questions in class at school despite glowing
bright red and sweating buckets each time. And I remained brave into
adulthood. Despite falling over at weddings, becoming paralysed at
Round Tables, rendered incoherent at vital business meetings and
having my throat clamp itself firmly shut when speaking in a
Westminster Committee Room, I tried. Eventually through years of
therapy and thanks to the links made for me by Dr Arthur Berwitz, I
succeeded. But that was a lifetime of change away from my
Levenshulme Scout days, where my rendering of the song Tea for Two,
rising to a shrieking, strangled crescendo was cruelly, but perhaps also
mercifully, curtailed by the cartoon-like use of a long shepherd's crook
that mysteriously emerged from the wings, took me by the neck and
tugged me, not too unkindly, out of the limelight, away from the gaze
of the audience, and into the shadows of obscurity.

...I was hauled off stage by a long shepherd's crook deployed from the wings.

That was in the winter. And I couldn't of course let them know how it had destroyed me so I waited until the spring to stop cycling to the Scout Hut evenings. But the Scoutmaster must have cared and he wrote, which of course I ignored, then he phoned, which I ignored more determinedly, and eventually, horror of horrors, one bright Saturday morning, he called at the house to discuss the situation with my parents. They of course were baffled and mortified to have "an official" calling about a problem youth, their son, and intruding into our tight-knit paranoid family world. Fortunately, I was reading a book lying concealed on the garage roof, accessible only by walking twenty feet or so along the top of the Sykes's wall – not something many adults could even attempt; apart maybe from our nimble Headmaster next door – so I was safe for the moment. After a few minute's conversation in the house, Father, Mother and Scoutmaster suddenly appeared in the garden, calling for me. I was shocked and alarmed – from several points in the garden they would be able to see me on the roof. And I would be called to account, quizzed and forced back into that hateful, painful group where my budding Show-Business career had been prematurely ended.

I crept up the roof and slid over the ridge, onto the Sykes's side of the building. But it was a long way down from there and the pitch was far steeper – but I was out of sight. They were calling persistently and I had to get far away as discovery and confrontation were utterly unthinkable. The Sykes's might appear and see me and call and give me away. I could see a route down into the Sykes's cobbled yard about eighty feet along the back of the outhouses and the greenhouse. I had to make the journey and so, risking discovery I shuffled along the back of the collapsing greenhouse, feet in the rotten wooden gutter and leaning onto the uncertain glass panes. It was very dangerous, but the danger carried no weight at all compared to having to explain to three adults that I was too shy to cope with the healthy social activities of a bunch of boy scouts – or of any other group.

Inevitably, Father, who was sometimes brighter than he appeared, spotted the shadowy figure through the distorting effect of a flourishing vine between two glass roofs and even recognised it as his second son. He called me and his calls became more and more strident as I, now in a highly dangerous position both remained determined not to be "caught" and was forced to concentrate on avoiding the very real possibility of plunging through the roof in a shower of Victorian glass. I shuffled on, just able through some of the clearer panes to see the astonishment on the face of the Scoutmaster, the anger of Father at being ignored and the social fear of Mother as she realised that, one way or another, I would be gone and she would be left to explain this bizarre behaviour to the Scoutmaster. I reached the escape route, clambered down into the next-door stable yard and with the incredulous shouts of Father echoing round the gardens made my escape through to the open farm land beyond.

Hours later, when it was dark, I returned. Little was said. I certainly never explained myself and life closed seamlessly around the incident, sealing it and all of its indefinable underlying early causes deep into my psyche.

The curse of shyness and crippling embarrassment struck not only at school, when I wanted to ask or answer a question, but also extended to simple tasks like shopping. I rarely shopped for me until I was thirty-five or so. I could not enter a shop and explain myself to a shop-keeper, particularly if there were other customers there. I couldn't order a drink at a bar or food in café without suffering extraordinary redness of face, perspiration and making a dreadful effort. Being passed over or ignored by a barman for a few minutes lost the pub a sale – as I had to withdraw and recover. My theory is that being the focus of Mother's and the family's attention was so life-threatening that I avoided all and any spotlight. Speaking out in a group was impossible; completely and utterly impossible. The best course was silence accompanied by obliging and polite nods and smiles that reassured people I was listening and taking part despite being a dumb-mute.

Imagine then my acute discomfiture and paralysis when, aged fourteen, returning at night from the Plaza cinema, sitting on the illuminated back seats of the completely full number Seventy-Five single-decker bus from Mersey Square to Green End, with a couple of pals and with a few local girls in furtive conversation about a local flasher in an archetypal flasher's old raincoat, who had accosted one of them, a certain Margaret Lamerton, one of the prettiest girls in Heaton Moor, who with eight or so mixed siblings (not Catholics but fathered by a vigorous Protestant Fleet-Air-arm officer), who was singularly unimpressed by the flasher's naked cheek - sitting further up the bus - that's the girls not of course the flasher. One of the girls in all innocence, and I know it was in all innocence because she later married me, said in a clear and crowd cutting voice, "Noel?" so as to definitely identify me to all the passengers; and only when she had their complete attention and they were all craning their heads round and staring fixedly in my direction did she continue;
"Noel?"
And she directed her question at me not because we had 'a relationship' of any sort but because the local kids nicknamed me 'Know-all' because I was a serious know-it-all.
"Noel" she called,
"What does – 'Will you knock-me-off' - mean?"

It was the seminal 'When Did You Stop Beating Your Wife?' Catch-22 question and the first time I had encountered the conundrum. Though only fourteen, and a good Catholic, I knew full well what it meant. I also knew or thought I knew, from the expressions on the frigid faces of all the passengers – mostly neighbours of ours – that they assumed I had just invited the innocent blue eyed girl, in her school raincoat, to do me that singular honour and to 'knock me off' at some convenient place and time.
 In normal circumstances, as the focus of so many burning eyes, I was not able to do more than mumble incoherently. Given the sexual connotations and the danger of saying anything at all in answer to such a loaded query, I was dumbfounded. I went a little pink. I went red. I glowed incandescently crimson. I started to sweat. I poured sweat. I flooded my face, neck and hair with sweat. And I couldn't speak. I was clearly and obviously guilty as charged – and had nothing to say in my own defence. Thus do miscarriages of justice occur: *"We must take your silence young man, - you twisted evil pervert – to be an admission of*

guilt. And sentence you to be taken hence to a place ...etc......" "Well. *You could see he was guilty – it was written all over his face".*

There were occasional respites and automatic remissions from the condition. Most noticeably when the testosterone started coursing through my veins or lymphatic system and the undeniable and instinctual imperative to find a mate swept over me I could go to a party, meet a girl, chat her up and be confident, intelligent and cheerful. But even then, drugged up to the eyeballs with natural hormones and in with the in-crowd, I rarely, if ever spoke out in a group of more than three or four people. Like a secret illiterate I was a secret non-speaker, a mute, and just as illiterate's do I developed hundreds of tricks to avoid having to speak out anywhere or anytime to anyone. When I had to speak out, the chances were that I went pink. The pink deepened to red. I got hot; very hot. I started sweating. I tried to control all these symptoms. People would back away from me in perplexity. I was not able to recall names or find common words. My inner world flamed red and all recall was lost. This could happen in a business meeting with clients, or with friends at home, or in a theatre, or at a sports event or anywhere.

I was most comfortable alone where speaking was not an issue.

(At the time, I believed that shyness was very important, but now I know that shyness is one of the evils one must try to overcome, that in reality to be shy doesn't matter—it is like so many other things to which one gives an exaggerated importance. Jorge Luis Borges.)

****

Chapter 15 - Llandudno

6th February 1952: King George VI dies in his sleep. His Majesty, King George VI, has died peacefully in his sleep at Sandringham House. The official announcement from Sandringham, given at 1045 GMT, said the King retired in his usual health, but passed away in his sleep and was found dead in bed at 0730 GMT by a servant.
He was 56, and was known to have been suffering from a worsening lung condition. BBC Archives

As Father built his solo-partner accountancy practice in Manchester, as sugar and sweets came off ration and as the gloom of the post-war depression lifted, Birch House was slowly redecorated, painting and papering out the miserable hospital inspired two-tone greens and brown dado line, replacing the black kitchen fire range with a smart oatmeal, anthracite fuelled Aga, covering increasing amounts of lino with rugs and carpets – and opening up the unused living rooms. Father, without any warning as he was wont, appeared one day with six modern paraffin burners that he stationed in the tiled hallway and on the main landing. They gave out a rudimentary warmth and filled the house with the comforting smell of un-burnt exhaust fumes. Their circular wicks needed daily trimming and the wells needed refilling twice a day – as did the hungry Aga that ate anthracite by the ton. Filling it from the top, through the central hotplates was perilous, man's work – as was riddling the red hot ashes out from the bottom door. Twice a week we let the Aga die out in order to de-clinker it. With skill and patience, the clinker could be extracted as one large circular piece of fused, burnt debris that glowed in interesting ways when re-heated on the gas cooker and then I mixed it with melted lead, just small pieces filched off the roofs and surely never missed.

Though as children in the early 1950's we never had underwear, and considered boys who did as weaklings, the new wealth also brought large supplies of grey flannel shirts, grey flannel trousers, grey woollen socks and grey V-necked jumpers with twin colour bands at the neck. Father would arrive home of an evening having stopped at one of his garment maker clients, with boxes of goods, in dozens, that were distributed by size. If it didn't fit – the culture was you would "grow into it." These ubiquitous school garments occasioned streets full of small children enmeshed in oversized navy blue Gabardine raincoats, with a desperate, shared hidden desire, like covered rhubarb, to grow rapidly. When their growth prayers were answered and if the new supplies were late in coming, gangly youths were suddenly in evidence, with long self-conscious legs gleaming between short grey trousers and socks reaching only mid-calf.

I several times solved the badly fitting raincoat irritation by the simple act of throwing the offending garment away over a garden wall as I trudged home from school – then feigning utter bafflement as to its whereabouts. Mother sort of guessed what I had done as she recalled the time in the war that she had sent me to the shops over the bridge from the house in Slate Lane, with a ten-shillings note, a fortune then, and with the ration books, and I was seen by some intrusive neighbour to toss the money and coupons over the bridge into the canal. Sometimes, when you are four, walking away from a problem is the most efficient way to solve to it.

As Birch House was spruced up and heated we could also afford holidays.

Most holidays were spent in North Wales at Llandudno, or its sister-town Colwyn Bay. Llandudno, defined by the Great Orme at one end and the Little Orme at the other, had a pebble beach, a freezing, grey sea that turned us blue and chattering with cold in three minutes and a children's boating pool where we often burned and blistered on the first day and then spent happy hours for days after, popping the blisters and picking away the dead skin, leaving raw pink patches that quickly blistered again. Sun creams and sun blocks had not been invented.

Llandudno or die! Our huge, old Austin Sheerline - Driven like a racing car by Father.

Though Father had not yet embarked on his racing and rallying activities he took every opportunity to practice winning. Every car journey was to him a competitive event. With a big family he bought big second-hand cars. We had a black Wolsey, the familiar 'forties police car. We had a pale-green Rover with a Viking ship on its nose. We had a great Jaguar, racing green with wide running boards and huge free-standing headlamps that Father and I toured Scotland in together – hiking up Ben Nevis and taking a fishing boat to Skye. We had an Austin Sheerline, an immense machine with built in under-floor hydraulic jacks and a secret emergency petrol tank that could be switched to from inside the car. These sedate family cars became high revving, Formula One racing machines in Father's hands.

A holiday started with the loading procedures, Father was tidy and precise;
"Shipshape and Bristol Fashion." as he put it.
Luggage for up to six children and two adults takes a lot of space. Father despised roof racks for aerodynamic reasons. At least two of the children, at any one time, suffered acutely from travel sickness, exacerbated by the smells of real leather, the real wood, the anxiety, the tension and, when in flight, the bucketing, pitching and rolling at maximum speed. Father, as driver and captain, had the most space. He needed room to hold his arms straight – as good racing technique demands, he needed clear space around him to ensure his lightning fast reflexes were not obstructed, and he needed clear views in all directions.

Mother was installed in the front passenger seat, apprehensive but silent at this stage. This was before the government decided to insult the inherent skills and good sense of all drivers by insisting on cars having safety belts, so there were no entanglements of that sort to be accommodated. Under her legs went a suitcase and on her lap would go the youngest child. The boot would be hard-packed with cases and slammed tight. The remaining children and luggage would be crammed into the rear seat and on the floor. Older children would baggsie a corner seat with window, though we were mostly too short to see out, and the younger ones would end up perched on suitcases in the middle of the seats. Sometimes we took the dog with us just to make up the numbers.

Mother became deeply silent and pale. Father checked the car, checked the house, checked the weather, re-checked the house, used the loo, then did a roll call and then started the engine. At which point Mother said tensely,

"You will drive carefully won't you Edwin?"
And he replied "Hrrrummphh!! Hrrumph!! Of course dear, of course."

Only in towns and built up areas was there a speed limit. There were no motorways, dual carriageways were rare and the ubiquitous lethal three-lane highways to death were highly regarded. On a modern map the journey from Stockport to Llandudno looks short enough and safe enough. In the late 'forties, on twisting country roads, through market towns, up hill and down dale, in a loaded car weighing two tons, with primitive brakes, puking, bitching children and an increasingly hysterical wife; it was a long, long way. Several times we made the thirteen-hour trip to Cornwall; and of course, back again.

But Father never wavered in his parental duty to get us to the holiday destination as rapidly as possible, dead or alive. On one return journey, with the car bucking and heaving with the terrified family, racing up the busy three lane Chester Road to Manchester, Father dancing the car past all lesser mortals and dodging into spaces two feet shorter than the car at seventy miles an hour, we were followed and were eventually stopped by a police car. The policemen looked perplexedly into the jammed interior. There was no question of exceeding speed limits, as there were none.
"Where did you learn to drive, Sir?" said an officer in a neutral tone, and before Father, shrinking into his seat, could answer…
"…We've been following for about five miles, and couldn't keep up, Sir. You passed four lorries back there into oncoming traffic, Sir,…" He paused then continued admiringly
"…And I'd swear the back of your car shrank as it went through the gap! Mind how you go, Sir."

Half an hour into a journey, as we left the relative sanity of thirty-mile-limits behind us and as Father swooped past all other road users at frantic speed, Mother's nerve started to fail and she launched into an endless critique of his driving and a continuous prophecy of doom.
"Slow down Edwin! You'll kill us all. You'll kill all these children. Oh my God, you nearly hit that van then. Look, he's shaking his fist at us. Oh My God, you're going too fast. If you don't slow down now Edwin, I'm getting out at the next police station and I'll have you arrested. Look Out! Look Out! Those lights are on red. Can't you see? Can't you see? Oh you're NOT going to try to overtake here are you. You're a madman. Stop the car Edwin – I'm going to turn you in. I will I swear it. I'll see you in prison for the way you're driving. Oh Holy Mother of God save us – look out! look out! he's pulling out…"

And on and on she wailed.

Father completely and utterly ignored her and our headlong flight continued, with squealing tyres, booming exhaust, opposite lock, braking on a sixpence and with all the excitement of Le Mans until an inner-seat child was sick. Inner because the outer children, before they spewed-up usually had time to wind down the window, stick their heads out and, if they didn't get their heads knocked off by a passing branch or fence or car, they could happily retch and watch the bile liquid spatter onto the rear wing and make its way with the full-speed slipstream round onto the boot. Most journeys ended with both sides of the car thus redecorated and two retching, wretched children in danger of falling out of the back windows as Father negotiated a double-chicane on opposite lock with masterly skill. But Father's fastidiousness overcame his racing instincts if a child threatened to spew inside the car. By long experience he had learned that sick over his luggage was unpleasant and took a lot of cleaning; so a heaving child without access to a window, could, in extreme circumstances, bring the express journey to a halt. We all piled out, shivering from the shock of continuous vomiting, for a breath of clean air with no sick fumes and Mother became silent again, gripping the passenger bar and staring palely and tight lipped into the far purple mists of the Welsh mountains still ahead of us.

We once made a similar racing family journey from Stockport to Rome and back- in two cars. But, that's another story.

I was car-sick for most of the time on most journeys. It was perhaps in an unconscious act of revenge for being made so ill that when we got to the boarding house, about half a mile back up a hill from the seafront at Llandudno, I hatched a cunning plan that still, many years later, fills me with merriment.

The house was pebble dashed, on a steep hill, and accommodated about fifteen people. There were no en-suite rooms in those days and, amazingly, there was just one lavatory between all of us. It was a small narrow solid room upstairs, sporting glazed lavatory paper, a puritan invention that never actually worked, with a little, boy sized, frosted glass window. For the sake of efficient airflow, the window was usually open just a little at the bottom. The guests were polite Englishmen and Englishwomen. Though on summer holiday, the men wore ties and sports jackets in the house and the women wore Lewis's prints. There was no noise. It was all very civilised and buttoned up. Only an inquisitive child would have opened the lavatory window wide and noted that due to the steep slope on which the house was built, while the little room was upstairs, the window sill was just five feet above the rear garden path.

After a full English breakfast, served to all at the same hour for the convenience of the landlady, I was away from the table and up to the lavatory, into the room. I locked the door, slid the window open and climbed out, lowering myself to the path. The lavatory; the one and only lavatory in this most lower-middle class English setting, despite being in Wales, was now empty and securely locked on the inside. Then I returned discreetly to the silent dining room – and waited. Soon the guests, whispering timidly, started to leave, giving little good-morning nods as they exited. After eight or nine had gone, I followed and joined the self-conscious little English queue forming on the landing outside the lavatory door. The average lower and middle class bladder and bowel is of durable construction and of copious dimensions. But they are not infinite and eventually crossing one's toes and clenching one's jaw and buttocks is no longer enough. But breeding and hierarchy is paramount in Britain and no command structure had yet been established – so despite the discomfort, the queue, queued. I was of course quietly quaking. They fidgeted silently. A long happy time elapsed.

Maybe it showed. Or maybe his natural authority emerged under the stress. Or maybe he had drunk more tea than the others. Whatever broke the dam, it was Father who first spoke.
"Who's in there?" he said sharply.
And within seconds several mature males of the primate species Homo-Sapiens were firmly turning, pushing and tugging at the door handle. One tapped on the door.
"Who's there? Are you alright?" then to the fidgeting and increasingly rebellious queue,
"Do you know who is in there? They might be ill."
Throughout these polite if firm exchanges, the adults were, unconsciously of course, counting on their fingers and placing each guest in their right locations. The missing person, would, by logical deduction, be occupying the lavatory. Logic failed. There was no such person. But still they were unsure. I quivered and quaked merrily but all behind a dead-pan face that even Richard could not have fathomed.

How Father realised that it had to be me, I'll never know, as he took the secret to the grave with him when he died at sixty-six, running, flat-out of course and in A-One health, for a train at Euston Station. But he twigged and after rapid fire questioning to ascertain the barest of facts, and, as timing was now of the essence, with all prisoner's rights summarily cast aside in view of the acute state of the emergency, I was frog marched round the house and ignominiously shovelled back into the window and on pain of death or far, far worse, I was pressured to unlock the Llandudno lavatory door. As they nodded and bobbed and were wholly occupied with the urgent business in hand uttering excruciating "after you; - oh no after you I insist" politeness-es, I escaped and ran to a distant place where I could at last howl for a long time with unrestrained laughter.

It remains my best practical joke ever.

***

Chapter 16 - Liliana and The Laurels

3 May 1951: King George opens Festival of Britain - King George VI has inaugurated the Festival of Britain and opened the Royal Festival Hall on London's South Bank. - The festival has been organised to mark the centenary of the Great Exhibition of 1851. It is intended to demonstrate Britain's contribution to civilisation, past, present, and future, in the arts, in science and technology, and in industrial design. - After a special service attended by the King, Queen Elizabeth, Princesses Elizabeth and Margaret and other senior members of the royal family, King George declared the festival open in a broadcast from the steps of St Paul's Cathedral. - Cheering and flag-waving crowds lined the route taken by the King and Queen to St Paul's from Buckingham Palace. BBC Archives.

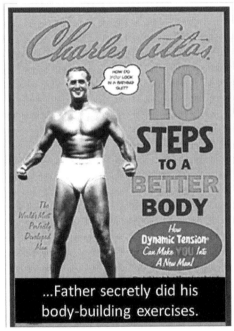

Liliana, an eighteen-year-old Italian beauty, came in 1951 from southern Italy to live with us for a year or so in the damp and cold of northern England, bringing with her a hint of the exotic and temperamental south. Mother, bringing up six children, was getting tired and father, getting wealthier, could afford an "au-pair" a domestic position which had just become a fashionable addition to many aspiring middle-class families. We puzzled for some time over the origins of the term, at first writing it as 'au pere' until mother forbade the very idea, consulted her books and informed us it meant, in French, 'on an equal footing.'

Like us, Liliana was a Catholic and – mother firmly believed, knowing something of the restrictions in poor but respectable Italian families, that Liliana would be a 'Good Catholic Girl' – of the very type that she was already introducing from the local stable of good girls, the plainer and more frigid the better, to her young sons, for the sake of our immortal souls – and therefore, presumably, it was supposed that even with an obviously highly potent, active and manly man for a husband, mother could safely assume that there would be no hanky-panky with the au-pair and no scandal in our household – thank you very much.

Father had improved his manliness, before and during the War, by assiduously following The Charles Atlas body building course, which applied "dynamic tension", muscle countering muscle, to turn a mouse into a man – able to punch beach bullies who paraded around kicking sand into the faces of wimps and weaklings. Father was not a wimp. We discovered his course manuals stored in the tea-chests in one of our six empty attics at the top of the house, along with his neatly preserved courses and notes from his studies to become a Chartered & Certified Accountant, his Home Guard Manual, his Fleet Air Arm officer's uniform and, of great interest, several Gas Masks with a Baby Gas Protector – essentially a round canvas kit bag with a window and a gas filter to breathe through. Fortunately, the Germans did not drop mustard or chlorine gas bombs on our cities – so the masks were unused. Father's entire life history was carefully packed into four or five tea-chests in one of the attics.

We used one of the front attics to space out cooking apples from our trees, in neat rows. Properly done, the bounteous harvest would provide apple-pies until February.

Now Father prepared three other attics, with electric wiring and lights, as a flat for the arrival of the Au-Pair – and he secretly practised his Charles Atlas routines.

Earlier that year, Father Burnley, the parish priest, came into the eight-year-olds class at St Winifred's one sunny morning, clearly with something of great import to impart. Sister Angela, a younger, stick wielding, mean and narrow nun who taught us, was all of a dither, hushing the children though we weren't whispering, dusting the top of her table, tidying already neat papers and brushing down her immaculate black habit. I was not only top of the class (Ann without an 'E' hadn't yet launched her challenge on my supremacy) but I was also very clued up on Catechism and the Testaments Old and New.

"I have come here this morning children…" intoned the priest earnestly,

Sister Angela
A strict teacher.

"...to choose this year's new altar-boys."

A religiously respectful hush descended and heads started to turn to identify the lucky boys who were about to be so honoured. Dust motes danced silently in the generous sunbeams that glanced across the room.

"Though many of you here would make very good servers at the Lord's altar..." Father Burnley continued evenly, "...sadly there is only space for four new boys." The respectful hush deepened. "I'll call out the names we've chosen." he smiled with an acknowledgment to Sister Angela who smirked and bobbed her head at him, "And then I'll ask you if you would like to volunteer to serve the Lord in this way."

Like a talent show presenter, he read out the nominations from fourth to first choice, "Laurence Delaney; Edward Shaw; Christopher Keegan; and Noel Hodson."

The class shuffled and smiled a bit. Even Sister Angela swept a congratulatory, yet still wary and warning glance over her charges. Father Burnley maintained his serious face.

"Now Laurence, would you like to be one of our altar-boys?" he asked warmly.

How could anyone say "no" to this holy honour, which probably included a Plenary Indulgence, a sure-fire Catholic passport to Heaven.
"Yes Father" answered Laurence, as did Edward and as did Christopher.

As a child I would normally do just about anything to comply rapidly, to be accepted, to fit in and most of all not to have to explain myself to an audience.

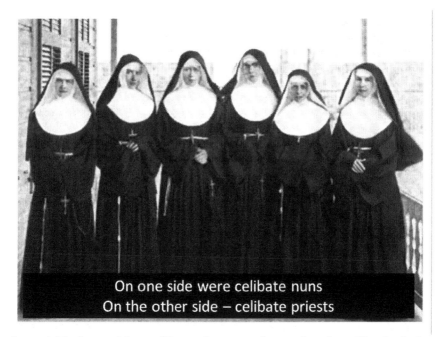

"...and Noel, would you like to be one of our altar boys?" asked the priest confident of the answer I would give.

He and Sister Angela were just about ready for the next step in these appointments and all but turned to their papers.

"No Father, I don't want to" I stammered in red and rising panic.

As the shock receded and they realised they would never get a coherent reason from me for this negative response, the nun and the priest repaired the damage by choosing another lucky boy – and the deed was done and ended.

Despite witnessing a miracle on a Catholic mass schools pilgrimage by train and ferry to Lourdes, source of innumerable healing miracles; we youngsters could only guess at the deep religious significance, indeed on a completely calm sea – obviously the holy miracle - of the violently rocking lifeboats, of the missing older girls and boys and of the outraged, priests and nuns, failing in their frantic panic and obstructing black habits to scramble up the rigging to the boats, to stop them rocking, we presumed. But no other Catholic miracle intervened in or changed the course of my life.

After school we, Richard, me, Peter and later little Martin, walked back to Mauldeth Road with the Keegans: Michael, Bernard, Chris and their little sister Angela, who was Peter's age. My pal Lawrence Delaney came with us part way, peeling off home up Hawthorn Grove, which eventually led to the Clay Pits; a no-man's land where young gangs from far and wide came to chance the ancient, derelict brick-works, deep pools, earthen hills and bicycle paths as steep and dangerous as the Big Dipper at Belle Vue.

First stop from school was our kitchen in Birch House where we carved up a fresh loaf of bread, if mother and Liliana were out of the way, spread the slices with a quarter pound of butter and half a pot of strawberry jam and thus refuel the energy wasted in school.

Then, if it was still light, as it usually was that late spring, we dispersed and made for our favourite playgrounds. For me the most alluring place was the Laurels, where we made dens, climbed ancient conker trees with the aid of six-inch nails and ropes and carved out secret pathways under the dense shrubbery and grasses.

The Laurels was three or four acres of grounds of a house bombed in the war – and cleared. No adults came to it and nobody tried to tame its natural growth. It had once had a large stable block with a yellow brick floor, still intact, and enclosed on two sides by a twenty-five-foot-high wall that still stood – and that we could climb, run along and leap from into a deep pile of hay that we had gathered in a corner of the one-time stable.

But one evening as I demolished my second strawberry jam, doorstep sized sandwich and made to leave, I was waylaid by Liliana, the first live-in domestic we had had; eighteen years old, Mediterranean, slender, and – yes of course – an olive skinned beauty, from Naples. As I've said, for her arrival, sight unseen, father energetically, looking younger, had had decorated and electrified the whole haunted floor of six abandoned attics at the top of the house and he furnished two of the adjoining attics, those with the best outlook, as a bed-sitter for the Au-Pair.

Father shed years
as he fixed the
attics for , sight unseen,
Liliana,
our Au "Pere"
from Napoli.
(Artist's fantasy)

Liliana had a proposition for me. We struggled with her limited English and my ability to guess her mimes but we got to the nub of it. Her boyfriend, George, was coming to see her in a few days-time; he would have afternoon tea in the garden, if the weather was good, and then take her out for the evening. Before he came she wanted me to teach her the lyrics to the popular song, _**They try to tell us we're too young,**_ sung by a Mario Lanza sound-alike or it might have been a song by the great man himself. In any case, Liliana wanted to sing it to her boyfriend – in English.

The deal was that I would get to meet George. It was enough - because George was a Commando, a Royal Marine Commando, on leave from fighting in Korea, and he would be in uniform, complete with his Green Beret.

So I listened to the radio, tuning in to Forces Favourites, to hear the song and then, instead of vanishing off to the Laurels each evening, I first patiently relayed the lyrics to Liliana and corrected her notes and words as she practised.

"They try to tell us we're too young..." she crooned huskily, as we imagined the thousand sweet strings which backed the singer...

"Too young to really be in love,

They say that's Love's a word,

A word we've only heard,

And can't begin to know the meaning of..."

She sang slowly and sadly, a Juliet separated from her Romeo by dried out, envious old women and jealous, shrivelled old men with medals and grey beards,

Then with operatic force she triumphed;

"And Yet – We're not too young - to know,

Our love will last - though years may flow..."

I wasn't at all sure what this 'Love' business was all about, but I faithfully coached her to sing the right words with a good English accent – northern accent of course. The mixture of back-street Neapolitan, modulated Mancunian, Mantovani's thousand strings, and my on-the-half-beat timing, made for a rather pleasing affect; which I thought even the toughest Commando would be swayed by.

And then she sang the last lines softly and longingly...

"And then someday, - they may recall,

We were not - too young - at all."

And an entire orchestra soared with us into an orgasmic celebration of longing, love, and life.

Once Liliana could manage the song on her own, I was off to the Laurels.

Our private nature park and playground was coming under a lot of stress that spring and summer.

Not only were the Keegans, three lads and their young sister Angela, spending more and more time there; with the unfair advantage that their house backed onto one of the lanes bounding the Laurels, but Michael Carroll, whose house in Priestnall Road backed right up to the Laurels' west hedge, took it into his head to wander in, without our permission.

On top of all these local interlopers, Jackie Wake and her friends also sauntered in on many evenings. Jackie, who actually lived opposite Leeman's field on Didsbury Road, a robust girl visiting the Keegans, even committed the unforgivable diplomatic blunder, in our territory, of wrestling my older brother Richard to the ground and sitting on him until he gave up the struggle; a public defeat which scarred his soul for decades.

It was during that same summer, before large new gates were fitted to the original generous and open IN and OUT driveways of the old house that an intrusive middle-aged man, wheeling a bike, took to watching us from the empty gateways. He lurked in the lane with his back to the Lawless's garden fence as we played at the far end of the untamed acres – and climbed the high stable wall, to jump off it into a thick pile of hay gathered in a corner of the walls. He turned up five or six times, in the evening, keeping his distance, but eventually, having waited for the younger children to go, leaving us seven to ten-year-olds to play on – the man ventured in and tried to ingratiate himself with us. His advances were unsuccessful – but somewhat sinister – so we told parents – who told the police, who sent a constable – who spoke to the man, who never came again.

And finally, also invading our space, two new boys, the Reeves, had moved into Mauldeth Road and although older than us, they several times explored the recreational possibilities of our sacred wilderness.

Wilderness? Well it had been for as long as we could remember - but no longer. Someone, none of us had seen who, had parked a small modern caravan in the stable block area – then drawn the curtains and locked it.

We quickly unlocked it and the older boys, led by Richard, found it a convenient place, particularly when it rained, to smoke abandoned stubs of cigarettes, in little wooden pipes, and to play cards – the start of Richard's long and profitable career in gambling.

But they, whoever it was, also fenced off the outlet to the Keegan's garage area and they fitted two sets of tall wooden gates at the wide IN & OUT entrances in the east wall opposite the Lawless's vegetable garden, and, insult piled upon insult, they had made the wall impassable by mounting a high chain-link fence along its top. Presumably the same someone, a few weeks later, erected several 'PRIVATE - KEEP OUT' signs, visible from the front and side lanes – which we of course ignored.

But we could no longer ignore the changes when, while our backs were turned, a substantial wooden hut, locked more securely than the caravan, was plonked in the south-east corner on top of one of our dens, obliterating two secret pathways. And then, without so much as a by-your-leave these same vandals, these wreckers, these alien invaders, mowed the central area and started flattening it and painting lines on it – to make a cricket pitch.

Aghast, we murmured more and more loudly against these creeping "improvements" to our Laurels. Who the devil were they anyway? But we were pacific – we bore the invasion with patience and mature calm. We continued, of course, to completely ignore the increasing number of PRIVATE signs that seemed to spring out of the ground like weeds.

The playing field or cricket pitch, or whatever they were trying to make, only occupied the middle of the Laurels, leaving the borders as wild and useful as ever. We moved our dens into the margins, reworked our secret paths through the shrubs and hidden piles of rubble and made new escape holes in the thick hedge along the long northern border with the allotments – in case we ever needed to escape that way. In short, we accommodated the unseen aliens, we compromised, and got on with our lives as before.

One late spring evening, when we were gracing their newly mown grass with an impromptu game of cricket – one wicket being the great conker tree, twenty feet round and patterned like a plane-tree standing on the allotment boundary – the other being a newly arrived, heavy iron roller we had sweated to bring into the middle of the pitch, the padlocked gates at the far eastern end suddenly swung open and an open backed van full of men, raced across the grass. We scattered, and the men, in fact mostly teenagers in cricket whites, chased us. But, fleet though they were and urged on by the older men as they were, we were in our Laurels, and we knew our land – and they couldn't catch any of us.

I slipped away towards the Priestnall Road end, and, unseen, climbed above the high shrubs up a tall thin sycamore tree, high into its topmost leafy branches overlooking the pitch. My friends scrambled over the south lane wall and vanished in seconds, and then re-appeared, resting their elbows along the top and watching closely. A few aggressive invaders ran at them again, and my pals disappeared – to return as soon as the cricketers gave up.

The newcomers, we were soon to discover, came from Heaton Moor College, a small boarding school up near St Paul's church, which garbed its inmates, many from overseas, in brown jackets and caps with a yellow badge. This was the very same school that David Hall attended most of his school life as a day-boy; bringing his Headmaster to the verge of a nervous breakdown as David would learn nothing of any academic worth - whatsoever.

Short of open land near the school buildings, they had, without any consultation with us, the rightful tenants, bought the Laurels for their playing fields. We learned this news that very evening as, tragically, Bernard Keegan, Biff, – why do these things always happen to the nicest people – had run and escaped but left his jacket behind, draped over the iron roller, where an eagle eyed teacher pounced on it victoriously.

The evil tutor held the jacket aloft and waved it at the row of faces along the wall. He even had the temerity to address us – though not me as I was hidden up my tall tree.

"Whose jacket is this?" the sports teacher demanded waving the nearly new garment in the air. "You'd better come and get it – hadn't you?" he warbled with pleasure.

Nobody moved. Would they take the jacket with them or leave it there? – It was already growing dusk and there was less than an hour of light left.

The jubilant teacher anticipated our thoughts. "I can always go through the pockets," he challenged, knowing he held the winning cards, "and I'll bet your address is on something in here."

Biff – the most kindly and best behaved boy among us – hauled himself reluctantly over the wall and walked bravely to meet his executioner – who grabbed him by the arm and took him aside for interrogation.

Another teacher was organising the cricket team to roll and mark a pitch. They moved our carefully sited roller, our wicket, seeming to lament the depression it had left – right in the middle of the green. Seeing it, the arresting officer shook Biff and pointed angrily. Biff could only shrug regretfully and say nothing.

They went and unlocked the new shed to bring forth a lining machine which was filled with whitewash and rolled along the margins, making neat white lines. As they came around the western edge, a gangly youth, a prefect I suspect, glanced up and spotted me up my tree. He got quite excited and made alarm calls which brought them all running. A crowd gathered round the base of the tree – and I was truly treed.

"You! Boy! Come down at once" ordered the Bernard-Catcher, intent on clearing out the whole damned nest of these ragamuffin trespassers.

Straddling a slender fork and clinging on to a topmost branch where I had been happily browsing new sycamore leaves (which are quite tasty as a spring snack) like a small contented primate, I considered my options. And then shook my head.

The teacher shook his fist, glaring up at me. The light was fading.

"Come down at once – or else" bellowed the teacher.

I knew all about bellowing. It was what I did to scare off bigger boys who threatened me – and my rages were so convincing that I could put whole gangs to flight. I had once rescued Richard from a thumping from Titch Noon, three years older than me and the cock of our school, by loosing one of my temper tantrums at him. Bellowing didn't count – I was better at it than this inexperienced teacher. I couldn't be cowed by my own technique.

I shook my head again.

The teacher furiously searched his pockets, producing a notebook and pencil which he held aloft and purported to write in.

"What's your name?" he demanded, "Give me your name, or I'll call the Police."

This did perturb me. I took another handful of new leaves to chew while I thought it through. The nearest police station – even if he knew where it was, was set back in the infants' school yard at the top of Balmoral Lane, half a mile away. The nearest telephone – unless he had the awfully bad manners to barge into a house and ask to use the phone, which was unheard of after six o'clock – and I guessed it was now after eight – was further on, outside the post office on Heaton Moor Road. And it was going dark. I once again relied on the old Lancashire adage: *When in doubt – Do nowt.*

I said nothing and looked unemotionally at the crowd below.

"I'll get him Sir!" volunteered one of the taller cricketers, grabbing at the tree trunk.

Come down here Boy!

The light was fading...

I knew that he wouldn't. He was twice my weight and would break the branches of this leggy tree – and plunge to his doom. I was forty-feet or so high.

The teacher, fatally for his bluff, hesitated. "If you don't come down immediately – we'll come up and bring you down!" he threatened unconvincingly.

"You and whose army?" I thought truculently; but wisely I said nothing.

They were having difficulty seeing me now as the daylight was slowly extinguished. I was wearing my ubiquitous grey shirt, grey pullover, grey trousers, grey socks and black – or off-black, almost grey shoes. My hair was mousey and my face and hands soiled – a greyish colour. I was well camouflaged. I was unconvinced by his promised action. I made no move.

The teenager in his white kit made to start up the tree, eager to show his climbing skills. The teacher held his arm and shook his head.

Had they been state school boys, he might have taken the risk of losing a few lives, but these were fee paying pupils, most with parents living abroad – possibly administrators in British Embassies and so probably important or well connected, or both. The teacher – determined though he was, couldn't risk having to explain to a bereaved parent about one of his precious charges plummeting to earth, to his untimely death, clutching this aggravating, small, soiled, ape-like creature in his arms.

And it was going – or damn it! - it had gone, dark.

Heaton Moor College decided to withdraw.

I waited ten minutes after they had driven away. Then I climbed down the tree, in the dark, slipped along one of our many hidden pathways, silently climbed the stable wall and made the difficult drop down the other side – into the lane by the Keegan's.

Though we continued to use the Laurels with impunity, keeping a weather eye out for the new owners; it wasn't the same. The wilderness had been tamed and we had lost our natural habitat. We had to adjust or die out as a species.

But the next Saturday I forgot the Laurels and the cricketers when Liliana's George came, in uniform as promised, for tea in the garden. He was young, tanned, handsome, good fun – a fully trained Royal Marine Commando, the toughest soldiers on Earth, and he taught me how Commando's use unarmed combat to vanquish their enemies and to kill with one blow. Within just half an hour I was transformed into a deadly, lethal weapon. If only I had had the lessons before the cricket team arrived to evict us.

Next time I saw her Liliana reported that the song had gone very well; she had remembered all the words in the right order. But just a week later, on a Saturday, her gratitude seemed to have evaporated.

Disenchanted with the conversion of the Laurels from wild jungle to suburban park, a gang of us were careering around the garden of Birch House for most of the afternoon. Even though it was a fine day, Liliana had to light a fire in the kitchen to help dry clothes quickly on the rack above. The coal fire wouldn't come to life and she stuck a long poker into its heart to lift the smouldering coals and let in air. Then she forgot it. An hour later the fire was intensely hot and the poker was incandescent.

She was pretty. Even at nine I could appreciate Liliana's beauty – in a detached, chaste, celibate and aesthetic way. But the older boys, just entering puberty, were more than artistically pleased by her; for reasons they could not comprehend, she excited them. They got silly around her. They said and did idiotic things to capture her attention – between booting footballs, climbing trees and throwing spears in the garden. As the afternoon wore on, they made excuses to go into the house more and more often. They offered to help her with the washing and ironing; they offered to make her cups of tea and they teased her about her accent and tweaked her skirt and apron strings – then dashed off laughing.

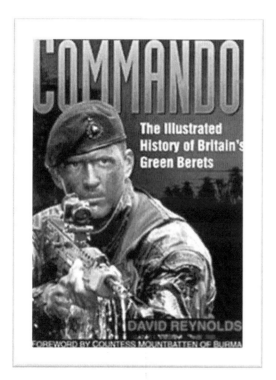

Liliana was getting cross. She shouted at them in Italian and made extravagant gestures with her hands – neck wringing gestures. She left the kitchen and busied herself in the scullery with the washing tub and the electric mangle which squeezed water from the wet laundry and grabbed unwary fingers. Four or five boys, led by the same ingénue, Biff Keegan, sneaked in and hid themselves under our large kitchen table, recessed into a big oblong window seat;

from where they could see her brown legs and could leap out and shout "Boo!"

But a bunch of pre and post pubescent boys are rarely still. They giggled in anticipation like little girls as Liliana carted in a stack of wet clothes and bedding for nine people, and carted out drier ones. They squirmed without knowing what made them squirm, they squeaked the chairs along the floor and they breathed heavily. In short they fidgeted.

What precipitated the attack, I don't know. But it was terrifying. The Mafia would have applauded Liliana's revengeful spirit that day.

The boys became excited around Liliana

Liliana suddenly snapped. She dropped the laundry, Splat! On the tiles, leapt to the fire – remembering to guard herself with a damp towel round her hand - and snatched the white-hot poker from the coals. Yelling in Italian, she lunged the three-foot sizzling bar under the table and waved it about wildly. The space under the table suddenly exploded with four youngsters hurling themselves back out of reach. One touch from that iron would be murderous and cruelly wounding. But they were backed into the alcove, the heavy table knocked askew and pressed against the window seats, leaving no exit – other than through the chair legs past the maddened Italian.

She lunged again, getting down on her knees so she could properly see the targets and thrust the glowing poker at them, one after another. Their scrambling and yelling turned to terrified screaming as this manic foreigner waggled her fantastically dangerous wand at the boys. They were not pretending. They were not giggling. They were truly and simply terrified.

I stood by the kitchen door and watched in horror.

As suddenly as she had started, Liliana stopped her attack. "OUT!" she shouted, adding a turbulent stream of rich Italian invective.

And they got out. They crawled out. They rolled out. They scuttled out. They got out any way they could, giving Liliana the widest possible berth and rushed past me.

She flashed a look at me. No memories of love songs or Mario Lanza showed in her eyes. I got out too.

The house was strangely quiet after that.

A few months later, in the autumn, Liliana left us. Mother said she had moved to another family in Rusholme. There was whispered talk of mother's fur coat going missing and of a visit father made to see Liliana in a police cell. And we never saw her again.

In the winter Liliana's place was taken by Bruno – the same age, from the same place, with the same olive skin. But Bruno was fat and uncommunicative. She sat a great deal. She chain-smoked and gazed into the fire for hour after hour after hour. She only moved when prodded by mother. She held no excitement, no mysterious promise for the local boys, whose awakened libido's reverted to a state of quiescent youthful arrested development – while father put back on the years he had briefly seemed to shed.

Heaton Moor was a more sombre village without the fiery Liliana.

***

Chapter 17 - Jelly and Gin

*8 Oct 1959 – General Election - Following the **Suez Crisis** in 1956, **Anthony Eden** the Conservative Prime Minister became unpopular and resigned early the following year to be succeeded by Harold Macmillan. At this stage, the Labour Party, with Hugh Gaitskell having taken over as leader from **Clement Attlee** just after the 1955 election, enjoyed large opinion poll leads over the Conservatives, and it looked as if they could win. The Liberals also had a new leader in **Jo Grimond**, meaning that all three parties would contest the election with a new leader at the helm. However, the Conservatives enjoyed an upturn in fortunes as the economy improved under Macmillan, and his personal approval ratings remained high. By September 1958, the Conservatives had moved ahead of Labour in the opinion polls - and won. - Wikipedia*

Mother, sporting a big blue Tory lapel badge and a bunch of leaflets, supporting her husband's bid in 1959 to become Conservative Member of Parliament for Gorton, which was a long held Labour Party stronghold, knocked on the door of a small terraced house in Ardwick. The man who opened the door, in collarless shirt and braces, was immediately familiar to and accurately identified by Mother as a stalwart member of the working class; familiar because she had been born and raised nearby, in streets like these. He, on the other hand, mistakenly immediately identified Mother as cosseted middle-class, a toff, playing at politics in her leisure hours, and here standing on his mean, humble and tiny soap-stoned doorstep to solicit his vote for her absent and equally privileged posh husband. He glared silently while she delivered her canvassing spiel – ending with "…and so I do hope you will vote for us in the election next month…?"

Then he launched into a verbal attack; vilifying this upper-class woman who dared to trespass in working-class streets of rows of Victorian terraced homes, which had no bathrooms, had outdoor lavatories and whose occupants worked themselves "to the bone" and an early death – to keep this type of self-styled Lady in comfort and luxury. He ended with "…Gerroff Missus, you've never done a real day's work in your life…" That was his second major mistake.

In measured tones of unstoppable powerful rhetoric, Mother explained to the hapless householder, trapped on his own doorstep, what her average one-hundred-hour week, fifty-two weeks of the year, with a family of six children to cook, clean, wash and care for, consisted of. She explained what washing powder and peeling potatoes did to her hands, what hanging out the sheets, fetching coal and taking out the ashes did to her back, what repairing clothes did to her eyesight, what living alone for six years of war while her husband constantly faced death on the Atlantic ammunition convoys, did to her spirit, "And what pathetic thing did YOU do in the War?"; what working in Longsight (next to Ardwick) from the age of five did to her childhood, and, employing her uncanny instincts about the signals her protagonist unconsciously broadcast as she lambasted him, with incisive knowledge and authority she demolished his role in the world, his lack of success, ambition and intelligence, his inelegant, stained clothing and frayed braces, his bad haircut, his unwelcome body odours, she criticised his height, bodyweight, flaccid muscles, skin tones, scruffy shoes, speech patterns – and finally his utter lack of political understanding.

Cowed and beaten, he did manage to mutter "Sorry Missus" before slumping in despair on his doormat. It is not recorded if the man survived the encounter – or crawled away and put his dandruff infested, work-shy head in the gas-oven.

Trying to turn Gorton into a Tory seat was an uphill struggle, doomed to failure. However, Mother and Father persisted; equipping our car with double loud speakers on the roof and posters on the doors – and driving around the mean streets of the constituency expounding on the virtues of Harold MacMillan, Anthony Eden and the other Conservative aristocrats who had a natural God given right to rule. Father won a bet to swim five miles in the local pool – which won him an article in the local press. Mother overcame her shyness and reticence to man (or woman) the loudspeakers, while Father drove slowly round the district he was raised in; stopping at pubs, clubs and churches to engage with The People. Their efforts were good enough to reduce the large majority of the incumbent Labour MP, Leslie Lever, from many thousands to a few hundred votes – an effort which was recognised by Father being elevated as a Justice of the Peace of Manchester. Mother even conquered her shyness sufficiently to join and rise up the ranks of Save the Children and other politically acceptable charities – and to attend Tory fund raising events – where infamously, drink was taken at lunch time.

We, the bemused children of these campaigning parents, sat silently starving near to death one summer Sunday lunchtime, staring at a fully set but food-less table, while Mother & Father attended a fund raising meeting. Mother had of course prepared a full meal before going out – which was on a low light in the oven, awaiting her dutiful return. She eventually came back, dressed for public politics and slightly oddly different from her normal self. She dished out the stew from the oven to her brood nest of helpless, begging offspring, which we ate in silence as Mother and Father talked more and louder than usual. Next, came the sweet or pudding. We always had a sweet at Sunday lunch.

Mother cleared the main course dishes into the scullery, came back with pudding dishes and spoons, went back to the scullery and returned once more with a large wobbling red jelly which she plonked in the centre of the table – and the centre of her quietly expectant children and husband. Mother stood over the table, raised a large serving spoon, looked slowly over the pudding-craving faces and said uncommonly loudly "Who'd like some jelly?"

None of us answered this obviously rhetorical question that required no response. Without question, we would all like some of the delicious jelly. Who wouldn't like a portion, a large serving of the jelly? Mother again eyed the assembled diners – her loyal family and again raised the large spoon. "Everybody?" she rightly and unnecessarily assumed. And she nodded with total certainty and smashed the spoon down – on the jelly – which spattered in all directions – landing in lumps across the table and on the waiting children and husband. Then she giggled.

Mother, it was explained later, had had a gin and tonic at the event. This was an extraordinary thing – on an empty stomach. We, our family, like the vast majority of families, did not drink alcohol – particularly at Sunday lunch. Mother was tipsy and we were speechless and in shock. The world had shifted on its axis.

***

Part Two – Teenage
1953 to 1962

Chapter 18 - Beauty and the Beast

Surgeons battle to save woman's arms after Alsatians almost tear limbs off in attack at unlicensed dog training kennels – Daily Mail

In 1953 the Lawless's, our next door neighbours, in the house between Birch House and the bombed out Laurels, having survived our casual psychopathic attentions for some years and after the amazingly agile headmaster, Mr Lawless, had visited retribution on a few of us, moved house. Where they went, we neither knew nor cared. The incoming family, Mr & Mrs Marsh and their two children, stirred much more and far wider interest.

Janet Marsh was a little younger than me. Her brother Kenny was just a few months older than me. Their father, dark haired like Janet, was a fearsomely fit and focused looking forty-something – travelling far and wide, selling precision machine parts. Their mother was very pleasant, fey, small, attractive and somewhat distracted. Janet, who at twelve attended the infamous Fylde Lodge School for Girls, a hundred yards or so away, was an athletic gymslip beauty. I was just entering puberty when they arrived and had begun to notice the unfathomable tensions between members of the opposite sex. As she matured, Richard, even though in a different and higher teenage league, couldn't and didn't fail to notice Janet. He received many more visitors at home from his male contemporaries, than previously. Dave Hall, a regular long time visitor to our house, I think fell in love with young, upright and straight laced Janet, who wore her dark hair short and her school clothes neatly pressed. For reasons I never understood, though we rarely spoke, Janet and I had a distance between us, which sometimes, at my most paranoid, I felt as an unspoken hostility.

I became good friends with the somewhat reckless and impetuous Kenny, who as we grew up pursued girls with single minded determined energy, which was more often than not successful.

As we matured, the major obstacle to wooing Janet, for all her would-be suitors of all ages, was a bloody big Alsatian dog, Sultan. Janet and Sultan were inseparable – chained to each other - with Janet strongly gripping one end of the chain and the inexhaustible muscular Sultan pulling at the other, intent on ripping out the throats of all who approached too close, friends and foes alike. One also imagined that the dark-eyed, taciturn, unsmiling Mr Marsh would not take kindly to overly familiar boyfriends sidling up to his well-built, virginal daughter. Fortunately, he was often abroad on business, leaving his testosterone driven son; small, strong, blonde and super fit, to explore life unimpeded by adult rules – and freeing Janet's admirers to lurk around and admire her.

Kenny, bright and schooled at the prestigious Stockport Grammar, would have a go at any sport; was good at them all and he took risks that more cautious boys, like me, might take days or weeks to consider before diving in. As a long time Heaton Mersey resident, when one weekend it snowed heavily and wetly, it was incumbent on me as host to collect a few pals, including Michael McCarron – one of thirteen McCarron children, and invite Kenny to go to our favourite steep sledging hill, Leeman's field. The field came up to the main Didsbury Road, next to St Winifred's RC school; from the road it fell sharply, at more than 45 degrees, down to a tree lined pond of two acres. Kenny had nicked his dad's new driving gloves – woven white cotton backed onto pale tan leather – fashionable and enviable cold weather protection.

The main fast run was disappointingly bare of snow, due to wet snow falling onto sodden ground and because of the wind direction. But a lesser slope on the right, from the school boundary down to the pond, had a pristine covering of gleaming white snow – and we went to the top of it. We five older hands who knew the field well, stood hesitantly at the top, with sledges parked. This short hill, we knew, and so did Kenny know, descended to a dell, backed by a smooth bank, beyond which it dropped suddenly to the big pond. In the dell, covered with deep snow was a small pond – more of a muddy puddle than pond, which when stirred in summer months by hunts for newts, frogs and creepy crawlies, emitted foul gases from trapped mud. Was the small pond frozen, and was the ice cover supporting the inviting snow, and was the ice strong enough to take a sledge? We wondered. If so, if well frozen, it offered an exciting skilful swoop down the hill, a fast skid across the icy pond, an up-rush over the bank, and a clever sideways turn to avoid a dive into the water beyond. And so we hesitated; tacitly coming to the intelligent conclusion that we should walk down – test the ice with a stick or stone – walk back up – and then …zoom!

Faster than our cautious thoughts could be formed into words, Kenny was off! He dived onto his sledge with a whoop; gripping the front with his brand spanking new driving gloves, and he careered down to the dell – at quite an exhilarating speed considering the cloying softness of the wet snow. Arms extended, head down, lying flat to reduce drag, Kenny hit the pond. The ice, such as it was, immediately disintegrated and at full speed Kenny disappeared through the virgin snow, leaving a veritable tunnel, and he plunged into the foul swamp mud below; which oozed back up the tunnel and blackened the banks.

By the time we reached him, the stench of marsh gases was already fouling the cold, but sadly not freezing, air and Kenny was dragging himself from the shallow stinking pit, still clutching his sledge rope. He was covered, mired from head to toe, to the tips of his still well protected fingers, in black, sticky, gaseous mud; and was in shock.

Somehow we bundled him onto the sledge, sitting, shivering and slumped forwards in dishevelled despair. The five of us manhandled the sledge to the top and pulled and pushed it round the contour line back to the main road. We dragged his sodden form through the fence and back onto the sledge and started the long walk back home, over the snow that was just firm enough to let it slide. Eventually we reached his home, 20 Mauldeth Road. It was about 4.30 pm and going dark on that winter's eve. His dad's new, black, polished, smart executive car, from which Kenny had "borrowed" the gloves, was in the driveway. We lifted him off the sledge, bundled him, stinking, shivering and dripping, to the front porch – leaned him against the door, rang the bell – and retreated.

From a safe distance, in the dark, we waited until the door opened and his, at first shocked, then concerned and then irate frowning Father dragged the boy inside and closed the door against the night.

Kenny never did give us the full satisfactory story of what dad said to son and what son said to dad – and what happened to the expensive gloves; so likewise, we will now draw a veil over the incident.

With the benefit of hindsight and age and great wisdom, it occurs to me that Janet's barely detectable hostility towards me and subtle distancing may have dated from that day. What more could we have done to save her big brother from retribution and disgrace? Perhaps we should have got him out of the country for a few years.

But, though at the time I was unquestionably not in the running for a sweet smile or kind word from Janet, courted as she was by many older, bigger, more handsome, richer lads than I – there was another incident which, again with the benefit of hindsight, from my now great age, I interpret as her not being entirely indifferent to me.

Janet and Sultan were inseparable, chained together.

About ten of us, girls and boys, aged thirteen going on fourteen, were gathered in the sun, on the five green flat acres of Fylde Lodge sports fields, a mile or so from home. Some of us wheeled bikes that suddenly seemed too small for these growing gangly youths, some smoked cigarettes, without coughing much, and some just fooled around. From the acres of allotments that separated the playing fields from the Marsh's house, came Janet and a couple of friends, complete with Sultan; unusually the dog was unleashed.

Our two parties were fifty or so yards apart when someone tweaked Janet's skirt or took her beret or some such juvenile excuse for contact – and one of her party threw a ball to us. The brute of an Alsatian chased towards us, then veered determinedly for no reason to race at me, growling aggressively, – and Janet suddenly shouted "Get him Sultan – Get him". As I've said, dog and girl were devoted and joined in psychic bonds which enabled Sultan to precisely know his mistress's mind. On came the dog at full tilt, mouth wide, snarling, bright white teeth seeming in excellent condition for tearing out throats, and jumped at me. I had a dog, at that time a large bullmastiff, and knew dogs and was not particularly afraid of them, and would not do harm to one. But this gigantic wolf hound was clearly intent on showing me how it could bring down a male teenager – and perhaps tear off an arm or two before biting out my throat. So, as it rose towards me, in mid-flight, I jerked my knee upwards and caught it squarely under its chin. Sultan's jaws snapped shut – on his tongue. Thus discouraged, he missed me and landed at one side, squealing like a baby – and high-tailed it back to Janet, tail between the legs and yelping with fear and pain.

My defensive action and the humiliation of her terrible beast did nothing to strengthen our non-existent friendship. As we rarely spoke, there was no reason for her to single me out from the crowd and set Sultan into kill-mode. Do you think that Janet had a secret thing for me – her neighbour and her older brother's friend? I'm sure that David Hall would have died for the privilege of being so focused upon; to be in her mind's eye. He would gladly have fed one or the other of his arms to Beauty and her terrible Beast. Better to be hated and hunted down by a slavering wolf than to be ignored by this desirable enigmatic Princess.

A year later, we had aged sufficiently enough to take ourselves off to the Pennines, by train to Edale, under Kinderscout, for a week's camping. Six of us, in three little tents, pitched in a farmer's field, by a tinkling stream, cooked and washed and slept – and walked about looking, inevitably, for footloose and fancy-free females of our age. Not that we had the slightest idea of what might ensue if we found such

1957 Edale.

Kenny was the only one brave enough to bathe in the freezing stream.

Kenny Marsh – bathing at our camp in Edale. C 1957

fair maidens. And not that there were any maidens, of our age, without alert, outward bound and stout parents or guardians, with equally stout boots, stout staffs and decidedly unwelcoming attitudes. But the endless optimism of curious, exploring maturing youths kept us daily at our hopeless quest.

Typically, Kenny was the only one of the six of us who was bold and tough enough to bathe in the very cold stream running past our camp, which descended from the bleak hills above. Clean and refreshed, ever optimistic, he led us out once more to search the deserted highways, sparsely populated camps and sleepy hamlets for elusive companionship and love.

***

Competing with Kenny Marsh's home as our favourite party venue, and especially blessed with liberal, fun loving parents, was the home of the Rider family, who kept "open-house" at Number 1 Elms Road, close by Heaton Moor Park where youths assembled in large numbers. The Riders comprised the remarkably pretty Eileen, Mrs Rider; Eddie, Mr Rider; and their six children – Tony, the eldest who seemed to have aristocratic heritage; Terry the next son, who conversely must have had a mongrel heritage; then Peter-John, my age, who became my close friend; followed by three girls – Mary-Jo, a blonde pale beauty; red haired and kindly Penny, and finally little Janine; who, as the youngest, was possibly a wee bit spoiled and indulged.

These eight, attractive, outgoing and social family members had many friends, spanning all classes and a wide age range – and all were welcome to drop in at their home, at pretty much any time of day or night. The doors were rarely locked and tea and toast was always freely available. For several years, I spent a lot of time with Peter-John, mostly at his family's hospitable house.

When we were old enough to drive, Peter-John suddenly got the keep-fit bug and organised several of us for early Sunday morning hill walking – and like our early previous camping trip, this was also from Edale village and up onto the high almost impassable black-peat-bog plateau of Kinderscout, where it was rumoured that dozens of walkers were lost and had died on that featureless, baffling, eerie moor. Our teenage outings were not so much walks as silent hooligan races. An hour's combative drive from Stockport brought us to the village square where we parked close by a dark green corrugated iron hut, which later in the morning, on our return would be open and serving steaming tea and bacon sandwiches – also hot and steaming. Behind the village pub ran a rapid river which rushed in a gully alongside the narrow rocky path down from the crown of Kinderscout. Serious walkers assembled in grim little groups at the pub; checked their life saving maps, whistles, compasses, rations, water, first-aid kits, hats, boots, laces, blankets, waterproofs and energy tablets, before venturing bravely onto the upland trails, where damp, cold mists could descend in minutes and maroon the unfit and ill-prepared.

We heretical teenagers arrived in our tennis shoes, plimsoles, or wearing wellies in wet weather, slacks, louche open shirts, some of us daringly without ties, tweed jackets, hatless and map-less. Being young gentlemen we walked sedately behind the pub – at about 8 o'clock in the morning for a hundred yards or so until we left the village

– then we jumped down into the river bed onto the rocks and smashed trees and, leaping dangerously from rock to rock, we raced up the mountain stream bed, spurning the carefully signed paths and risking life and limb with every leap we conquered the river, its gullies and its waterfalls. The narrow river, which as we climbed, became a stream and then a set of springs which cascaded from the great flat millstone rocks piled one on the other at the top, with wonderful views over the Edale and Hope valleys to the south and, to the north, over the uninviting, dangerous, black peat bogs with their deep defiles.

At the top, Kenny, Peter-John, Goulash, I, and a few assorted other early risers, reassembled on the great rock – admired the view, got back our breath – and then raced down the precipitous path. Again, but now in full view, we leapt from rock to rock to hassock to rushes to mud patch, in a pell-mell descent, back the way we had come. Typically, near the bottom, half a mile up from the pub we encountered and sped silently by the sober parties of real outward-bound, fully equipped hikers, who had started out at the same time as us, labouring up the footpath with their eyes set on the distant pinnacle rocks, half a day away, that we had commandeered a few minutes earlier. Occasionally, in fine weather, we diverted up the valley sides to ponder yet again over the wreckages of planes downed onto the moors in the war – and swapped tales of our respective dad's roles in beating the Hun.

Straightening our hair – usually soaking wet as it rained a lot then and still does today, and tidying our jackets – we arrived back at the humid, warm corrugated iron tea-shop and claimed our rewards – pint mugs of tea and doorstep sized hot bacon sandwiches. And each time, every Sunday, consuming this well-earned breakfast, we declared it without reservation or fear of contradiction to be the best food we had ever ate and the greatest feast on earth. Another hour's rapid drive back to Stockport and we were home by midday.

It was about this time in our lives that Kenny's dad spent more time abroad and Kenny opened their house to packed teenage parties, ushering in an era of frantic overly-familiar exploratory hot fumbling. And Kenny, with his dad away and a compliant mother, also made room for our noisy skiffle group, orchestrated by Peter Tattersall; with me and my unusual out of rhythm half-beat, on the washboard; Tats of course on the guitar; and Biff Keegan on the tea-chest double bass.

**

Chapter 19 - Cherub

1959: Buddy Holly killed in air crash. Three young rock 'n' roll stars have been killed in a plane crash in the United States. Buddy Holly, 22, Jiles P Richardson - known as the Big Bopper - 28, and Ritchie Valens, 17, died in a crash shortly after take-off from Clear Lake, Iowa at 0100 local time. The pilot of the single-engined Beechcraft Bonanza plane was also killed. Early reports from the scene suggest the aircraft spun out of control during a light snowstorm. – BBC News

Michael Howard lived with his canary, Cherub, which was comfortably middle-aged, rotund and very yellow. Cherub sat quietly and contentedly, observing its small world, on a perch in a wire bird cage of no particular architectural merit, hanging above and close by the kitchen table. This is Cherub's tragic story. For readers with deeply sensitive souls, who are easily disturbed by bleak tales of death and dishonour, you may wish to look away now – skip this story and turn to the next chapter.

Michael also lived with his three-years older sister, Rosemary, who kindly taught me, in 1959, after I was rejected from the Osborne Bentley School of Dance, how to Jive like Elvis Presley and Rock like Bill Haley, a social skill that has served me well ever since; and Michael lived with his father and mother, Mr and Mrs Howard, in a nineteen-thirties, semi-detached, mock-Tudor, part timbered house, standing narrow and tall, on rising land, behind the tree line, well back from the pavement of Priestnall Road, about two hundred winding yards from the infamous and magnetic Fylde Lodge School for Girls, whose buildings dominated the wooded crossroads at Priestnall Road and Mauldeth Road.

Michael, like the house, was also narrow and tall, sporting black hair, oiled with *Brylcreem,* as were the coiffures of all male teenagers in those days, and illicitly allowed to grow longer than the mandatory military short-back-and-sides, which enabled Michael when safely out of parental sight, to flick his hair up and back in pale imitation of and in secret homage to the dark, back-swept look of Elvis. But, uncertain as was his admiration for the Teddy Boy style of the day, it meant that he never combed his straight locks quite determinedly enough for his hair to stay swept back for more than a minute or two and, inevitably, his quiff fell limply forwards and straight across his eyes, to be flicked back moment by moment with his fingers – like a nervous tic – which the girls seemed to find quite attractive.

Taller than his pals, Michael compensated by stooping slightly, sometimes lending him an anxious, hand-wringing appearance. He was an amiable lad, more likely to negotiate than to challenge, with a modestly reliable talent as a card player. My older brother Richard, who played cards with professional skill and dedication, had established a fashion for intensive, schoolboy games of three card brag, pontoon (blackjack) and five card poker, often hosted, for hours and hours, in one of the many unused rooms in Birch House, our haunted Victorian mansion on Mauldeth Road, a hundred yards from Fylde Lodge.

The Game, which was played for real money and from which Richard, winning often, was saving for a two-month Continental hitch-hiking holiday, involved everybody, who was anybody, in the district. As new players heard of it and joined in, The Game grew both in numbers and in stakes. Vital pocket-money was won and lost, leaving some bereft of funds for the coming week. One or two of the older lads had left school early at fifteen and were earning wages, apparently giving them the power to outbid and out-brag the others – but usually losing far more than they had imagined they might and thus enriching the frugal but astute young scholars; giving the lie to the street urchin's taunt *"If you're so clever Mister! Why ain't 'cha rich?"*

Some of the young players were coining it in.

Wealthiest of all, wealthier than the legendary Croesus (I was forty-five before I discovered the saying was not "As rich as creases;" which never made any sense to me – but "As rich as Croesus"; you know - the classical Greek millionaire) and more profligate than Timon of Athens, (he's from Shakespeare) was Willy Mason.

Willy was perhaps a year older than Michael and me, which placed him halfway from our age to my older brother's age, who in turn ranked in maturity alongside local legends such as Terry Rider and - her name can hardly be written without tremors of post pubertal excitement - Susan Grenouille, the fabulous siren of Fylde Lodge School, blonde of course, rumoured to dress like a film star, even mid-week, travel from her modest home into Manchester and meet men, grown men, in the bar of the Midland Hotel – the poshest hotel in the region – to allegedly, so my mother and her friend Mrs Carley knowledgeably averred, indulge in unspecified practices that fourteen-year old youths could only dream about. Willy, painfully thin, faintly blue in the face and as tall as Michael, lived in a large detached, mock Tudor house, on the opposite corner to Fylde Lodge.

The Mason's garage at the side of the house was directly across Priestnall Road, visible from the Head Mistress's first floor Oriel window.

Willy's dad was very, very rich; so rich that he gave Willy twenty-pounds a week pocket money – when the average respectable young teenager would be lucky to be given half-a-crown. To translate this amazing differential, there were eight half-crowns in a pound meaning Willy had one-hundred-and-sixty times as much as his pals and as much as, for example, a thirty-year-old office manager earned in

Manchester. Willy not only had cash to burn but his father let him, even as young as seventeen, drive his cars. Willy, notoriously, crashed two Rolls-Royces in one year, destroying them beyond repair. Terry Rider claimed to have seen the wreckage of the Mason's white Rolls Royce, on Kingsway in Burnage, a modern dual carriageway into Manchester city. He also maintained that Willy was too rich and too thin - so thin that when he stood sideways you thought he'd gone home.

"It was a total bloody mess." Terry assured his goggle eyed audience. "A smoking, smouldering ruin; A complete bloody write-off; Nobody but nobody could have survived inside that car. It was a pile of scrap squashed flat!" And he surveyed his captive audience satisfied that he had them in the palm of his orator's hand.

"It was completely silent. Nobody said anything. Then something moved. A bit of tin shifted and fell off the pile onto the road with a big clang. The only recognisable bit left of the whole car - the only piece you could tell what it had been – was the exhaust pipe..."

Someone sniffed derisively.

"...No honest it was; just the exhaust pipe..." grinned Terry "...There was this great crumpled heap of metal and steam and smoke – and sticking straight up, like the mast on a ship – was the exhaust pipe..."

"...As God is my judge – nobody could have lived through that crash. There was no room in the car left for anyone to be in it..."

"...then..."

Terry waited a moment as his audience shifted inwards, nearer to him. "...And then – there was this little extra puff of smoke came out of the exhaust pipe. Honest it did. ...and it formed a smoke ring that drifted up in the air..."

The collection of boys and girls were smiling, anticipating the next twist in the tale.

"...And I sniffed it. This smoke. And I'll swear to God – on my mother's grave (his dear mother was very much alive) – that it was Turkish, Sobranie tobacco..."

Willy smoked expensive Sobranie cigarettes.

The fabulously wealthy and ever so painfully thin Willy only smoked Black Sobranie cigarettes, a brand which claimed to be made in Russia, which was unlikely. They came in a marvellously expensive pack, were wrapped in matte black cigarette paper with gold leaf tips on each tube – and smelt of exotic, rich, Turkish, sun dried leaf.

"...and the exhaust pipe shifted – just a fraction. And another smoke ring came up from it. ...Honest it did. And then, from this scrap yard of a car, out of the exhaust pipe..."

We all knew that only Willy was slender enough to emerge from a car exhaust;

"...came Willy; Honest to God; as real and solid as I am here."

Terry offered his arm in an exercise of dubious logic, for any doubting Thomas to hold or prod, in a pseudo-scientific substitution for the real Willy. But there were no doubters.

"...and he was unmarked. No oil, no bruises, nothing. His hair was still waved like a girl..."

Willy had fair crinkly hair which he brushed hard back on his pointed head where it crouched in unwelcome, small, harsh, blondish waves.

"...and he was smoking; wearing his dog-tooth jacket..."

Willy characteristically wore a Dunn and Company black and white checked, double breasted jacket of the very best worsted – and usually with a flower in his top button hole – and always with a colourful bow tie.

Terry had his audience gripped; all grinning and waiting to hear the dénouement.

Willy's Pink Cadillac.
"More like docking an ocean liner than parking a car"

"...But the extraordinary thing was..." said Terry, his face at its most serious, credible and astonished, "...the ash was still on his cigarette."

Several lads guffawed, not entirely believing the miracle that Terry had witnessed.

"No. As God is my Judge! I'll swear that it was. He rose up out of that exhaust pipe like a Genie out of a bottle. Not a mark on him. Smoking a Sobranie – and there was a quarter-inch of ash still on the cigarette."

Before the year of the white Roller, when Willy was too young to drive legally, his dad had an American car, a fabulous Juke-Box of a car in pale pink and gleaming chrome, which Willy took on short illicit runs up to the local shops. This behemoth wallowed on its soft American suspension making it difficult to steer and manoeuvre and particularly irritating to park in the garage at the side of their house – opposite the Headmistress's window. The crossroads were slightly offset in a dog's-leg that narrowed between the Mason's and Fylde Lodge, forcing the Mason's to slow the pink blancmange vehicle to two miles an hour and reverse several times in the street to bring it home to rest. It was more like docking an ocean liner than garaging a car.

Willy found a quicker route. He adopted the habit, before the headmistress, the local police and his father intervened, of hurtling back to the crossroads, huge, pink and wobbling, ignoring the necessity of the dog's-leg, and looking to neither right nor left, as other vehicles were statistically unlikely, not impossible but in those days unlikely, to be on the roads, driving straight ahead into Fylde Lodge, through the tall, thin privet hedge; hand-brake turning the ludicrous machine through ninety-degrees on the Headmistress's small private lawn, before bouncing over a shallow rockery through the other hedge, down the kerbstones – straight across the narrow road – into his garage;

without, so urban legend reported, losing the ash on his Sobranie cigarette, eternally perched, absolutely horizontal, in the centre of his lips.

Thus did Willy's reputation go before him and the tales of his unlimited wealth and mediocre gaming skills, ensured he was invited, politely press-ganged, into as many of the card games as possible. Being impulsive, Willy played emotionally – and so lost. Willy's immense losses, which made not a jot of difference to him, leveraged up the stakes of The Game. No longer could Richard command the arrangements of where and when – and with whom – it would be played. Terry Rider introduced a newcomer, Mike Hobbs, a short, thickset and quiet boy, who played well – and won – and won and won, as did Terry. Richard silently dropped out of games when Mike Hobbs played, particularly those at Willy's house, where Willy might lose ten or twenty pounds – fortunes for teenagers – and Richard set up alternative games, reverting to schoolboy stakes and to his winning strategy of imposing on the players a form of sensory deprivation, locked in a darkened room for uncountable periods of time, hunched over a card table with a single light and chain smoking; inducing disorientation, dehydration, dizziness and ultimately the will to live – or win - and not allowing anyone to leave the game until he, Richard, was in profit – but he won fairly and squarely; he never cheated.

It was some months before Willy learned, and was justifiably enraged, that the unreadable Mike Hobbs had a father on the stage; a father who was a conjuror, specialising in card tricks. Willy stopped playing cards and went off alone to write-off a few more cars. Without its financial mainstay The Big Game sputtered to a halt. But as The Game splintered, other youths saw the opportunity to play host and place themselves at the epicentre of Heaton Moor society. Michael Howard, whose innocent and inoffensive parents spent weekends away, offered his kitchen as a gambling den. Cherub, the canary, cocked its little yellow head and watched from its vantage point perched above the table, with one bright eye, as the white, black and red cards flashed across the table top at the regular games.

We all smoked; not expensive Sobranie but cheap Woodbines, Senior Service and Players cigarettes that we could buy in packets of five, un-tipped, unfiltered and, of course, lethal. Ten or more of us packed round the russet and black flecked Formica kitchen table, concentrating fiercely on the cards and the cash for five or six hours. Tea was brewed every hour on the hour and served dark and strong with two spoons of sugar – builders' tea – in large mugs which clustered around the wide ashtray at the edge of the table immediately under Cherub's cage. Pennies, thru'penny bits, silver sixpences, half-pennies and even farthings were tossed into the kitty along with larger coins, two-shilling-pieces, half-crowns and, when the stakes skyrocketed, an occasional and rare reddish-fawn ten-bob-note.

From its bird's eye view in the suspended cage, Cherub watched all this unaccustomed traffic on the table, its bright eyes gleaming and fluffy head bobbing quietly, seemingly unaffected by the invasion. Below, it saw a bunch of schoolboys in their weekend gear, emerging, as they grew older and larger, like butterflies from the chrysalis of school uniforms, flaunting long trousers from Burtons in grey or blue flannel and fashionably narrow. Tweed sports jackets, navy blue blazers and crew-neck sweaters were popular – and all males wore a tie, or, if they had the sartorial nerve, a silk cravat at the throat. Hair had to be sleeked, with *Brylcreem*, and from every top pocket peeked a well-used, oily, comb – some clean, some that looked like they could, if accidentally dropped into a Lake District reservoir, take out the whole population of Manchester.

"Does it talk, Mike?" asked another Michael, Mick Farmer, who reared hawks in his small suburban semi, nodding in the direction of Cherub and blowing a friendly lungful of blue cigarette smoke at the brooding yellow blob, which hiccupped once and coughed a brief shoulder shrugging cough.

"It did – sometimes," answered our host "…but not recently. Not in the last year or so. I haven't heard it say anything…"

The card school regarded Cherub dispassionately, tacitly accepting its rights to be there and acknowledging the bond between Michael and this puffed up little resident. Cherub felt the shift in attention, looked back at us sharply, shook itself before settling its head deeper into its shoulders and shuffled a few embarrassed steps sideways on its perch.

The games were intense, weekly or sometimes twice a week we gathered in the Howard's kitchen, huddled round the table under its cage and played – and smoked – and drank tea – and smoked some more. The air was laden with smoke and natural boyish odours; this being before the days of male deodorants. On some days Cherub seemed depressed; chunking its little head deeper than usual into its rounded shoulders, peering sadly over its breast feathers and shuffling back and forth along its perch. Sometimes it just sat in a silent, perhaps condemnatory, little yellow heap, with its eyes waiting for the invaders to finish and go – and leave it in peace. Everyone liked the little scrap of life and did their best to cheer it up. Between hands, players might pick up a sunflower seed the bird had dropped on the table and hand feed it, offering the tasty morsel to its polished beak. Or they would refill its water dispenser and induce it to sample a few drops. When it remained particularly immobile, we discovered that blowing a cloud of cigarette smoke at it elicited a cute, tiny cough, and maybe stimulated it to flap its wings – though we never saw Cherub lift off in joyous flight. But the nicotine did seem to give it a moment of new energy; encouraging more players to puff smoke at it and then emulate its shoulder shrugging cough.

It was in the winter of nineteen-fifty-six or thereabouts, four years after Elvis exploded onto the scene, that Mr and Mrs Howard went away again, leaving Michael and his sister, Rosemary, in charge of the house. That Saturday afternoon the card school assembled at around three o'clock, happy to get in off the cold streets and sit shoulder to shoulder over steaming mugs of tea with the warm orange glow of cigarettes, glowing stronger as smoke was drawn deep into the lungs, creating a camp-fire atmosphere in the kitchen, while light faded from the thin northern sky. Lonnie Donegan was singing sadly from the sitting room on his 78-inch vinyl disk, played over and over by Rosemary, telling the world that "It takes a worried man to sing a worried song – I'm worried now, but I won't be worried long."

The players were very sharp that day and very focused. Nobody paid much heed to Cherub as it sat in its now customary sulk above the game. The light faded and turned to darkness. Michael switched on the electric light over the table, whose shade cast a shadow over Cherub, consigning the little canary to obscurity as the game ebbed and flowed energetically beneath it. After the second or even third mug of tea, the pace slackened and one or two players stood up to stretch – and to light another cigarette.

Cherub, it was observed, had its head buried even more deeply into its shoulders than usual and seemed infinitely more depressed than ever. It perched, as birds are wont to do, its minute claws clutching its favourite bar in the centre of the cage, almost a perfect ball of vivid fluffy yellow, with its eyes closed. Davy, known as Crockett, a big strong lad, from down Didsbury Road, with a tender heart and bruised knuckles, wiggled his finger through the bars and tried to engage Cherub in conversation. Cherub stayed determinedly asleep. Two or three of us tried the mouth to beak re-energising that had worked so well over the past months and blew clouds of smoke in Cherub's face. But Cherub ignored the gifts and stubbornly remained immobilised.

Michael was alerted to the bird's uncooperative behaviour and he took up an authoritative and commanding position in front of the cage. The game was put on hold as we all gathered around. Michael spoke to the family pet – in pet like phrases. Out of deep respect we shall draw a veil over this one-sided conversation, the text of which may detract from the seriousness, sadness and tragedy of the moment. But still Cherub did not respond.

Michael picked up a wax fire spill from the side of the kitchen stove and used it to gently prod Cherub in its proud little feathery chest. At the first and lightest touch – Cherub toppled from its perch. The little mite, still gripping the rail which supported it, swung backwards away from the prod, in a graceful arc until it was suspended upside down, like a tennis ball with feet, and, thus orientated, its claws lost their grip and it plunged, shockingly and as it transpired, finally, to the bottom of its cage.

A deep silence gripped the company.

The silence persisted and it was now our turn to be immobilised. Slowly we turned to look at Michael and perhaps to assuage his overwhelming grief.

"Bloody Hell..." muttered Michael, seemingly more alarmed than grief-stricken – but then death affects people in many different ways – so we stood in silent respect and said nothing.

"...Bloody Hell..." he said more loudly, "...they'll be home soon..."

We then began to understand that, while he must have been deeply and forever saddened by Cherub's secondary smoking demise, Michael, in a saintly kind of a way, was more concerned at his parents' grief over the tragedy than his own. At least, that is how we chose to interpret it.

"They'll kill me..." he continued, seemingly now a little less concerned for his parents' feelings, "they'll bloody kill me." And he looked around the room wildly for inspiration before searching our eyes for a miracle that might bring Cherub back to life.

We all shrugged. What could we do?

One player with great and immediate initiative started to clear the tea mugs and wash them in the sink. The rest stood as before around the cage which had now become a funeral bier for Cherub. Cherub lay on the bottom of the cage in the archetypal pose of dead birds, flat on its back with its minuscule feet up in the air. Michael's face registered frozen horror and rising panic. We began to realise the earnestness of his emotions and some of us started to think.

"You could..." hesitantly offered Kenny Marsh, a Stockport Grammar School boy who was always quick off the mark, and being Grammar School was officially and inarguably brighter than Michael who only attended the inferior Mile End School,

"...put it back on the perch, and pretend it never happened..."

Michael looked at first as if he had been punched in the solar-plexus and was still groaning inwardly at the pain, but then he straightened up and a gleam of hope sprang from his eyes. He said nothing, but inserted his nicotine stained hand into the cage and grabbed – quite tenderly – the yellow corpse and plonked it back on the central bar, adjusting its claws around the pole.

Cherub promptly fell off.

Michael placed the dead bird even more firmly on the perch. It stayed in place, looking no different than when life still coursed through its dear little corporeal form. We all breathed again – very slowly. Michael held the cage in one hand and ever so carefully closed the wire door and with the skill of a reformed safe-breaker, eased the spring catch to lock it. The spring clicked!

Cherub – the smoked canary.

Cherub fell off again, on to its head then performed a head-over-heels to end up with its feet once more in the air.

Michael's eyes were starting from his head and he incessantly flicked his quiff back from his forehead.

"Let me try..." said Biff Keegan, who as a prized goalkeeper was known to have a safe pair of hands. He also came from a strong Catholic family and was a zealous altar boy at Saint Winifred's church, and might, if we stretched our imaginations, therefore have much needed ethereal connections with the powers of creation. He handled the bird with reverence and skill and with his large fingers folded the tiny claws around the pole. "They're getting stiff..." he reported. "...It might stay on."

Cherub sat on the perch. Biff eased the cage door shut – and Cherub sat on the perch. We all moved a step away. And Cherub sat on the perch. We smiled at each other in relief and turned to congratulate ourselves. And Cherub still sat on the perch.

We all relaxed. Michael started to breathe again and we understood it was time for us to get out before Mr and Mrs Howard returned. From the living room the final notes of The Platters harmonising *'Yes! I'm the Great Pretender'* faded and turned to scratchy bumping before the inward spiralling gramophone needle triggered the lifting mechanism and switched it off. The living room door opened, there were footsteps, the kitchen door opened – and Rosemary came in.

"Hi.. Hello.. Just leaving" and so on and so forth, we all mouthed politely, urgently keeping our gaze off Cherub's final resting place. Rosemary crossed the kitchen to fill the kettle. She lit the gas and put the kettle on the stove as we started to slink away; she turned and cooch-i-cooed at Cherub, wiggling her fingers through the bars.

Cherub fell off.

Michael, not widely celebrated for his repartee, was uncharacteristically quick; "What have you done?" he shouted in distress, "...what have you done to Cherub?"

We let ourselves out the front door into the winter darkness, turning up our Humphrey Bogart raincoat collars, as Rosemary stood in shocked silence trying to formulate a suitable response to her impertinent younger brother. Possibly out of reverence for Cherub, the smoked canary, we never played cards at the Howard's again.

***

Chapter 20 - Marjorie Barlow

SEX-STARVED - 1960: Lady Chatterley's Lover sold out. Bookshops all over England have sold out of Penguin's first run of the controversial novel Lady Chatterley's Lover - a total of 200,000 copies - on the first day of publication. DH Lawrence's sexually explicit novel was published in Italy in 1928 and in Paris the following year. It has been banned in the UK - until now. Last month, after a dramatic and much-publicised trial, Penguin won the right to publish the book in its entirety. For those who can manage to find a copy, it is available in paperback for 3s 6d. Rush to buy. London's largest bookstore, W&G Foyle Ltd, said its 300 copies had gone in just 15 minutes and it had taken orders for 3,000 more copies. BBC News.

While Terry Rider was preparing to serve Queen and Country and making Britain safe to live in, and would be lucky to avoid a Court Martial for losing his tank; in 1957 I was thirteen going on fourteen, as was Peter-John, and we were far too young to drive cars, which were in any case completely unaffordable. I was getting to school in Hale Barns, seven or eight hilly miles away, by bicycle on most days – or in really bad weather, in two hours by bus. Stockport and its suburbs were well served by buses, if you were happy, that is, to be back home in bed before ten o'clock.

It was, however, buses or no buses, imperative for us to be out late on weekends as, in those far off days, the days when Vera Lynn was still a major star, Anne Shelton sold thousands of vinyl records of *'Lay Down Your Arms and Surrender to Mine'*, Frankie Vaughan winked provocatively at our women and Alma Cogan waggled her cleavage at the men-folk, via the twelve-inch, black and white TV screens, we had to learn to dance or lose all chance of ever joining in the teenage mating rituals. So, come buses, storms, poverty, parental bans, homework or terminal illness, we somehow or another completed the journey from Heaton Moor, down into Mersey Square – often on the Number 75 single-decker, red North-Western bus – then by foot or bus, a mile or more up from the River Mersey and out on the main road south, to The Osborne Bentley School of Dance.

Both Osborne and Bentley seemed lost and forgotten in the mists of time. Peter-John, in his stern way, attributed their permanent absence to the same cause as he was learning to explain when, dressed very like his father, he worked on Saturdays at Tompkin & Rider, Shopfitters, his father's firm in Smithfield Market, in the centre of Manchester.

The telephone would ring, Peter-John would answer it curtly; "Tompkin & Rider..." he snapped at the offending customer, supplier, employee or wrong-number.

"Can I speak to Mr Tompkin please?" asked the caller, trying to by-pass this obviously hostile and unwelcoming youth.

"No!" Peter-John retorted.

Somewhat taken aback by the abruptness, the caller typically paused and then fell for it "Why NOT?" they snapped back in anger.

"Because he's dead. Died in nineteen twenty-seven. And we don't want to dig him up," said Peter-John, pressing the heavy black bakelite mouthpiece down onto the chromed disconnect buttons. And then he'd smile grimly to himself at his private joke.

They lost a lot of new customers that way.

But, reckoned Peter-John, Osborne and Bentley had suffered the same fate as the unlamented late Mr Tompkin years before we discovered the School, as we never saw hide nor hair of them in all the times we graced their establishment. *(...but see Appendices)*

This was not a school for modern dancing. This was formal ballroom dancing. Events which we might attend and, if incredibly brave, lucky and bold, ask a girl to dance – and sweep her around the floor like Fred Astaire with Ginger Rogers, were organised by schools, churches, or the Liberal Club, or the Young Conservatives or, horror piled upon horror, might be Masonic-Lodge "ladies" evenings or "safe" gatherings for the children of the Catenians, the Catholic answer to Free-Masons, and at such events, the music was pre-War and the dances were those of the adults – quickstep, foxtrot, waltz and so on. Jazz did exist in dangerous clubs for far older people, in sleazy dives in Manchester – where Jazz-Dance might be on the menu, or Jump-Jive that was just coming in. Rotund Bill Haley with his Kiss Curl and Rock-Around-The-Clock had not arrived and Elvis Presley, in our parents eyes an unbelievably lewd, writhing and incoherent manifestation of the Anti-Christ *'Its rubbish - You can't hear the words'* and his treasonable Rock'nRoll was, though only a year or two or three away, yet to materialise in the universe. So, if we were going to be able to curl a manly arm around a girl's waist and feel her silken arm over our shoulders, we had to learn to quickstep.

Girls and Boys, heading for the dance school, travelled in single sex groups, eying each other across the bus aisle or the pavements, with deep suspicion and fearful misunderstanding.

Pauline Mallalieu, Margaret Lamerton and Jennifer Greenlees, an inseparable trio, perhaps with Diane Watkins from Princess Road, caught the 75 bus at the bus-stop before mine, where I waited with Kenny Marsh and maybe with Elizabeth Mc'Coy from round the corner, and Tats – Peter Tattersall from Cleveland Road. My eldest brother, Richard, who had graduated from the Dance School a year or two earlier, might come along just to show us how the professionals did it.

The bus then wound its way up Clifton Road, where Marion Heighway, styled like a forties film star, the intriguingly pneumatic and enigmatic Anne Diamond (if her mother let her out) and the obviously intelligent Tony Wagstaff, might clamber on. The bus then went along Heaton Moor Road, collecting Steve Court, from the shoe-shop, and the schizophrenic Paul, who years later minced along Heaton Moor Road in shocking leather trousers tightly laced up the back; before the bus turned right into Parsonage Road opposite St Paul's, the local Church of England, to bus stops where Leon Marshall the wealthy Lithuanian tailor's son; possibly Michael Farmer in bow tie, yellow waistcoat and outrageously decadent suede chukka boots, without his hawks, and the much admired Tes Tyler, admired by the girls that is; we boys knew him as 'Testical' Tyler which reflected his single minded drive and biologically graphic tales of conquests, joined the crowd.

Pulling out from Parsonage Road the bus left Heaton Moor behind to descend southward on Wellington Road, the broad main road from Manchester, two miles down to Mersey Square, where it parked at the bus station, in the overpowering shadow of the two-hundred-foot high, long, brick, Victorian viaduct which spanned the river and bestrode the cobbled Square and the complex of roads which snaked under its many arches; carrying trains from Manchester to Derby and thence to London.

There was once a competition to estimate the number of bricks in the vast bridge, but nobody could get near the right answer, everyone grossly underestimating its immense bulk, so the competition was abandoned; with no authoritative answer ever published.

Other buses from the east side of Heaton Moor and Reddish Road trundled down Wellington Road, or came from the west side, down Didsbury Road, to empty more teenagers into Mersey Square – Peter-John in his dog's-tooth-check jacket; the beautiful, prematurely ripe Pat Fudge, Goulash, Malcolm Holt and maybe the budding chemist, Roger Woods (inevitably 'Woody') if he wasn't going to miss an episode of the Goon Show, Jeff Osborne and, before he got his first motor-bike, Graham Fish. Michael Solomons, whose Greek father owned a tea and bacon sandwich café in Mersey Square, wasn't allowed at that age to mix with girls – but he made up for it later. Jackie Wake, and Peter Reagan the policeman's son, strangers to each other, might catch the

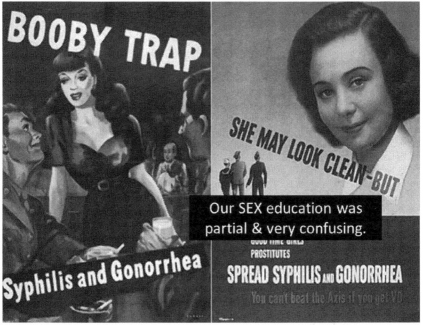

Number 80 Bus, along with the boy I sat next to at school, Roger Clarke from Queens Drive - all at the same bus-stop by Leeman's Field, on its way down Didsbury Road to Mersey Square.

From Mersey Square, come rain or shine, swathed in school mackintoshes, or for the more fashion conscious, in belt-less white, buff and khaki raincoats, with turned up collars, that Humphrey Bogart and Edward G Robinson, as incessantly smoking gangsters and private detectives, flaunted on screen; the groups from Heaton Moor toiled up out of Mersey Square, taking the white steep Art-Deco steps by the Plaza Cinema, past the side entrance to Stockport Baths, with its miserably cold swimming pool, where, as Primary School pupils we had been taught to swim, courtesy of Stockport Council, by being hauled, blue, shivering, snotty and swallowing gallons of cold chlorine and water, on the end of a rope, with the lady teacher's posh, loud encouragement, loud enough to drown our death gurgles, to "Push and Glide – And Push and Glide – And Push and Glide" before those of us who survived the ordeal escaped, shivering, to buy a hot Oxo beef drink, a chocolate Wagon Wheel and to try and recover.

And hence out onto the main road opposite Stockport Infirmary; walk up past the Town Hall, go another mile or so, mostly uphill, and pile into Osborne Bentley, still keeping a safe distance between the sexes – as the girls could not be sure that male spermatozoa, lurking, they were reliably informed, on all public lavatory seats, did not also leap great distances from the trousers of precocious boys and wriggle through the girls' wool and cotton skirts, to spitefully impregnate them; and, equally, boys were unconsciously concerned, due to mystifying, misunderstood and gruesome public health posters, that females accidentally or deliberately distributed terrible venereal diseases which made male equipment curdle, break out in boils and fall off, along with their noses, lips, eyes and hair before finally consigning them to madness and a horrible lingering death.

For romance – we HAD to learn to dance like our parents.

But in spite of this almost certain knowledge of almost certain impending disgrace, dishonour, disease, death, and eternal damnation, the genders nevertheless drew closer and closer as they crossed the Dance School threshold – above several small shops near the Stockport Road turnings to Bramhall and Offerton. The Osborne Bentley School of Dance[1]

The instructress, Miss Marjorie Barlow, was we assumed, also the present owner-manager. It had been some decades since she had truly been a Miss; and at some sessions a silently compliant, husband-type figure lurked round the door to the office and generally tried and failed to look useful. Miss Barlow was, blonde of course, ageless, tall, muscular and slender, tightly packed into a pencil-thin silvered dress with a small flared pleat on the back hem to enable long Tango steps. She was at least as tall as me and, with six-inch stiletto heels, complimenting her clearly defined and muscled legs, calves and ankles, and with her hair wrenched upwards into a high tight knot as if by an unseen hand from heaven, she loomed above me in her several determined attempts to lead me, indeed force me, round the training room, stepping correctly like a show horse at a gymkhana.

Miss Barlow also, at times, carried a black, silver topped cane in the manner of a Russian ballet mistress. The upward pull on her blond hair stretched all her features towards the ceiling; ears, eyebrows, forehead, eyes – outlined in dark blue – cheek bones, pointed chin, neck and, not least her fine long nose. Thus tautened and strung she could not but help looking down her nose at crumpled and uncertain creatures, such as I, who had the temerity to imagine we might one day lead such a beautiful, groomed, painted, graceful and high spirited dance partner, out under the swirling multi-faceted ballroom light and into the envious and admiring gaze of competitors, judges, friends, enemies and suitors alike.

The whole business baffled me.
We were split into boys and girls and set against each other on opposite sides of the studio. In groups and individually, Miss Barlow took us through our paces, dictating which girl should dance with which boy, selected on some aesthetic criteria and judgements of her own, making choices which almost always failed to please any of the pupils.

We dressed, out of school uniform, like small copies of our parents. The Western World was on the verge, the nervous, jitterbugging edge, of the teenage explosion of self-expression. We were the War Bulge, the War Babies, The Baby Boomers, who resulted from the hurried, often unsatisfactory and ill-considered relationships between millions of troops, going off to die, and popping back on a forty-eight-hour pass for a quick knee trembler on the canal towpath - and the girls they left behind.

A post-war school class was typically fifty to sixty youngsters, with boys in short trousers to the age of twelve or thirteen. Everything was rationed after the War, requiring money AND ration coupons to buy the most mundane items, including cottons and other clothing materials. But the depression was about to end, ration books were being torn-up, employment was soaring and a new confidence started to course through society.

...and forward,
One Two
to the side, One
Two
Turn, One Two.

I just couldn't get it.

In tiny bedrooms, in mean back-to-back slum houses, linked by alleyways and shared outside lavatories, post-pubertal youths were absently squeezing their blackheads with nicotine stained labourers' fingers, as they studied with fierce concentration a prized photograph or yellowing newspaper illustration of handsome male heads crowned, as they would be crowned, with thick, long, greased hair, swept back behind the ears, grown down the cheeks into solid Edwardian sideburns, curled up and tweaked at the nape of the neck - the infamous 'Duck's-Arse' or DA - and pulled forward at the front to hang frond-like out over a quizzical forehead, with the eyebrows and scalp

The DA (duck's arse) hairstyle.

permanently raised to lift the bobbing construction, giving the wearer an aggressive, in-your-face, *'are-you-looking-at-me; or-chewing-a-brick? – Mate'* look, mixed with the apparent fear, signified by the raised eyebrows and furrowed brow, that somebody or something indefinable was about to clout them hard on the top of their heads. Eyes were at all times narrowed to sinister slits, not only to put the fear of god into all law-abiding citizens but to reduce the amount of smoke invading the eyes from the de-rigueur burning cigarette, dangling, at the same angle as the front quiff of hair, from an often protruding and dangling lower lip. Shoulders were raised, vulture-like to fend off the expected blow from above.

The fashion, yet to appear, evolved as an outright rebellion against the War inspired short-back-and-sides, polished shoes and ubiquitous dark grey civvies suit. The protective shoulders were padded heavily, inside stylishly long jackets in light colours, trimmed with velvet collars, which, for the serious Teddy-Boy, was further trimmed, behind the velvet, with razor blades, as a surprise for any opponent who foolishly tried to grab such a fashion-icon by the lapels, preparatory to drawing him forwards and "nutting" him and breaking his nose, cheeks and teeth, with the opponent's forehead. To complete the desired outline, the wide shouldered upholstered jacket worn over a ruffed shirt with a bootlace Mississippi gambler's tie, narrowed as it descended to just above the knee and was fastened at the navel by a cuff-link type double button. This narrowing was then extenuated by black drainpipe trousers, just twelve-inches around the ankles – but somehow contrived to still carry the military crease that all trousers had to have – the ends of which were clearly marked by the shocking announcement of bright pink, green, red or yellow, *Lurex*, glowing socks.

The tapering effect, from BIG hair, oiled and bobbing and endlessly preened with a comb that redistributed the grease, down to the enormously broadened, padded shoulders, and down, down, down in a 'V' to the black twelve inch trousers, was now complete – and – it was felt by some leaders of fashion, overdone; leaving some of the larger youths seemingly balancing on neon hued tip-toe and about to topple to one side or the other. This rather delicate and inherently unstable stance was corrected by creating a solid platform at ground level, a sort of ballast or foundation around the feet, of the famous 'blue suede shoes' with inch thick crepe soles, making them 'brothel-creepers' which outraged every ex-military man and their brave wives, which was the whole of the adult population, as not only did the offensive shoes not have breathing leather soles – which our parents knew would cause a plague of jungle-foot-rot and trench-foot, but the hairy suede exteriors, even if one could with extreme self-control ignore the fact that they were coloured – "For God's Sake!", were just that, hairy, and could not be polished; could not be burnished and made to shine with daily applications of black Cherry Blossom shoe polish. And, the shoes were decidedly large, counteracting, counter-pointing and counterbalancing the carefully contrived ensemble above.

Thus was the end of civilisation and the inevitable coming of Armageddon and the cast of Apocalypse, the Horsemen of the Apocalypse, the Ten Headed Beast – and most excitedly anticipated of all, The Scarlet Harlot - pronounced, to the generations which had fought and died in the First and Second World Wars to preserve the nation from the barbarian hordes.

In case any thought to mock them, in their novel clothes and *Brylcreemed* hair (I always thought they looked very fetching myself), when the Teddy-Boys emerged in large numbers, they armed themselves with flick-knives from Corsica, bicycle chains from their now redundant bikes – have you ever tried pedalling a bike in drainpipe trousers and an Edwardian long jacket – and cut-throat razors from barbers shops, and embarked on expeditions of mindless violence which dissuaded even the most liberal and kindly observers from presuming they understood the inner-motives of the new teenagers. The rampaging youths quickly established a reign of terror and NO-GO areas in the cities, mostly by attacking each other and less often by beating up poncey youths from Heaton Moor, on our lawful way to spend a good citizen's evening at the Church Youth Club or the Young Conservatives Association. They quickly learned that cut-throat razors could cut throats and kill people, which, with the extant threat of the Death Penalty, they hadn't intended, so the razors were then bound with tape, leaving a shallow cutting -edge that inflicted terrible wounds, but did not bite so fatally into vital arteries.

Despite their bizarre clothes, oily dripping hair, single syllable vocabulary, brothel-creeper shuffle and expressions of bewildered fear and rage, these Teddy Boys attracted girls – we noted. Their girls wore tight sweaters, often polo-necked, wide and tight waist bands, lampshade skirts over two thousand yards of pink tulle, the same lurid socks as their consorts, flimsy ballet slippers in red or black, large, hoop earrings and pulled their hair up into tight pony tails that bobbed and swung as they walked. The Teddy-Girls were in general pacific creatures, not expected to indulge in mindless violence like their boyfriends nor to attack innocent and virginal youths, as did the Mill girls, the thousands of women who worked in Stockport and Manchester factories and, it was rumoured, in their tea breaks ambushed unwary male visitors, subjecting them to all sorts of unspeakable abuse, which the average fair youth could only dream of.

We, in contrast to the Teddy Boys, dressed like our parents with some concession to film culture and television images, where white or cream mackintoshes with complex upturned collars and tight, tied belts, eventually gave way to belt-less raincoats, still white and with turned up collars; collars which served as windbreaks for us to light our lonely, moody, night time cigarettes – with a Swan match.

To assuage the loneliness and to try to find out what IT was really all about, we once embarked – and never again – on a blind date.

***

Chapter 21 - Fixed Wheel

The saddle must be set so that the legs can reach full stretch at the end of each down-stroke; and the heel should be pushed down also – to avoid cramp. – Racing Cycling Manual.

Following in Father's footsteps and carefully coached by him, I learned early how to cycle as fast as a professional. Father, being manly and having in his youth won innumerable across-Britain cycle races, spurned gears on bicycles. Sturmey-Archer gear hubs were simply impediments that reduced speed and added useless weight.

Derailer gears were essentially a foreign, possibly even a French invention for weaker men that messed up the smooth running of the chain, collected mud and were susceptible to damage. I did eventually succumb to the decadent addition of gears but when young I cycled like Father on fixed-cogs. Our bikes, light enough to lift with one finger, were fitted on the rear wheel with the smallest possible cog making the highest possible gear – with no free-wheel. Feet were securely clamped into pedal toe-caps. Once started, slowly grinding forward on the high gear, legs had to pump to keep up with the revolutions of the driving pedals. These were constructed of sharp metal and woe-betide those whose feet slipped off the pedals, flailed around and were whacked with the unstoppable force of those merciless scythes. Nobody in those tough, thick skulled times, wore a crash helmet. The technique to climb steep hills, which abound around Stockport, was to press with one foot and to pull with the other. Thus the combined power of two athletic legs was employed and the hill was easily surmounted. Coming down was an adventure. As the machine went faster and faster down, for example, the five miles of Long Hill from Buxton to Hazel Grove, our legs had to stay on the pedals and revolve ever faster or risk being cast-off, chaos and a mighty crash ensued. The speed of descent was controlled by the legs. With all the braking power that two legs had, there was need of course for only one brake; which was on the front wheel.

Equipped and trained, I could roam the urban lands and get out into the Pennines to zoom up and down hills that defeated all but the brave. And thus, when I was eleven, had failed my Eleven Plus and was consigned to a school for idiots, some seven miles away, I had an independent means of transport. Most days I cycled from Heaton Mersey to St Ambrose College in Hale Barns. Every day classes began with our Form Master, Brother Leonard, a committed, youthful and red necked, black-cassocked monk conducting a Latin Class. For this first class of every morning we had to memorise Latin vocabulary. There were fifty-two boys in the class.

The robust Brother Leonard took the register at nine o'clock sharp. Then, without preamble, he plunged us into the hell of daily examination. Each hapless child row by row was asked to translate a single word. If they failed, they had to move to an area at the front of the class. Every morning about half the class failed the test. Once the victims were identified, Brother Leonard, in a godly, regretful sort of manner being a religious person, drew from a long pocket in his black cassock an inch-thick leather strap. Today such straps are only seen in barber's shops where they are used to sharpen cut-throat razors – strops – or might be found in museums dedicated to collecting instruments of torture. The monk took each hand of each failed pupil, raised the heavy leather and whipped it down with all his strength on the open palm. It was done efficiently and in silence so that punishing twenty-five children occupied no more than five minutes. It was a point of honour among the boys not to utter a sound, but all were injured, all were alarmed and all spent the next ten minutes nursing their swollen palms. None of us enjoyed Latin. Or indeed any subject at all.

Six of the best, on each hand, took a lot of nursing. One infamous day a poor youth, Peter Naylor, then slightly befuddled from a recent cracked skull sustained in a road accident, was beaten so much by an enraged Christian Brother for reasons we never discovered, that he had be taken to hospital and kept off school for a week.

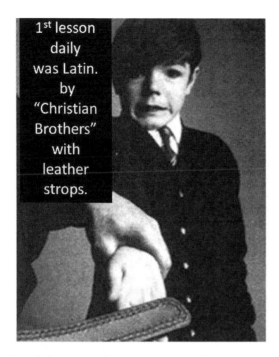

1st lesson daily was Latin. by "Christian Brothers" with leather strops.

All the teachers employed the same teaching methods to a greater or lesser extent – except in the daily religious knowledge class. And so we lived and learned in fear, all day, every day. There was just one teacher who could actually teach without beating the children. He was also an Irish Christian Brother, who, it was rumoured, had been a mathematics tutor at Cambridge, or somewhere like that in the soft South, and had come to us to recover from a nervous breakdown, which, we surmised, Southerners, all indigenous populations south of Manchester, were prone to. He was intelligent. Faced with fifty-two fifteen-year old fifth-formers, heading for their 'O' levels, few of whom could add up and take away accurately, never mind calculate a simultaneous-quadratic equation, this tired but enlightened man quietly said he would teach no-one who did not want to learn and he faced out the entire class until he had commitment. He never shouted, he never lost patience and he never beat anyone. In dramatic contrast to all the other subjects, all these boys passed their Maths O level. It's amazing what the love of God and good scholarship can achieve.

Apart from the harsh regime, the school was deadly dull. We had no frivolous subjects on the curriculum. No Art. No Music. No Drama. No Poetry. Not even Hymns; and no chapel or church. The food served at lunchtime was always grey, largely inedible and served in a squalid dripping shed. With the constant threats of the strap, the appalling food and a secret penchant for banned cigarettes that my friend and constant companion, Roger Clarke, supplied from his mother's corner shop, my duodenal ulcers played up most days. Particularly after lunch, I sat in considerable pain for much of the afternoon. But it kept me quiet.

Getting out and going home by bike was a treat. I crammed everything into a large saddle-bag, jacket, cap, books and all and zoomed away, sweating freely, on my fixed high gear. The objective was to get home before my fellow pupils who lived near me and used the buses. They took a school single-deck bus into Altrincham then caught the double-decker number-eighty bus, wreathed in smoke and nasty with condensation, to Stockport. Theirs was a triangular route by powered omnibus.

My bike route took me straight down-hill from Hale Barns, through country lanes skirting Timperley, which are probably now subsumed into Ringway, Manchester Airport, across and through the vast Wythenshaw council housing estate, down the long northern border of Wythenshaw Park, (incidentally passing my grandmother's home) across the dual carriageways of Princess Parkway, into little used streets at the back of Northenden and along a lonely footpath by the foaming, fermenting threat of the River Mersey - eventually emerging through the green wooded park of Fletcher Moss and up into Didsbury, by Ye Olde Cocke Inne where my route re-joined the bus journey. Then I cycled to the clock tower at Parr's Wood, and made the steep climb up Didsbury Road to Heaton Mersey. At fifteen I could do the journey in a very creditable sixty minutes, while the buses and queuing absorbed twice that long. What depressed me, and all my classmates, at the point of getting home, was we every evening had four hours of homework to do – and if it wasn't done it was back into the endless routine of being strapped and berated, in God's Name, until the tasks were done. This punitive schedule defeated some of the pupils who then entered an altered universe of constantly being behind, beaten, more frightened, less able to work, further behind, beaten and ultimately, failed. I thank God earnestly that the school did not have a sixth form where I could stay on for a further two years.

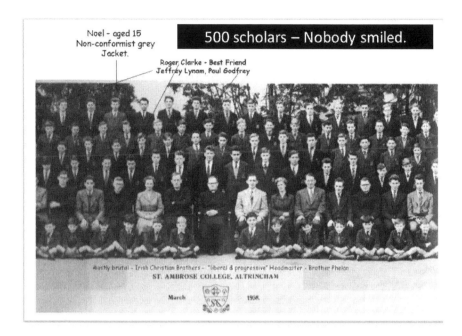

We were, however, very good, possibly the best in Lancashire and Cheshire, at school rugby. My position, as I was in my first two terms still square and robustly built before the ulcers took their toll, was as a sturdy prop forward and I was unwittingly picked for the school team which meant having to drag myself to school on many winter Saturdays. Before I had come to the shocking realisation that most Irish Christian Brothers were nature's thugs, and not the contemplative, blessed monks as I had once assumed, I was stunned in one of my first rugby training days, spent mostly in a hot and fetid scrum, trying and failing to push over a strong wooden fence, to be told by the normally reserved, neat and pale Brother Ryan, replete in his black monkish cassock, that when a ball went loose and a bold player dived to own it, and clamped his hands around the prized leathern egg, that the gentlemanly player's response was to 'Stamp on His Bloody Fingers', thus bringing the ball quickly back into play - perhaps to the advantage of one's own team. Such sporting violence was completely beyond my capabilities – but for reasons I have never fathomed, I was retained on the school team.

Fortunately, I was no good at cricket and tennis so in spring and summer my weekends were my own.

Going back to school by bike in the mornings, I again raced the buses, and determinedly arrived at full pelt, usually on time, sweating copiously, donned the highly compressed, body odour absorbent school uniform, a jacket of blue and red stripes like an upper-class prison uniform and visible at one mile, then sat in class steaming gently and smelling like God only knows what. Assaulted daily by the unmitigated, undiluted body odours of fifty-two unrepentant, English teenage boys may have explained why the Irish monks beat us so soundly and so often.

Our religious studies were delivered daily by our Form Master, the strong armed, youthful, red necked Brother Leonard, who spoke with a thick Irish brogue and had a simple faith in Catholicism. Hellfire and damnation were always close to the top of his agenda and though we ploughed through the old and new testaments in my five years at the college, there was little room for debate; although as I've said we were spared the rod during Religious Instruction. Odd really as there might have been more justification for whipping little heathen bastards for not remembering their Catechism, than for forgetting the capital of New Guinea. Any faith, vocation or calling I may have once had, was eradicated by my experience at St Ambrose College, Hale Barns.

Who, by the way, was Saint Ambrose? He created a lousy school.

There was no bullying in the school, probably due to the common enemy of arbitrary and instant corporal punishment from the monks. We were not sexually abused. The Irish Christian Brothers were simple, good, sincere, if horribly misguided men. I know of no child of my time who was interfered with in any way, discounting the daily beatings which were simply an accepted, traditional part of the school system, by any nun, priest or monk.

*****

Chapter 22 - Finishing School

"I left school at the age of twelve – and went out to work. It never did me any harm."
My Father - Edwin Hodson.

1959: Hovercraft marks new era in transport - A revolutionary new form of transport which can operate on sea and land has been officially launched in the Solent, off England's south coast. The Hovercraft, which has been described as a cross between an aircraft, a boat and a land vehicle, was invented by boat-builder Christopher Cockerell. Dubbed a "man-made flying saucer", the hovercraft is propelled on a cushion of air created by its own fan power.

At five years old I walked about two miles from the house we had for two years in Derby Road, across Heaton Moor, to Didsbury Road, bordering the hill down on one side to Heaton Norris and on the other, to Parrs Wood, to attend St Winifred's RC Primary School. For a small lad with short five-year-old legs, it was a long and tedious journey which I uncomplainingly made twice a day, there ...and back. My abiding memory is that next door to us in Derby Road lived a retired army officer who collected guns that were pinned to the walls of his well-ordered house – from flintlocks to modern revolvers – which we were allowed to admire but not touch. The house in Derby Road was my second and larger home – a step up from Audenshaw, Ashton, thanks to Father's increasing income.

When Father returned from active service in 1945, he gave up his job as an accountant at the Gas Board and started his own Accountancy Practice in central Manchester, financed by Lloyds Bank, King Street. With a jovial nature, a natural effortless talent for mathematics and a sporting determination to win, he quickly recruited several hundred clients, hired a small team, gave his clients a year's credit to pay their fees (as did most businesses), sold tax efficient pensions and insurance, in an era when Sur-Tax and Super-Tax peaked at 98%, and slowly became modestly successful and well-off; moving his family up the housing ladder.

A year after I started school, we moved to Heaton Mersey into the cold clammy haunted Victorian pile of Birch House, sold cheaply in the post war recession by Radio Three music presenters, Mr and Mrs Green, who could no longer afford to heat, repair or decorate it. They left musical instruments, a high class radiogram with a supply of steel needles that picked out music from the shellac grooves of hundreds of brittle classical 78's discs, and a large collection of beautifully bound albums, boasting all the best classical orchestras, singers, soloists and children's records – including Sparky's Magic Piano.

An advantage of this cold, gloomy, draughty house was that it was nearer to my school, about one mile, halving the boring walk. Even so, the repetitive journey along the same old dusty streets, past the same old neat homes and well-trimmed hedges did drag on my spirits from time to time, and on warm days increased the intolerable burden of carrying my oversized dark blue gabardine rain-coat. I dealt with that problem, at least once and I recall, probably twice, by tossing the offending garment over one of the well-trimmed hedges, onto somebody's well attended flower border; never to be seen again. Apart from those two acts of silent and unseen temporary insanity, I was a model pupil.

The class I joined in 1947 numbered about fifty 1942-3 war babies, all on healthy if frugal post-war rations, tightly controlled by government coupons issued in Ration Books, supplemented by thick, sweet State orange juice and sweetened thick condensed-milk, which ensured we did not over-eat but were growing-up with strong teeth, bones, regular bowel movements and vanishingly few lice – parasites that were hunted down and destroyed by regular visits of the School Nit Nurse; who examined every pupil's head for the tiny lice eggs, nits, which attached themselves, or were lovingly attached by their mothers, to single hairs on our expanding scholastic skulls. Bathing, immersing ourselves in lukewarm water in condensation filled chilly bathrooms, and actually washing our hair, was an occasional duty and ritual, performed perhaps on a Friday evening, applying carbolic soap to all body parts, and hair, not only to clean the skin and scalp but to also kill all and any unwelcome minuscule visitors. The powerful acids and alkalis in the soap were unkind to eyes, wounds, grazes and healthy skin – and best used sparingly. Scrubbing brushes, flaying the skin with harsh bristles, were commonplace – until supplanted by slightly less abrasive loofahs – claimed to be natural sea plants shaped like cucumbers woven from wire-wool – but probably in fact surplus instruments of torture from the Spanish Inquisition.

Thus cleansed and deloused, my first class of fifty bewildered five to six-year-old pupils was taught by young red haired Miss Halissey; who with vague and distant kindness drummed into us by rote and repetition the Alphabet and our Times Tables up to twelve. I will never forget that "Twelve Twelves are A Hundred and Forty-Four". How on earth does the computer generation manage life without those two permanently imprinted on-board vital tools – The Alphabet & The Times Table?

Our continuing health was guaranteed the next year, in 1948, when socialist Prime Minister Clement Atlee, who had displaced our great war hero Winston Churchill, and the new Health Minister Aneurin Bevan, after tortuous negotiations with the medical consultants and general practitioners, "Stuffed their mouths with gold" as Bevan put it and achieved the world's first National Health Service, the NHS – free to all citizens – paid for by an additional tax on wages, called National Insurance Stamps. It was this NHS, in its first year that pumped me full of penicillin and miraculously saved my life from that infected, potentially fatal, Mastoid bone.

The last harrowing national epidemic that threatened us Baby Boomers and older children was poliomyelitis, infantile paralysis, or simply Polio, which lurked in swimming pools and other shared facilities. In passing, Polio casually crippled and paralysed its victims, sometimes consigning them to wheelchairs for life. The worst affected could not breathe unaided and were housed in iron-lungs, clumsy mechanical pumps which moved their chests. We all knew of children who had caught the disease and were invalided for months or years. One of my neighbours, Roger Wood, had caught Polio, but slowly recovered his full strength, which he then spent on illicit and dangerous chemical investigations in his bedroom and on learning most of the jokes and goofy voices from the Goon Show.

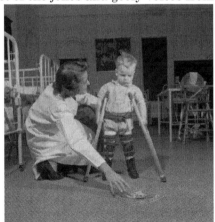

The disease was curbed, contained and almost eradicated by two vaccines – both discovered and developed by two rival Jewish doctors; in Europe delivered as a drop of clear liquid on a sugar cube and in America by injection. From 1954 onwards, all schoolchildren and millions of adults worldwide were inoculated with the Salk-Vaccine or the Sabin-Vaccine – and the dreaded Polio was vanquished. Doctor Salk refused to patent his world saving vaccine – gifting it to poor and rich alike.

There was **intense** rivalry between Sabin, shown here, and Salk over who would first develop a vaccine. Sabin dismissively called Salk "A kitchen chemist". Sabin's oral vaccine with live weakened virus eventually won out over Salk's shot with dead polio virus. Sabin too was Jewish.

Later – we Baby Boomers, as we reached teenage and sexual maturity – were terrified out of our wits (but not sufficiently to cool our irrepressible ardour) by horror posters that had been crafted in World War Two, to dissuade troops from casual "carnal knowledge" and protect them from another awful epidemic but never mentioned disease, The Clap. These posters, displayed in all public toilets and similar locations, depicted otherwise blameless men and women, often still in military uniform, who had foolishly and sinfully Eaten of The Fruit of The Tree of Knowledge (carnal knowledge) and contracted syphilis or gonorrhoea or both – or simply pubic lice – resulting in their noses, mouths, tongues and, we can assume, their privy parts, rotting away until they died horrible and shameful deaths – thereafter to be cast into the Eternal Fires of Hell and Damnation. These rotting features were drawn with all the poisonous and demonic artifice that could be summoned, sparing no detail of the certain fate that awaited

us. These public health messages were, for the vast majority of us, the only sex-education we would ever receive.

The 1950s and 1960s had record numbers of teenage pregnancies. It would have helped to have been told how babies are made and born. But everyone was too shy to discuss it. My blessed mother had six virgin births.

St Winifred's RC Primary School never, of course, mentioned sex; or knew of its existence. The school did however educate us five to eleven year olds in hellfire and damnation, spiced with a bit of Heaven and charitably leavened, for any presumed innocent, pre-Judgement Day non-Catholics and un-baptized babies, with Purgatory; a very grim punishing, time-limited, waiting room for The Last Judgement; and with Limbo, a not unpleasant, bland, in-between place for lost souls. I was never sure about how long we (souls after death) had to remain in these places – or how our living tutors gained their knowledge of these after-life locations and conditions. But, setting aside the unanswerable questions – we were thoroughly educated in religious knowledge.

From St Winifred's, aged eleven, I progressed, as I've reported earlier, to the boys only, private St. Ambrose College, located in the much posher district of Hale Barns, Altrincham, and staffed by those Irish Christian Brothers armed with leather strops. By bus it was a two-hour journey; into Altrincham centre and out to Hale Barns on a dedicated school bus. Here, again in a class of fifty-two pupils, and to repeat myself, I learned to play rugby, as a sturdy prop-forward, and learned a little Latin; before contracting my long undiagnosed painful duodenal ulcers which over the years reduced me to a stick like figure, with a grim visage that successfully masked the stabbing pains which arrived two or three times a day.

My illness was not helped by the awful inedible school lunches. I survived largely on illicit pies from the off-limits village shop, financed by cycling to school and keeping the bus fares, and a small bottle of milk, supplied free daily to all post war school children. To avoid an excess of enthusiastic, painful strapping and caning, I was a diligent scholar, usually in the top three of my class. Nightly, we had 3 to 4 hours of Homework to do – or, we craftily realised, if we stuck to the two hours' bus journeys, on the top of a crowded smoke filled North-Western bus, we could enjoy an illicit cigarette and co-operate over difficult tasks and dash our homework onto paper in a bus-shaken hand, that was just about legible to the teachers – and complete about two thirds of the homework before arriving home.

I came near to death one evening, cycling home, on a narrow stretch of busy road, when a long lorry negotiating oncoming cars, ground past me at low speed almost pitching me into the high kerb. As its tail passed me – I thankfully pulled out a little and got behind it. Shock, Horror! It was towing an equally long trailer, with just enough space between them to fit my bike. Then, with me trapped between kerb, lorry and trailer, the rig speeded up. It is a tribute to remarkable acceleration and schoolboy fitness, that I kept up long enough to live until the road widened and I had the space to get back near the kerb – where the twin lorry passed me. Of course, we never wore crash helmets.

Old Trafford

By my fourteenth year I had mastered travel by bike and bus, and as a passenger in dad's car of course, but trains were something of a mystery to me. Heaton Moor boasted a commuter station, going north-west a few miles to Piccadilly Station in central Manchester; and going south-east a hundred and fifty miles to Euston Station London; but I had never travelled by train and had no knowledge of how and where to buy a ticket – return or single, day-trip or season, express, direct or slow, at what times, or where I would be when we reached the destination station; or how to get back from there. Relying as I did on an innate sense of direction and the position of the sun, rather than on maps, timetables, street and village names, and travel books, and living in our odd family that never discussed anything at all, I remained suspicious and wary of The Great Iron Horse that Crosses the Prairie – all trains were then steam driven – and so I avoided them. But, at school I gathered that numbers of my classmates travelled daily from far off places by train into Altrincham, where they caught the school-bus.

So – when one of them arranged tickets for the 1955/56 football League semi-final replay in October between Blackpool and Manchester United, at night, under the ground's new floodlights, and figured out how we could get there after school – by train; I set aside my paranoia and trusted that these seasoned travellers would get us there. And indeed, the experienced train-and-connecting-buses users led the way, that wet and freezing evening, to Altrincham station by bus; then onto a packed train going to Stretford and Central Station Manchester, which stopped en-route at Trafford Park. From there we followed the crowds, mostly men and boys, wrapped in warm and waterproof clothes, some with torches to pick out the

potholes in the cinders. This was not only my first train journey, but it was also my first professional football match – even though we all pledged allegiance to Manchester United, I had never seen them play. Added to the mounting excitement was the prospect of seeing the legendary Stanley Mathews, then the greatest footballer on Earth, playing for Blackpool. Teetotal, vegetarian, and I guess in reality a non-smoker, he played world-class football until he was fifty – then retired and opened a bicycle shop in Blackpool.

In the dark, the rain and the cold, we queued to get through the narrow iron turnstile gates and being an hour early we established a prime place on the concrete terraces – positioning ourselves immediately in front of one of the steel crush barriers, with it protecting our backs from crowd surges, we hoped. With our coats buttoned up to the neck and hands deep into our pockets, we stood fast in our place as the stadium filled with men from every occupation – dockers, builders, engineers, office clerks, coal miners and all manner of jobs. We stamped our feet to stop them from freezing into blocks of ice. Fifteen minutes before kick-off, the floodlights were tested – and seen to work, then switched back to low – as electricity was so expensive. Being young, lightweight and small, we were glad of the crush barrier taking the weight of the packed crowds behind.

It was a great match and we were close enough to the pitch to see aging Stanley Mathews' deep concentration, almost a meditation, on his intricate manoeuvres as he weaved his way through the defenders – and his completely calm detached toughness when our team tried dirty tackles on him. He was unbeatable at the beautiful game. But Blackpool wasn't unbeatable and United won the game; all players being muddied, bruised and bashed – except Stanley Mathews who looked as if he'd taken a Sunday stroll round the grounds.

The game ended and the crowds surged towards the great double gates, thrown open to get us all out without injury or delay.

As we were funnelled towards the exits, my pals and I were separated and the packed spectators were pressed tighter and tighter. Suddenly and without hope of resistance I was turned round backwards, trapped by larger men and was, thank God, lifted up off my feet – the dreadful alternative would have been to be crushed downwards and trampled in the stampede – and I was carried backwards, held by the shoulders of the crowd for twenty or thirty yards or more, until the crowd cleared the gates and spread out across the cinder apron outside the stadium. I made a graceful touchdown and turned to face where we were going.

As the crowd thinned and dispersed; thanks to our highly visible bright maroon and blue striped school caps, my classmates reassembled – identified our buses or trains home and said our goodbyes – until the next day when we met at school to be flogged at nine-fifteen, as usual, for not having thoroughly learned the Latin vocabulary set by our Form Master for that night. I guess though, that Roger Clarke, who I shared a desk with, and I, on our bus to Heaton Mersey, did bury our heads in the Latin lists – and so probably avoided the daily punishment meted out to the dim-witted and petrified.

St. Ambrose College finished after O Levels at 15 or 16 years old and cast us out into society to make our way in the wide world.

Just before our O Level exams, replacing the politically canny and jovial Brother Phelan, we got a new and grim little headmaster, who experimented by limiting us to taking 5 O Levels and so - after suffering six or so confused, confusing, short-lived, linguistically challenged French tutors - I and most of my fifty fellows failed French, and I won just four O Level Certificates of merit. The new headmaster, Brother Foley, (or was it "Folly") then immediately had a "nervous breakdown" and was shipped back to Ireland. But, armed with my three-terms a year school reports, which, unlike today, publicly ranked us from best to worst, from dumbest to brightest, or in my case as most cane and pain averse, in summer 1959 I left school, went home and, in the absence of any careers guidance, or indeed of any conversations at all about my future, I took myself off to The Stockport Employment office, with Pauline, and via the job offers on their wall, applied to train as a Structural Steel Engineer at Banister Walton Ltd, Central Avenue, Trafford Park Industrial Estate.

In the short transition between school and factory, I instantly rejected everything St Ambrose College had ever taught me – crammed into my head through tedium, illogical philosophy and cruel treatment. I refused to be brainwashed and bullied by the brainless. After all – I determinedly danced on the half-beat. Eighteen months later I rejected The Catholic Church.

Trafford Park, close by Salford Docks, once part of the large estates of the noble De Trafford family, had become the largest industrial estate in Europe – which The Luftwaffe had tried to bomb out of existence. Its culture was and is most accurately and artistically depicted in the Andy Capp cartoons. Among the factories were a few mean streets of Victorian terraced houses, homes for the few remaining families marooned in and dwarfed by vast industrial compounds, spewing out every sort of deathly pollution and brain numbing noise. The average life expectancy of residents was 38 years; at fifty they were old and broken by the crippling environment.

Andy Capp & Flo Famous residents of Trafford Park, Salford. (Life expectancy 38)

It was also home to the greatest ever football team, Manchester United, years before the club was commercialised by the Edwards Family, resident in Cheshire, who made their first fortune from a chain of butcher's shops and international trading in meat; followed by a larger fortune from incorporating and selling the football club. The already famous stadium, Old Trafford, was just half a mile from Banister Walton and in my last year at school, it housed the world famous Busby Babes, who were wiped out in the February 1958 Munich Air disaster – to be rebuilt by Matt Busby to achieve even greater fame over the next decade. In 1968 when Richard speculated in property deals and joined the Manchester night-life scene, he befriended one of the most famous players, George Best, as a heavy drinking partner; but that's another story.

Manchester United - Busby Babes, average age 22, went down in Munich air crash February 1958.

The engineering drawing office, with windows of hazed frosted glass, designed to avoid us being distracted by glancing outside, was on an upper floor, one large room which was home to thirty chain-smoking engineers, drawing in Indian ink and calculating on ivory or cheaper bone or plastic slide-rules (prior to pocket calculators or PCs). We worked out the stresses, strains and strengths of steel bridges and building frames. I wrestled quite successfully with the slide-rules, the mathematics, copying structures and with erasing drawing errors with a razor blade to scrape off the rubbery Indian ink. When approved, I reproduced the drawings on a large Gestetner copier, producing table-sized blue hued plans – known as "blueprints". The steel was in our huge sheds next door, being stacked and hauled about by overhead cranes, and bolted and welded into transportable sections – as instructed by our team in the drawing office. A railway line ran through our site, connected to the whole world. Ocean going cargo ships still sailed into Salford Docks, along the Manchester Ship Canal, fifty miles from the Atlantic port of Liverpool.

The clocked-in-and-out work-day, plus Saturday morning, was 8am to 5pm, or actually till precisely 4.56pm, which generously allowed us four minutes to run down a railway line to the central cinder surfaced bus-station, by the gates of GEC, whose thousands of engineers invaded the buses at 5pm. Our four minutes of grace created a level playing field for us to join the bus-queues. It took about an hour for any bus to clear the two miles of cobbled roads to the Trafford Park boundary. Our Managing Director, whose office was below ours, was sometimes to be seen scooting down the tracks, briefcase in hand, to the bus station, alongside the rest of us.

On the other side of my office, across another railway track, was the Works Canteen, where we ate a free lunch, including steamed-jam-roly-poly and custard, in thirty minutes. Beyond the canteen was a high double wire fence, surrounding several blackened acres where thousands of old tyres, of every size, were stored – and burned day and night to recover their wire frames, with the stinking black smoke labouring into the, usually wet, dank, sky. The air and ground pollution was appalling. I guess the nearest tree was probably 5 miles away – and dying a slow horrible death. The industrial estate was not a pretty sight. Perhaps our frosted glass windows had been fitted by caring managers, to protect our nature loving sensibilities.

My commute, from home to factory, was two hours in smoke wreathed buses whose ceilings dripped with brown stained condensation – the combined breath of forty or so heavy smokers. I left home at six in the morning. As an apprentice engineer I attended building and mathematics courses every evening at Stockport Polytechnic, arriving back home at 9pm. The pay wasn't good. It's grim Up-North.

Trafford Park – World's largest industrial estate (nearest tree 5 miles away and dying a horrible death)

I soldiered on for six months until a severe heart problem (my girlfriend emigrating to New Zealand) caused me to re-evaluate my life plan and I took "temporary" work at Father's accountancy office (his unspoken cunning plan for me all along), next door to Manchester Cathedral, where I was coerced into helping with a staff crisis (at the office not the Cathedral) and ended up aged nineteen as a precocious office manager in a central Manchester accountancy practice in a profession I had little aptitude and no liking for. Richard, who had chosen accountancy and had the appropriate talents, overslept aged nineteen, and missed one of thirteen papers to qualify as a Chartered Accountant, he passed the others with merit, but there was no question that he might re-take. Father spurned education. But, he was later also shepherded into Father's business and, some years after, brother Peter also joined us. Father's joke to his business pals was that he was breeding his own staff – and there was a deep truth in his never discussed system. He really felt entitled to shanghai his kids into his solo-partner practice, where, if we never formally qualified, he would remain the indispensable, unchallenged top-dog, for life. I think he, whose own dad had abandoned them when my father was only twelve years old, justified his manipulations as being a good parent and providing us with a future as accountants, and himself with a lifelong pension – despite our personal, undoubtedly foolish contrary inclinations or talents. Father's long term dream was to buy a very large house which we would all live in together – a tribal home.

Thus, I became an unqualified accountant – and my education was complete. But, sadly for Father, Richard unravelled all his commercial hopes and dreams, when he, Richard, discovered the unmatched excitement of gambling by phone from our shared office, a lifetime's salary lost or won in 3 minutes on the global commodities markets; and drew Father into his non-too-safe net.

Only Martin challenged Father's contempt for education ("I left school at thirteen and it never did me any harm") and after winning a wrestling match in The Morning Room at Birch House, when he hurled Father into the never opened drinks-cabinet. He studied law at Manchester University; and went on to build a Lincoln's Inn practice of 50 people.

***

Chapter 23 - Blind Date

"Ultimately the bond of all companionship, whether in marriage or in friendship, is conversation, and conversation must have a common basis, and between two people of widely different culture the only common basis possible is the lowest level." Oscar Wilde

20 Jan 1961: John F Kennedy sworn in as US president. The Democrat John F Kennedy has been sworn in as the youngest ever elected president of the United States. The 43-year-old Roman Catholic was inaugurated as the 35th president on a snow-covered Capitol Hill in Washington. He takes over from the oldest president in American history, General Dwight Eisenhower, who is bowing out aged 70. The president's Republican rival, Richard Nixon, who came a close second in the race for the White House, also attended the inauguration ceremony.

Goulash, Peter-John and I had somehow contrived to meet three girls from the youth club on Wellington Road on the understanding that we would all six go to the Savoy Cinema and sit on the back row.

Goulash was by far the tallest of us, with golden red hair, a willowy stance, a precocious light blue three-piece suit and, thanks to his dad sharing his tales of the world of Sporting Club men, with a deep understanding of adult night-life. I was the next tallest, thin like Goulash, authoritative on factual matters, plain of face and, still confined to my school blazer, considered to be a bit boring. Peter-John was easily the most handsome of us, with a straight nose, wide grey eyes, fair wavy hair, a square determined jaw, good clothes and a confident manner – but he was short of stature and brusque. The three girls, who we met by Martin's Bank at the top of Shaw Road, were Angela Crook, the tallest of them, their leader, pretty, neat and slender with a hint of an early preference for twin-set and pearls; Sandra Dodgeson, smaller than Angela, wearing a pale yellow and black striped shirt-waister, intelligent and attractive, who cocked her head on one side and spoke quickly – like a little robin; and lastly, short, rounded, none too bright, plain, not smelling like a rose and badly dressed, was a girl we shall call Dilly.

Goulash's most valuable asset was his talent for humorous stories. He could make girls laugh. And it was a well proven fact that once you got them laughing – you were there! Not that in 1958 any of us were at all certain about where "there" was. He also had the most natural opening chat-up patter – his name. Everyone called him Goulash. He was indubitably Goulash. Most people didn't know his real name. He introduced himself as Goulash and, as we never went back to his home, nobody heard what his mum and dad called him. Even the shyest and most reserved of fourteen-year-old girls who had been time without number warned from the womb to the Osborne Bentley School of Dance to Never Talk to Strange Men, could not resist asking "Why Goulash?" To which he had a selection of answers to suit any audience and any occasion. He was also tall and not bad looking in a freckly sort of a way.

As we walked in the gathering dusk and light rain up Heaton Moor Road to the Savoy, Goulash and Angela immediately hit it off.

I liked Sandra. She was quick witted, wore little make up – I couldn't bear greasy make-up - and was not manipulative or moody. Although she deferred to Angela, she had a brave streak of independence and was no pushover. She was pretty and she could think. I think she liked me. Shyly, we found ourselves walking side by side.

Peter-John was used to getting the best. Small but perfectly formed, the strong silent type, with a good turn of speed on the dance floor and expensive clothes and good manners, he usually got the girl he wanted. But the dice that evening had been cast too quickly and to his consternation he found himself at the back of the queue. At least Dilly was shorter than him, making him appear taller, as they came together by default and walked ahead of us; Peter-John setting his inevitable at-the-double-pace which we all had to keep up with, and Dilly reaching out for his hand which he wordlessly snatched away.

In the Savoy, in the Circle, we made it onto the second to the back row, all six of us parked our raincoats on the back of our own seats, lit cigarettes despite the expense, to prove we were not kids, and settled down to wait for the exciting moment when the lights went down – and we could pretend to watch, through the fog of tobacco smoke, the antics of the Three Stooges followed by Jack Hawkins grimly saving the nation in The Cruel Sea - while in reality our attention was wholly focused on surreptitious breathless advances and sharp retreats of our questing hands, as they silently investigated the mysteries of The Opposite Sex. We might even kiss.

Peter-John however was stonily still. He was adamantine in his determination to be alone. He set his grey eyes under his black eyebrows in a ferocious glare, fixed for the duration on the screen. He kept his elbows in, lest they should touch and so invite Dilly, and his hands were glued to his lap. When her podgy little hand tried to creep across their shared arm-rest he brushed it aside with a dismissive, expressionless gesture that brooked no response. When he lit yet another cigarette he declined to offer one to Dilly. While she bent her head cutely, to gaze up into his strong silent face, he stared straight ahead, refusing to acknowledge her existence, never mind to meet her small hopeful eyes. Dilly was not easily dissuaded, she could handle rejection; even when she had the temerity to lift her short chubby arm high enough to stroke the back of her escort's neck – no easy move for one so vertically challenged – which he angrily ducked from and pointedly turned up his jacket collar to prevent further incursions, Dilly was not deterred.

At a very, very quiet and tense part of the film, when the seas had for a moment stopped roaring and the waves ceased their crashing, and all the sailors were dying and imagining their tearful loved ones at home and Jack Hawkins was staring despairingly into the darkness, Dilly, with all the wiles of the fairer sex, almost climbing out of her seat, leaned closer to Peter-John than ever before, in fact leaned on him and tried to seduce him with a stage whisper which carried around the whole cinema, "Oh Peter-John…" she wheedled, "I'm so cold," and she shivered pitifully.

For the first time, her beau, her date, her male, her man addressed her, turning to look her in the face and to disengage her arm that had slipped, kitten like, for warmth and protection, under his. In his normal voice, perhaps less abrupt and in his terms somewhat kinder than expected, but nevertheless a stern voice that echoed around the stilled cinema, jarring the whole audience out of its pleasurable lachrymose mood, he replied, "Then put your coat on – you potty bird."

Even Dilly started to get the message.

The Savoy – Heaton Moor Road. Films viewed through a fog of cigarette smoke.

On our way out, Goulash and I clutching Angela and Sandra, and Peter-John legging it up the road to outdistance a puffing, enamoured Dilly, posters were excitedly advertising the revolutionary coming of Rock 'A' Round The Clock staring tubby Bill Haley with his kiss curl, and surrounded by a gyrating bunch of leering, long jacketed, drain-piped trousered, brothel-creeper shod Teddy Boys – whose coming would announce irreversible changes to the post-war world; but not quite just yet.

In a year or two, even we of Heaton Moor would be influenced by the Edwardian look, but that week, tripping over our collective feet at Osborne and Bentley, and subject to ration-coupons from the Ministry of Supply, we dressed like our parents, misunderstood sex like our parents – and for a short time, tried to dance like our parents.

Richard could dance. He could quickstep and tango and foxtrot and waltz as well as any hotel gigolo, with any female. Peter-John, handsome, smartly dressed and curt, quickly picked up the movements and could scud around the ballroom in his well shone shoes. Even David Hall, with his large feet, could place them in the required positions and lead a girl, who had to dance backwards, in reasonable safety. Malcolm Holt and Tes Tyler, both tall and dark, could glide across the floor with swooning girls in their arms, completely safe from any threat of trampling. All the boys and girls seemed to easily copy the intricate little steps demonstrated by Miss Marjorie Barlow and whichever male she picked to be her temporary consort – often my brother Richard.

But I really couldn't quite get it.

Lead with the left foot, and step-one two, to the side one-two, with the right one-two, slide one-two, and turn one-two and sweep forwards one-two.

The girls, any who dared risk a dance with me, always had a foot in the wrong place at the wrong time. They had delicate little shoes, when steel toe-caps would have been more useful, and they complained loudly and often when I trod on their unprotected toes or kicked their shins backwards with a vigorous initial move into the Blue Danube Waltz or Victor Sylvester's Foxtrot or Sir Malcolm Sergeant's more upmarket musical contributions – famously and ponderously lauded by Stockport's Lord Mayor after a noteworthy classical orchestral evening – "I'd like to thank Sergeant Malcolm and his Band for a wonderful …etc." - to the abiding shame of all educated Stockport citizens.

I liked music. I liked to sing. I wasn't crippled. But the steps refused to come in the right order or places.

After a few weeks of lessons and with an unmistakable decline in girls attending the school as they were systematically stomped, kicked and sprained by my unusual techniques – Miss Barlow herself devoted almost a whole determined half hour to one-to-one tuition, my arms raised as if on a rack with our hands clamped one to the other and a gap between us, wide enough for us both to see what my feet were doing – and, I now suspect, quite consciously to prevent my uncontrolled actions from jeopardising Miss Barlow's priceless dancing feet – were they insured I wonder. But even with the expert herself, devoting herself to my conversion and salvation, I remained baffled.

At last the dogged, dedicated teacher gave up the challenge.

"Noel…" she announced so the whole class could not fail to hear, in a high, temporarily exhausted and imperious voice, "Noel… …I can do no more with you." And then she damned and dismissed my dancing days for eternity, adding in the same loud, penetrating tone, "…You dance on the half-beat!"

And she threw me out of the school; in the middle of a session.

I walked alone down the hill into Mersey Square; stood irresolutely at the Number 75 Bus Stop; realised I had just missed a bus and anyway I wasn't in any hurry, as I had nowhere to go, nothing to do and no-one to do it with – and I trudged home up Wellington Road, eventually down Parsonage Road, round the back of St Paul's to the lane at the bottom of Shaw Road; across the Shaw Road farm, by the pig-pen, along Clifton Road – and hence, about two hours later, onto Mauldeth Road and home.

A failed quickstepper; a lethal waltzer and a discarded foxtrotter.

And, I still don't know what she meant. What is the half-beat?

***

Chapter 24 - Gangs

When you're a Jet, you're a Jet all the way
From your first cigarette to your last dyin' day!
When you're a Jet, let 'em do what they can
You've got brothers around, you're a family man!
You're never alone, you're never disconnected, you're home with your own
When company's expected, you're well-protected!
Then you are set with a capital J
Which you'll never forget till they cart you away
When you're a Jet you stay a Jet.
– West Side Story - 1957

This was the era of Teddy Boys who had earned a well-deserved reputation for utterly mindless violence.

Heaton Moor, middle class, middle aged and respectable, stands on high ground between Levenshulme to the North and Mersey Square to the South. Towards Manchester centre, next to Levenshulme is the still notorious district of Moss Side that in those days boasted city gangs based on two ice-cream parlours, Sivori's and Scapaticci's. In Stockport, Mersey Square in the shadow of an overpoweringly high brick viaduct, abutted the lethal territory of the Gorsey Bankers and other dark areas that spawned fashionable thugs by the hundreds.

The culture was explained to us, my civilised teenaged friends and me, by Graham Fish, our Heaton Moor racer, with a good brain, big heart and a completely mad passion for speeding crazily on motor-bikes – in those days without a crash helmet. 'Fishy' naturally wore black leather and was never far from his giant, gleaming machine.

He was famous for many spectacular adventures; such as the tale of the irate car driver who swerved across his line as they both descended Long Hill as it plunged down the Pennines towards Stockport. And such as when he spent some weeks in hospital recovering from "road-burn" caused when attempting to escape from a Wolsey Police car at high speed, (it was impossible for Fishy to NOT travel at high speed) down Wellington Road towards Levenshulme, past the McVitie biscuit factory; when he had to swerve, and the bike skidded from under him, leaving him to slide a long way on the tarmac, creating a much admired black skid mark on the road as his leathers scraped on the surface, which turned to red as the leather disintegrated and skin, muscle and bone were exposed.

Graham was short and thickset, with a broad swarthy face. His hair was black, long, wavy, and flicked up and back with *Brylcreem*. His world bridged the respectable community of Heaton Moor and the frightening gangland of Teddy-Boys. One summer's evening he described a 'West Side Story' encounter in Mersey Square between two Stockport gangs, intent on mutually assured destruction.
"The Granelli's came down the steps behind the Plaza..." Graham recounted to his wide eyed fans gathered on the pavement outside the Conservative Club on Heaton Moor Road.
"...and the Gorsey's were already there, in the bus station. They all made for Solomon's Café and met on the road under the archway..."

"How many were there, Fishy?" breathed one of us, all pseudo Rock'n'Rollers to a man – and to a girl.

" 'Bout fifteen in each gang." Graham obliged. "...and they were all tooled-up. Knives, chains, and the lot."

"...there were three or four of us bikers just by the café window – you know; on that cobbled bit before the bridge..."

We all obediently nodded our understanding of the scene; even those who hadn't a clue where he meant.

"...and we were keeping our heads down. No point in getting ourselves cut up... It wasn't our fight"

Again we all nodded in solemn and sage agreement exhibiting all the wisdom of seasoned street fighters. Stances subtly shifted to puff out chests and display bigger biceps. The girls with us adopted bored faces but stopped talking and moved in a little closer.

"…and they faced each other off. You know, strutting and jabbing."

Graham was enjoying his storytelling role.

"But they were nervous. Very nervous." He said authoritatively. "You see; neither gang had their Cocks with them. Without the gang leaders, they don't know what they're getting into…"

We remained respectfully silent, acknowledging Graham's unique behavioural knowledge.

"…Suppose – you see – they start scrapping and then just one of the bosses appears? They'd be in deep shit. So, instead of getting stuck straight in, they started testing. From about ten feet apart…"

Fishy indicated the distance with his hands and slicked his fingers through his forelock. "…There was this mean looking little fella with the Granelli's. A knife man I reckoned, with a scar down here…" he drew a finger across his cheek and down onto his neck – a long and ugly scar, we knew; probably an old razor cut.

"…and he darts forward, real pugnacious, and says slow and menacing 'We knows Red Mack'. Then he darts back before anyone can punch him." Graham is a good mimic and we are transported to the battle front by his tale.

"Then a big fat guy from the Gorsey's; a scruffy lad in a Donkey Jacket, lurches out and he says, a bit thick and nervous…" We know Big Billy – so don't mess with us' …and he steps back fast."

"That was a good card to play…" continued Fishy. "I know Big Billy and there's no way I'd get into a fight if he was around; he's probably killed a few blokes in his time."

"…But then the Granelli's lad is back in the ring, and he says 'Balls, mate. Big Billy's in Strangeways. Everyone knows that. But Red Mack could come through that arch any minute – now' and he points behind them, really confident."

Graham chortled. "…But then another Gorsey comes up – and Scarface runs back, and the Gorsey shouts 'You just watch it Mate. Big Billy came out last week and he can take Red Mack anytime. Anytime you want. In fact he'd take the whole bloody pack of you "And he runs at the Granelli's and they all back up like this..." Graham acts out a gang of cringing thugs in retreat.

"...Then one of the Granelli's turns back on them and says in a real low voice 'Big Billy might take Red Mack, but we know Killer Crane' And all the Gorsey's start back in fear – 'Killer Crane; that mad bastard' they say and they all retreat back to the traffic lights..."

"....Then! just when you think the Granelli's will run them out of the Square – A Gorsey comes back at them. 'Killer Crane, Huh! Killer Crane. That's Nothing – That makes no difference' he yells. 'We've got Mad Dave's dad...iiiieeeeeeeee"

This last scream was added gratuitously by Graham to illustrate the fear injected into the proceeding by the terminal threat presented by Mad Dave and his dad.

"...And so..." giggled Fishy, engrossed in his own story. "...the Gorsey's won the fight. The Granelli's couldn't think of anyone more fearsome than Mad Dave's dad..." and he laughed wildly.

"So they never fought?" one of us asked impatiently.

"...They rarely do." Graham answered. Then suddenly very serious he said "But nor would you if you knew Mad Dave – he's a real nutter. Smash you to pieces in a few seconds. And his dad; Well..."

Graham reflected heavily, all joking gone. "He's about the barmiest bloke you'd never hope to meet. Ex-wrestler. He once turned a car full of blokes over in Kingsway. Nearly killed them all. On his own. Talk about strong."

Graham's humour re-emerged, "...No they hardly ever fight. It's a Who-knows-Who competition. This time the Gorsey's won it. And they all know some bloody frightening blokes."

"But – if you see them coming. Get out of the way quick. They'll think nothing of carving you up just for fun. ...And your girl-friends..." He added spinning towards the girls at the back of the group.

Seeing that he had everyone's close attention, including all the girls' and being smart enough to know when to make an exit – Graham leapt onto his bike – kicked it into immediate and roaring life, stood it on its back wheel in a cloud of smoke and rubber – and screamed across the pavement, onto the road, still on the back wheel and raced away – into the setting sun, screaming his trademark scream.

How did he fare in later life? Graham Fish achieved his dream of racing bikes, entering the Isle of Man races several times – and was killed in a racing accident, still young and undoubtedly screaming with glee as he hurtled to his last Finishing Line. The Teddy Boys all grew up, quietened down, and took steady jobs, wives and made children, then were afflicted by lung and heart diseases caused by coal-dust, smoking and asbestosis. A few champions still wear their sleek Brylcreemed quiffs and ducks'-arses thinning hairdo's above lined and bewildered faces, wondering where their strength and pension funds have gone.

***

Chapter 25 - Physical Education

5 Aug 1962: Marilyn Monroe found dead - Screen icon Marilyn Monroe has been found dead in bed at her Los Angeles home. - The 36-year-old actress' body was discovered in the early hours of this morning by two doctors who were called to her Brentwood home by a concerned housekeeper. - The doctors were forced to break into Miss Monroe's bedroom after being unable to open the door. She was found lying naked in her bed with an empty bottle of Nembutal sleeping pills by her side. - The local coroner, who visited the scene later, said the circumstances of Miss Monroe's death indicated a "possible suicide".

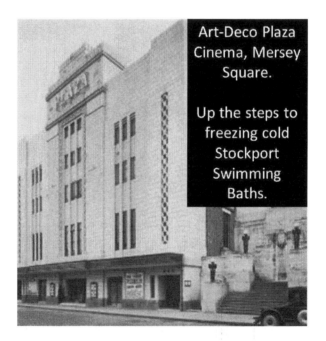

Art-Deco Plaza Cinema, Mersey Square.

Up the steps to freezing cold Stockport Swimming Baths.

Sex education in 1958 simply did not exist. Boys and Girls, Catholic or Protestant, curious or unconcerned, learned about sex secretly, behind the bicycle sheds and only through direct, fumbling experience. At primary school any suspect bits of the body which had to be referred to, due perhaps to near fatal accidents, were given coded names delivered by adults in whispers with terrified blushes. For our First Confessions, aged seven, preludes to our First Communions, a sweating, stammering religious instructor might manage a strangled utterance to a class of six and seven year olds about "self-abuse", leaving us completely perplexed and providing the basis for massive misinformation, which accompanied us throughout our lives.

The only available hints about sex were found, firstly, in the Bible, the biggest selling book in the World, in which Onan spilled his 'seed' on the ground, precipitating God's wrath and the incontinent wiping out of entire cities, and where Mary contrived to have a 'Virgin' birth, and where Moses, on God's authority, forbade his people to 'Covet Your Neighbour's Wife' or 'Commit Adultery' and in which various populations were 'raped' – each retelling of which threw our teachers into such states of guilt, embarrassment, excitement and confusion that sensitive children could not fail to realise they were concealing something of great import. Secondly, we had surreptitious recourse to Encyclopaedias. Father had bought, at considerable cost, both the full sets of Children's and Adult's Encyclopaedia Britannica, about twenty large volumes, bound in red leather. They were housed in a new bookcase, in the rarely visited Lounge. Father never opened one of them – but they did help us, the children, with our legitimate and illicit research.

Medical Encyclopaedias were obviously the most informative, with explicit fold out diagrams of the cut-away human body – and, as we became old enough to track down specific topics, where 'masturbation' and 'self-abuse' though still not explained, was expanded on to include its scientifically attested medical consequences, including blindness, deafness, low-moral-fibre, deformity, Socialism and physically wasting away with important bits dropping off.

Urban legends and hints from older children were the most reliable and trustworthy fonts of wisdom. We quickly learned that after puberty, girls and boys kissed. That was number One. Number Two was an experimental feel of the girls' breasts – on the outside of the clothes – and the other numbers marched inexorably on to ever higher states of intimate excitement, to ever lower states of moral turpitude and to esoteric knowledge, all the way up to Seven, which rhymed with Heaven. It was commonplace, in every strata of society, to remain without full 'Carnal Knowledge' up to nineteen or twenty years old. The sexual-revolution of the Sixties was inconceivable – if you will excuse the pun.

The birds and the bees.
The explanation of sexual reproduction. In old fashioned times people were embarrassed to discuss sex, let alone tell children. So they used Mother nature as a metaphor to portray sex as a natural thing and not a crime punishable by eternal damnation.

"Now Philip, It's your fortieth birthday and I feel you are ready to know about the birds and the bees." *1950s Anon*

One day, descending the front staircase, when I was sixteen or so and something of a man of the world, I intercepted my older brother escaping from a conversation with Father in our living room, into the welcome darkness of the echoing, large, tiled hall.

"Yeah, Yeah. I'll tell him." Richard was calling back into the living room as he hastily pulled the door – shut, with huge relief at having escaped. With the ESP and instincts that families have, I knew that the 'him' being referred to was in fact me.

"What'cha going to tell me?" I asked as Richard plodded thoughtfully up the stairs.

It transpired to our extreme astonishment that father had been persuaded, for reasons and causes which we could never have fathomed, to ensure that his sons had a sex-education. He had cornered Richard in the living room one winter's evening before we had slipped out to join one or another of the large groups of teenagers who assembled on street-corners, at park gates, outside the Savoy Cinema or in any one of their parentally vacated homes. Father, having waylaid his nearly eighteen-year old first male heir, had stood, red faced, looking down at the carpet until the silence became unbearable. Then he had to launch into Lesson One.

"I suppose..." he mumbled, perspiring lightly despite the cold air, "...that you know all about the ...er ...Birds and Bees and ...er ...that kind of thing?"

Richard, as acutely embarrassed as his father and only two years from siring his own first son replied "...er – Yes."

Father was deeply relieved and allowed himself to breathe again and to take a few tiny steps around the pattern on the carpet. But he had more yet to do.

"...And..." he pressed on with the sort of determined courage that won the war, "...that your brother, Noel..." we had several brothers so it was necessary to be specific, "...knows all about it?" he asked hopefully, almost pleadingly.

Richard and I had never discussed sex. The very idea was unthinkable. But Richard had to get out of the room as quickly as possible. So, on the basis of what he knew about the company I kept, he made a reasonable assumption. "...Oh! ...er...Of course. Yes."

Father was now immensely relieved. The tension that was threatening to crack the walls of the house dissipated. He let out an audible sigh of relaxation. And Richard turned to leave, opening the door behind him. Father heroically completed his painful parental duty, "...Oh! And let Noel know we've had this chat – tell him what I've said."

It wasn't much of a sex education, but it was more than Pauline ever had. Her mum and dad never once mentioned the word. Her father never appeared outside of his bedroom or on a beach with a shirt button undone or without his tie fastened at his neck.

A few months after the bus incident, Pauline and I embarked on a Romeo and Juliet affair which was almost as dramatic and tragic as the play.

Pauline was slender and very neat. She was born thin because of a fierce diet her tiny mother was advised to follow throughout the pregnancy in the War while her father, Derry Mallalieu, was away with the Ghurkha Regiment in India fighting against the Japanese, and she never put on weight. She looked uncannily like Audrey Hepburn, only prettier.

An only child, she lived with her mum and dad in Cleveland Road, next door to Jennifer Greenlees and, when she was eleven, she moved to a new detached house at the end of Princess Road, overlooking the Heaton Moor Golf Club links. At twelve she attended Oriel Bank School, an eight-mile bus journey away near Bramhall, near the Osborne Bentley dance school.

Pauline's constant companions were Jennifer Greenlees, another only child whose grimly prayerful parents, who deliberately omitted "...as we forgive those that trespass against us" as they did not consider forgiveness to be their duty, owned a greengrocery and florist shop; and, making up the young trio, the aforementioned flasher's friend, Margaret Lamerton, whose experiences of living in a very large family must have counterbalanced the solo-child experiences of Jennifer and Pauline. Margaret and Jennifer went locally to Fylde Lodge, in a class two or three years below the legendary sex-bomb, Susan Grenouille.

At thirteen they all three swooned over fourteen-year-old pop-singer Paul Anka, who belted out, in a nerve jangling, high falsetto, the hit song *'Oh Carol, I am such a fool'*. Pauline was distressed by and utterly failed to understand her father's sudden outburst against the sainted Paul after only a hundred and eighty-two repetitions of the blessed song, played at full volume on her portable phonograph, one sunny weekend, before the plastic, 45 revs per minute disk began to show signs of terminal wear.

At fourteen, she was completely mortified, in bed at ten o'clock, when it was still light outside (Manchester being far enough North to enjoy a few evenings of almost Midnight Sun), to have her parents, having enjoyed a few cocktails at the new and fashionable Bampton House Club, parade into her room accompanied, trophy like, by the infamous and incomparably sophisticated Susan Grenouille, only three years her senior, dressed if not to kill then certainly to seduce and looking like a Vogue icon; and from her ignominious position under the covers, to be shown off to the condescending Susan, like a pet cat.

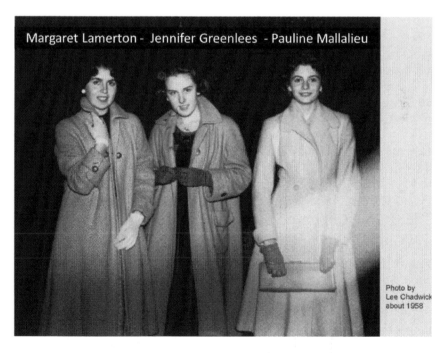

Margaret Lamerton - Jennifer Greenlees - Pauline Mallalieu

Photo by Lee Chadwick about 1958

The next year, when they were fifteen, the Famous Three, Pauline, Margaret and Jennifer, tacitly competed for a date with Tes Tyler; tall, dark, lean and muscular, and, I suppose, – handsome - to accompany him to the Mile End School dance. Pauline won the prize but her triumph was sabotaged by her mother's determination for her to wear an expensive Little Bo Peep dress, in baby blue, more fitting for a twelve-year-old's birthday party than for a night of teenage romance – and perhaps passion – leaving her to be upstaged by Margaret and Jennifer in tight sweaters and swirling knee length skirts – and to be consigned to the wall-flower seats in the school hall.

But - Never again!

The next year, at sweet sixteen, Pauline was lucky enough to meet the new, irresistible, testosterone charged me, and I, drawing on my one-to-one tuition in Jive and Rock'n'Roll with Rosemary, Michael Howard's older sister, and despite Marjorie Barlow's cruel rebuff at the dance school, I taught Pauline to Jive, in her two inch high heeled shoes, enabling her in turn to swing her fashionable shirt-waister skirt, worn over a dozen paper petticoats stiffened with sugar and water paste, and to flick her shining pony-tailed hair and flash her eyes, in the centre of several local parties, and thus to be the envy of all.

My good friend and Lonnie Donegan look-a-like, Peter Tattersall, Tats, who organised us into a skiffle-group at Kenny Marsh's house – with me on the Washboard and Biff Keegan on the Double-Bass tea-chest - was earlier that year going out with Pauline. We were all sixteen and about to leave school. Tats foolishly went on holiday with his parents and asked me, in the uncertainties of local teenage life, to keep an eye out for his girl. I nobly did that and invited her to a party, a rare party that we had at Birch House, and I walked her home afterwards.

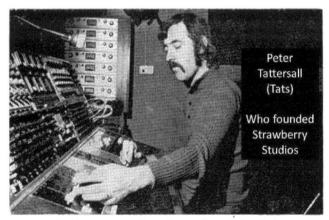

Resident engineer, Peter Tattersall, at Helios desk

As we sat across from each other in Pauline's living room, inevitably drinking tea as northerners endlessly do, I heard tinkling music that I couldn't locate the source of. In the partially lit room as I cast about, I noticed a light around Pauline that shimmered intriguingly and beautifully. I said nothing about it but the light persisted and grew stronger until she was surrounded by an inexplicable living rainbow glow. The music was strengthened but very slightly. I said absolutely nothing. Such visions certainly did not happen to up and coming drain-piped teenagers in the Rock'n'Roll era and certainly not to Heaton Moorons.

I may have been seeing and hearing things but I was schooled in the ancient northern wisdom "When in doubt – Brew Up", which we already had done, so I moved on to the next wise, more powerful imperative, "When in doubt - Do nowt."

So I did nothing. I made no move, drank my tea politely and went home.

Had the romantic lights and music intensified, and had, say, little green fairies and elves started to drop from the ceiling and lead me in dances round the room, I would have employed the final protective spell of the trio of wisdom, with complete confidence in its archetypal Mancunian power.

"When in Trouble **and** in Doubt. Pack your bags and F***' off Out."

But the third spell wasn't required. And, without remarking on the magical illusion I had experienced, I went home to bed.

Richard was away on his long hitch-hiking Continental Tour, entirely financed from his card-games, so I had the bedroom to myself. I then sat up for hours writing to Pauline. I was very smitten and hopelessly in love. Tats returned and rapidly and obligingly moved on to another beauty and after a few weeks Pauline and I started courting, spending every possible minute with each other.

That summer, we walked out together. We were inseparable. We took the train out towards Macclesfield, got off, or alighted, in the village of Adlington and had a picnic in the long grass of a wide and deserted hillside meadow – and the sun shone all day; not that we would have noticed if it didn't. I lifted Pauline over gates, hedges and fences that she seemed unable to climb or traverse without calling on my manly strength.

We were devoted. Shopkeepers started to take us for brother and sister. In private, we kissed a lot and passionately.

After two or three months of bliss, as summer waned and autumn approached, Pauline was looking downcast – indeed she looked deeply worried. Within an hour or so of walking hand-in-hand through the dark, deserted leafy streets of Heaton Mersey, she told me what the problem was. I was appalled. I was shocked. It was beyond my powers to deal with. What, indeed, could we do? What had we done?

Her period, a function of which I had only the vaguest concept, had not, she claimed, arrived. Her period was three weeks late. I learned that it had not always been unfailingly on time, forever and ever as it were, but over the last year or so, from fourteen to fifteen, it had been punctual and reliable. And now it was late.

How late is late? We speculated. Three weeks was very late. There was only one logical conclusion. She was pregnant, she was having a baby!

Or was she? I was convinced that she could not be – but Pauline's will and conviction were very, very strong. I started to believe her feminine instincts.

For days, we agonised about what to do; who to tell; who to ask.

Mauldeth Road, where I lived, was old established with tall trees and rhododendron bushes backing the long Victorian garden walls. We lived in Birch House, which logically had birch trees in the front garden and a raised shrubbery behind a thirty-yard wall. Next to us was the Sykes' house, with great old shrubs leaning over their sixty yards of wall. Then, on the curved corner of the street, as it turned north and down towards Burnage, there was a long, long wall, supporting a veritable sea of rhododendrons hiding the house and its grounds. The house, which I had never seen, had two curving driveways through the dense shrubs, and was occupied, so Pauline had discovered, by Doctor Curtis.

A doctor would know what to do.

We waited until six-thirty for the autumnal darkness to descend, Pauline donned her red, double-breasted greatcoat – for the feeling of security it conferred. Then we walked up from Princess Road, round the corner, and passed the great dark bushes and the doctor's house.

We walked as far as the Fylde Lodge crossroads, then turned and walked back, again passing the doctor's house and going on round the corner, down as far as the next long curve where on the right, opposite the farm, Mr Cox, owner of Park Wireless, who had made a million out of renting the new-fangled televisions, was constructing a fine modern house. We saw no-one, and turned again, hearts pounding, and walked back up Mauldeth Road under the tall beach trees as the darkness thickened.

We turned into the doctor's driveway. "Is this your family doctor?" it occurred to me to ask, seeing no brass plate or any signs of medical establishment. But, no, it wasn't. Pauline had just heard that a doctor lived here. He didn't know her. She didn't know him. The house came into view. It was Victorian, not as tall as the other large houses so probably a little younger and it looked less forbidding. It had three wide, shallow steps leading up to a large lighted porch, with the door on the right out of view. By silent agreement, I stopped in the driveway, in the dark, well back from the house and Pauline went on, up the steps to the front door. After a moment's pause she rang the bell.

We waited. A light came on and shone through a stained glass window in what I took for the hallway. A figure, a woman, passed the window and opened the door. I gathered that she was the housekeeper. She did not immediately respond to Pauline's request to see the doctor. She took in this slender sixteen-year-old in her child's red military coat, and noted a boy lurking halfway down the dark driveway. She put two and two together. There was no surgery here, this was his home, and the doctor was having his tea. But the housekeeper said, "Come in."

Two figures crossed the little window. The hall light went out.

I waited in the dark. I waited a long time.

After two or three eternities, while I contemplated the meaning of fatherhood and wondered how one went about getting a house and paying a mortgage, Pauline emerged, saying thank you to the doctor and shaking his hand politely. She joined me. We held hands and walked away.

"Well?"

She began a halting explanation "…He said that that if you've never put your …thing…" we both blushed and thanked the darkness for its cover "into me …into my, …you know…"

Well that was just it, I didn't know; and it had seemed pretty universally unfair, a gross miscarriage of justice, to be becoming a father – without having had the allegedly sublime pleasure of knowing of the much vaunted, much vilified, much banned, much misunderstood, much maligned, much sought after, much ill-defined, much valued, soul-destroying, mortally damning, mysterious - 'carnal-knowledge'.

She pressed on awkwardly "The doctor said that if we hadn't – you know put your ...thing... into my thingy-m'jig, you know..." she hurried on; "...then I couldn't... You know... be... ...well be... You know... ...pregnant."

What she said the doctor had said had a certain ring of logic about it.

Even prior to the benefit of father's informative sex lesson, via Richard, I had been wondering how, just how, girls could get pregnant through several layers of thick clothing – with no naughty bits exposed.

It could only have happened in the Fifties in Heaton Moor; or of course, two-thousand years earlier in Palestine, in Nazareth, with angelic intervention, in One-BC. Thus endeth the natural history lesson and we pressed on with our magical affair.

Tragedy was however looming. Pauline's father, at a turbulent point in his life, had left for America and Pauline's mother was alone. Her mother's father, Pauline's grandfather, the wealthy and indomitable electrical engineering boss, the trouble-up-at-th'mill Harold Bailey from Crown Point, Denton, decided they should sell their house and go and live with Pauline's Aunt Edith and Uncle Ernest in Auckland, New Zealand.

As they left to go by passenger liner to the utterly inaccessible other side of the world, I wept for several days and nights, wandering the highways and byways where I could be alone to grieve; to the silent consternation of the thirty chain-smoking engineers in the Trafford Park drawing office when, tackling my first job, I turned up for work looking swollen faced and distinctly odd.

So Pauline, whose periods were restored a few days after our visit to Doctor Curtis, sailed out of my life, forever it seemed. But I wrote; first to every port of call on their voyage, then daily to her in New Zealand – and she replied daily. So love, the Royal Mail and my compositions defeated all and Pauline and her mother came home after six months, again by boat. Pauline was courted by any number of exotic young men on the ship and came back utterly changed, grown up, a world traveller. As a gesture of universal justice, she took up fashion modelling, ditched me for my other best friend, Peter-John, and after just a few months in England, went with her mother to join her father in the equally inaccessible America, hotly pursued by the loyal Peter-John.

Years later, Pauline suddenly turned up in Manchester and phoned me. Here she was, a sophisticated New York beauty, still looking like Audrey Hepburn but with an American well fed bloom to her, now formally engaged to a wealthy Yale graduate, who went by the ridiculous name of Joseph Sigmund-Hanson the Third, and about to get married. Well, I ask you – how could anyone marry into such a name? She ditched the Yale man, went back to America to pack her things and came home to join me on twelve pounds a week in Heaton Moor, where she quickly won back her natural slenderness on a low protein northern diet.

There are few more alluring lifestyles on the planet that compare favourably with living on a pittance in a damp bed-sit in Broomfield Road, Heaton Moor; not if you properly analyse all the factors.

***

Chapter 26 - Tank Corps

The **Centurion**, introduced in 1945, was the primary British **main battle tank** of the post-Second World War period. It is widely considered to be one of the most successful post-war tank designs, remaining in production into the 1960s, and seeing combat in the front lines into the 1980s. The **chassis** was also adapted for several other roles, and these have remained in service to this day. Development of the tank began in 1943 and manufacture of the Centurion began in January 1945, six **prototypes** arriving in Belgium less than a month after the war in Europe ended in May 1945.[110] It first entered combat with the **British Army** in the **Korean War** in 1950, in support of the UN forces. The Centurion later served in the **Indo-Pakistani War of 1965**. Wikipedia

When not playing rugger, one of David Hall's haunts for his regular visits, probably his most frequented drop-in house, was the Rider's.

Terry was the second child. All the Riders were on the short side; some were "small but perfectly formed". Terry was short, quick witted and disreputable. Where Tony the First Born, dressed like a Lord and conducted himself with haughty decorum and was a valued Committee Member of Heaton Moor Cricket & Tennis Club, Terry was simply – scruffy and uncommitted. Where Peter-John dutifully joined his father's building and shop-fitting firm, Tompkin & Rider, long established in Smithfield Market in the centre of Manchester, Terry went his own way – often on a downwards sloping path of least resistance. Where the proud, kempt father Eddie Rider, descended from a family of wealth and position which had owned The Manchester Ice Works, a Rolls Royce and a Chauffeur, kept fit, retained his own well-groomed hair, and was able to hoist a two-hundred-pound barbell with one hand – Terry was weak, unkempt, prematurely balding and dissolute.

But he could tell a good story. None better. On the same summer evening that David Hall was regaling the regular customers of Lillian's Café with the touching scene of him taking leave of his Headmaster, a story we'll get to later in this book, suitably accompanied on the jukebox by Johnny (Cry) Ray crooning *'Just-a-Walkin'-in-the-Rain'*, repetitively selected from the stored 78 inch vinyl disks by a young tortured soul with more silver sixpences than sense, Terry had recently been demobbed from the British Army and was sprawling at a yellow *Formica* topped table with four or five pals, under Lillian's shrewd but tolerant eye.

As David eventually straightened up and giggled no more; taking on an altogether more dignified air, Terry picked up David's theme of outraged authority.

"My… hee-hee-hee… My Commanding Officer…" Terry chortled, already incoherent with laughter at his own memory.

Terry was, to his horror, just old enough, three and a half years older than me, to have been in the last year of National Service. Of all the none military types on the face of the planet, Terry, the most non-military of all, had been called-up for two years into the ranks of the British Army, still feeling victorious from the Second World War, fighting in Korea and, rightly, jolly proud of their reputation – until Terry joined-up. The service that was lucky enough to embrace him to their welcoming bosom, after he had been taught how to walk, dress himself and speak to superior officers, was one of the Tank Regiments. Terry was bright. Brighter than he liked it to be known – and the army quickly spotted his potential and, despite demolishing a few military structures with the tank's gun barrel, which was so easy to forget when turning corners, within a few months of training they had elevated him to Tank Commander. Terry thought his promotion was a gas – hilarious.

The tale Terry told us was set on Dartmoor, a high expanse of trackless unfenced moors in the south part of Devon, famous for impenetrable mists, The Hound of the Baskervilles in the Tales of Sherlock Holmes, and infamous for its grim and inescapable prison – where 'life' meant life and desperate prisoners were incarcerated behind forty-foot-high granite walls. The Moor was then owned by the Ministry of Defence, as it still is, and was in regular use as a training ground and artillery range.

Terry's tank with its crew of four good and true men, along with twenty or thirty other tanks, probably the redoubtable Centurion Tank, were all ferried by road from their base in Yorkshire to an army camp on Dartmoor, where the crews were given orders for their next training exercise. Terry listened intently – acutely alert, with no need to take notes.

The Commanding Officer explained that they were to rise at dawn the next day; groans greeted this order; and were to drive out onto the moors, on a north-westerly bearing; then spread out and take their own routes. The tank commanders would have to be especially careful of rocks, troughs, pits, mine shafts, wild horses, civilians, trees, swamps, cliff edges – and all manner of perilous obstacles which could endanger the vehicles – and the crews; though the crews were replaceable and therefore expendable. Few National Servicemen found this latter remark very funny.

Terry's laughing, wide spaced, Irish-blue eyes gleamed with interest. The Moors to him, a man from Heaton Moor, were no different to the Peak District and the high, peat bog plateau of Kinderscout, where as a youth he had often romped. Mists, fog, rain, muddy ditches, stone embankments, sheep and other wild-beasties were meat and drink to a northern lad like Terry. He just managed to restrain his right foot from lifting itself up nonchalantly onto his desk, to display dangling laces and ingrained mud that would have made a drill-sergeant-major explode.

"What is absolutely vital - chaps..." They still said 'chaps' in those days as if officers and men were – comrades - pals.

"...is to realise this incorporates a map-reading, orientation and navigation exercise... in strict radio silence..." the Commanding Officer swept his gaze across the tank commanders, seeking keen, intelligent understanding. He pressed on anyway – his boundless faith in the human race and the brave British Tommy, only slightly diminished.

"...so decide between you who will go where, which tank to which position, this evening, then tomorrow watch your compass, mark your charts, read the heavens and make damn sure that you know exactly where you are."

Didn't they have road signs in Devon, wondered Terry. How backward can you be?

"When you get to what you consider – this is a test of initiative that will count towards promotion – chaps – what you consider to be a strategically important controlling position over this North-South route here..." he swept his hand over a large map of the moors and a meandering faint pony trail, "... able to see the enemy coming, and lie concealed, waiting for the beggars; then dig-in..."

"What!" reacted Terry – "I mean, what do we dig in - Sir? What do you mean dig in - Sir?" at least he was listening, if not yet fully comprehending. He wisely bit back a clever joke he could have made about enemy ponies attacking thirty fully armed tanks.

"I want you all..." replied the commanding officer, "...to camouflage your tanks..." he added, narrowing his eyes and firming his jaw to show this was no longer a game – this was The Real Thing!

"...so that they can't be seen from the ground, or the air – and can't be picked up on radar. We'll be testing you from a Spotter-Plane."

"Permission to speak - Sir! Won't radar detect any metal objects the size of tanks – Sir?" snapped out tank commander Two. "Whatever we do with nets, shrubs and the like? - Sir?"

The Commanding Officer smiled. It was an 'I-have-got-a-trick-up-my-sleeve' smile that the men found somewhat sinister and disconcerting. "Not..." he confided, "...if you bury the tank... Eh! Hey! What!"

Terry's eyes opened as wide and round as the proverbial saucers. He couldn't believe what he had just heard. Was this Commanding Officer stark, staring mad? Was he an escaped loony? Had he ever driven a tank? Had he ever even walked round a tank? Did he know just how BIG a tank was? Had he the slightest idea what he was talking about?

"...All except the gun turret..." the utter loony was saying as Terry began to recover from shock. "...we want the gun turret to be free, able to turn and of course fire! So that has to be disguised – camouflaged – and kept level. It's up to you MEN how you do that."

"Sir!" shouted Terry, never backwards in coming forwards where work, demarcation, his comforts, rewards and well-being were concerned. He had to find a non-impertinent way of putting this which would not draw any hostility and blemish his record. It was an easier option commanding a tank – which he could ride in – than slogging about the country as an infantry-man, carrying all the equipment needed to wage a major war – on his back. "Sir – a Centurion Tank is a large item – Sir, and, er – do we have any special tools provided – to enable us to bury it – Sir?"

"Good question Rider..."

Terry let his jaw hang loose as he congratulated himself on his good question and cheerfully waited for a sane answer to his good question.

"No! – Standard kit only. Use just what you have on the tank. The usual stuff. No special equipment."

Terry's jaw – and the mouths of several of his co-commanders, fell open in theatrical disbelief and protest; which the Commanding Officer could not fail to notice and correctly interpret. Their hurt expressions kept just on the right side of a charge of insubordination.

The tank crews learned, as the Commanding Officer wound up the briefing, that they were to locate their strategic positions by lunchtime – twelve hundred hours - at the latest, dig the tanks in, up to their turrets, just the five of them, by six o'clock in the evening, eighteen-hundred hours, using the tank itself, the spades and shovels it carried – and their hands, muscles, sinews and brains. Camouflage the turret, by nineteen hundred hours, walk two hundred yards away from the spot – and check that the tank was truly invisible; then secure the machine, pack their kits – and walk back to camp in the dark – to arrive, if all went to plan, by ten o'clock, or twenty-two hundred hours – at the latest.

What about the tanks? - asked several men in unison - who will drive them back to camp?

They accepted the unwelcome reply in truculent silence. The tanks would stay where they were – So they had to be sure to immobilise them. They were to walk back; God knows how many miles, to camp that night. Sleep if they could. And then the next day, up at dawn again, trudge back across the bleak moors to dig their vehicles out – clean them off and drive them back to camp by midday – if they were lucky, in time for lunch.

"Bloody pissing hell…" said Terry to his crewmen who, non-hero's to a man, were not particularly willing to die for their country – or even to suffer marginal discomfort. They did not relish the hikes back and forwards. They spent the next few hours figuring out how they could carry the least kit back to camp – and out again the next day – and how they could take a position, separate from all the other tanks, to shorten the walk. Terry went into a huddle with the other tank commanders and came away satisfied that he had bagged a prime battle position for his tank, with the shortest possible walk involved. He then evolved a cunning plan for the burying process - involving a pretend sprained shoulder, much brave and regretful wincing with heroically borne pain, and his utterly fair and attentive supervision and useful advice as the other four crew members wielded spades and carted rocks and earth, to hide the two-thousand-five-hundred cubic feet tank, excluding the turret. From his labouring experience on his father's building sites, Terry reckoned that each cubic foot would just about fit onto a size ten spade, which made …two-thousand-five-hundred spade's full, divided fairly between his four men – was six hundred and thirty-three each. And somebody, namely himself, would have to organise it. Thus counting, he was lulled into a deep and restful sleep.

The next morning the mists were thick, clammy and wet on Dartmoor as twenty Centurion Tanks, cleaned, equipped, fully-loaded and potentially lethal, roared off in the early pre-dawn light, long aerials topped with small triangular flags waving with the motion, in a disciplined line some forty feet apart – each guided by a smartly uniformed, helmeted and be-goggled square-jawed, grim faced commander visible from the waist up in the gun turret. As they passed the sentries, each commander saluted stiffly. The British were coming. It was a sight that still managed to bring a lump to the Commanding Officer's throat.

That night, some very late that night, the men returned on foot, ate ravenously and collapsed into their bunks. Another dawn broke and the forces were up again, dubbin'ing their boots, adjusting their webbing, buttoning up their battle dress against the insistent damp fog, slinging their rifles and checking their charts and compasses. After a quick and silent breakfast from their iron-rations they slipped away, one hundred young soldiers, trained to deadly effect, disappeared out into the mist in groups of five, following each another stealthily for the first miles, then taking their own courses to recover their concealed tanks.

The Commanding Officer watched the tail-end-Charlies evaporate into the early light then he turned towards the officers' mess to get himself a real breakfast. Shortly before lunch the first tanks rolled into the camp, parked, were swiftly hosed down, oiled, refuelled, the odd spot of paint applied to a flesh wound – and the crews made rapidly - pleased with their successful mission – to the mess hut to have a large and hot meal. The Commanding Officer counted them in one by one.

At five o'clock, after tea and scones, he was getting a little nervous. At seven o'clock with the light beginning to fade and a good supper and a sun-downer beckoning, he felt a bit angry – and anxious. At nine o'clock

– or twenty-one-hundred-hours as it was written in the reports, the Commanding Officer sent out search parties.

Close to midnight, as he sat alone in his office, all his officers having retired to bed, a Jeep squealed to a halt outside his door and a sergeant burst in.

"Sir – Sir – We've found them Sir! All's well, Sir. No injuries."

'All's well that ends well' thought the Commanding Officer. He would have hated to lose men on his watch. He relaxed with a sigh – it had been a long day.

"Very good Sergeant. You must be tired. Why not turn in Sergeant? But I'd better just see the men first."

The sergeant hesitated. He seemed to want to add something. But then decided better of it. "Yes Sir. They're outside Sir. In the Land-Rover Sir."

"Then get them in man. I'll log their safe return and we can do a full de-brief in the morning."

Again, the sergeant seemed hesitant. And he was a man not given to hesitation. "...Er, Yes – Sir."

The five men, the tank crew, led by Terry Rider, shambled into the office, clearly tired and dispirited. The Commanding Officer was still basking in the reassuring knowledge that they were alive and well. He decided not to be too hard on them tonight. But he was intrigued.

"Well, Rider. All present and correct?"

"Yes – Sir. The men are fine - Sir" snapped back Terry; springing smartly to attention; but clearly with some great pain in his left shoulder.

The Commanding Officer was touched and proud that one of his men, after, what ...nineteen or twenty hours in the field, had the spirit and energy to respond so – so – militarily.

"At ease Men. Glad to have you all back in one piece. We were beginning to worry about you."

The men slumped a little, not meeting his eye.

"You are alright – aren't you? No injuries. That shoulder looks a bit painful Rider."

"It's nothing Sir" said Terry, shrugging the allegedly sprained shoulder bravely. "A day's rest is all it needs – Sir"

"Good – Good. Well, why don't we all turn-in then...?
...Sergeant – dismiss the men."

As the sergeant took a deep breath preparatory to bellowing orders at the absolute bloody shower he had found wandering aimlessly on a road heading vaguely towards London and certainly away from the camp they were supposed to be returning to, the Commanding Officer suddenly interrupted. He raised a single finger in the air.

"The tank – Rider – the tank. No damage there I hope?" he asked narrowly. These new Centurion Tanks were bloody expensive and it would be his neck if something hugely costly had got broken.

Terry, just turning to leave, sprang back to attention, drawing himself up to his full five feet seven and fixing his Irish eyes into their most honest and heroic gaze – as at a distant heavenly vision. "No Sir – nothing wrong with the vehicle – Sir" he shouted reassuringly. The Commanding Officer started to relax again. It really had been a long day.

"...As far as we know – Sir."

The Commanding Officer whipped around. And almost snarled, his gentlemanly languor and avuncular attitude gone in an instant. "What the hell do you mean Rider – As far as you bloody well know?" And he leaned forward, threateningly – almost bullyingly.

'Is he going to hit me?' Terry wondered. But rapidly reassured himself by visualising part of the Army manual guidelines, which he had read, on striking, or more pertinently, not striking, the lower ranks, including Corporals who have temporarily mislaid a tank.

He raised his two hands in the placatory gesture he had used once before, to reasonable effect in as much as it had deflected a blow to his head from a short plank, when explaining to his father how he and his team had dropped the uniquely curved plate-glass window they had waited seven months for, as they fitted it into the frontage of C&A's new Market Street store, which as it dropped - onto the pavement – had shattered into a thousand, maybe even a million, small pieces.

His hands thus raised pleadingly, he cocked his head in another placatory gesture and opened his big eyes in innocent, blameless appeal.

"Couldn't find the tank – Sir!"

Then, as he saw the shock and horror his statement had wrought on the previously sanguine features of his Commanding Officer, he added hastily "...But the tank is fine Sir. It's come to no harm."

The Commanding Officer sank to his chair. Gazing up with blank disbelief at this small northern, still cheerful, National-Service man who had been sent by God to torment and destroy him.

The boys and girls in Lillian's, as the sun sank behind the odd white, marble, Grecian bus-stop shelter at Wellington Road traffic lights, to a man were rolling with helpless laughter as Terry yelled and giggled and hooted. Dave Hall slapped his huge hands time after time against his thighs and did his silent double-bend dipping motions.

"You...   ...You didn't lose the bloody tank – Terry?" he guffawed rhetorically. "...You couldn't have lost the tank. Not a whole bloody tank?" and he slapped his thighs in uncontained, unrestrained merriment; and bent double again.

Terry was grinning manically – ear-to-ear – and he constantly fluffed his thinning hair as he giggled and giggled and giggled. He could barely speak. His breath was in very short supply.

"We ... We ... never found it" he screamed, falling across the ash tray on his table and beating the *Formica* with his fists. "Day after Day – I'll swear to you – we went looking for that bloody tank. Planes, helicopters, scout cars, platoons on foot. It's never been found..." and he hollered and hollered with laughter.

"But where is it?" someone had the sense to ask, "You can't LOSE a tank."

Terry couldn't answer – so we all waited, grinning and giggling as he writhed in amusement. Eventually he drew sufficient breath, "It's still out there – somewhere. It's yours if you can find it. If you want a tank – get out there and it's yours…."

"…I've still got the bloody key somewhere. Whoo! Whoo! Whoo! Hee! Hee – Hoot! Hoot! Haw!"

And with this he was unable to say more, having to be revived by being walked around the pavement outside until he regained enough strength to light a cigarette and slump back at the table into a shoulder giggling silent memory, a not altogether un-fond memory, of his Ex-Commanding Officer.

***

Chapter 27 - Big People

6 Aug 1961: Russian cosmonaut spends day in space - The USSR has launched its second cosmonaut into space just four months after Yuri Gagarin made his historic venture. - Major Gherman Titov, aged 25, has amazed the world by spending the whole day in orbit over the Earth aboard his one-person Vostok II spacecraft. - He has been sending messages to every continent saying "I feel splendid." - Sources in Moscow say he is due to land tomorrow morning after completing about 20 orbits around the globe. BBC News

Peter-John, was not as bad tempered and curt as his abrupt manner and rapid walk implied; except when dealing with his beautiful blonde sister, Mary-Jo, who was just a year younger than he. Like all the Riders, Peter-John was small but, unlike his father and two older brothers who were big men with short legs, he was, as was his pretty mother, 'small but perfectly formed'.

As we matured from schoolboys into teenagers and then into young-men, Peter-John, who had for years been the good-looking, strong, silent type, enhanced his sex-appeal and pal-appeal by more and more often driving his father's excitingly new and expensive cars and, when a car was not available, Peter-John had charge of a Tompkin & Rider builder's van. His twenty-four-hour command of a serious vehicle, of any type, with wheels and an engine, placed him in a higher realm than all of his contemporaries.

Even Leon Marshall from Parsonage Road, whose father owned several tailors' shops and who sometimes allowed Leon to drive his automatic 2.4 Jaguar, which Leon proved, on nearby Wellington Road, could accelerate from nought to a hundred and back again in a few seconds, burning off only an inch or so of rubber while carrying up to six 'speed referees' to witness the feat, was as a child compared to Peter-John's adult right to his own transport.

Big Fred, without bothering to breathe any harder, picked them up two at a time.

The van, always replaced after just fifty-thousand miles, so almost new, was part of Peter-John's work equipment, enabling him to travel from site to site, officiously ferrying men and vital building supplies from the Tompkin & Rider offices in Smithfield Market to the outlying areas of Manchester.

When a lorry was needed, Peter-John wasn't licensed for large vehicles, so he pressed Big Fred into service. Big Fred, a loyal and long term employee was, well, big. We stripling youths, daily testing our physical strength and endurance and regularly measuring our bulging or not so bulging biceps, enhanced by cunningly folding our arms and applying our knuckles to push them out, could only regard Big Fred and his feats of natural strength with awe.

Where ordinary men might hoist a hundredweight bag of cement onto the back of the lorry Big Fred effortlessly loaded three at a time. Where common labourers cleared sand and rubble for hours with a size eight shovel Big Fred good naturedly wielded a size fourteen. When two of us youths huffed and puffed and struggled manfully to lift a roof beam onto the lorry, Big Fred, without bothering to breathe any harder, picked them up two at a time. Big Fred was strong, and in the immediate environment of Tompkin & Rider, the only person Big Fred feared, apart from his boss Eddie Rider – was Big Nellie.

Despite the similar soubriquet, Big Nellie and Big Fred were not related. They were however of similar size, probably of similar weights and even, with suitable allowances for gender, were quite similar in appearance. Big Nellie and her large extended family owned a fishmonger's warehouse in the market, just a few doors away from Eddie Rider's first floor offices.

Peter-John, in his usual terse, tearing hurry, but even more so this Thursday spring morning, whisked three young passengers, who wanted to get to Manchester, in a small Standard 10 pick-up, from Heaton Moor to the company offices, en-route to accompany Big Fred in the lorry with a load, an urgent load of course, to a site in Moston.

With four of us packed into the two-seater cab, all of us smoking and flicking ash out of the quarter-lights, it was necessary for survival to have the main windows open – firstly in order to breath and secondly for safety purposes, as it was through the open windows that Peter-John, driving as if the survival of the human-race depended on our punctuality, forewarned pedestrians, cyclists, horse-drawn carts and other drivers, loudly, firmly and non-too politely, of our passage. He also blasted the horn a great deal. We covered the six or seven miles into Manchester centre on the main roads at a steady pace, around fifty miles an hour, through crowded streets where all other vehicles were travelling at fifteen or twenty miles an hour and were often stationery. This took some skill; skill that only a grim faced teenager, with three laconic po-faced friends, determined to show no emotion of any kind, could muster.

The pick-up-truck, carting a tall cement mixer in the back, charged and weaved and braked and twisted and turned and squealed and raced through the morning traffic. The streets around Smithfield were narrow and cobbled, packed with traders' vans and cars and wagons parked in every bay, on the cobbles and on the pavements; and with shoppers of all ages and sizes carrying bulging string bags and brown-paper parcels tied with string. They blocked the alleyways solid – but they did not slow our headlong flight. Peter-John's highly effective technique was to drive at obstructions and people, at high speed, horn blaring, lights flashing, face set in a death mask, and to only divert from his chosen route at the last second if the obstruction proved to be immovable and indestructible or if the pedestrians stumbled and fell beneath our wheels with cries of despair, pleading for their lives.

Dogs were given right of way. Peter-John liked dogs.

Smithfield Market, Manchester.

Where the cobbles were blocked, we drove on the pavements, where parked vehicles intruded into our path, Peter-John gently nudged them out of the way with the pick-up fenders, caring little, in fact caring not at all, that the inoffensive vehicle would be trapped in its new position for eons, until uncovered in some future age by zealous archaeologists. Where a pedestrian wandered down the street in a pleasant dream, Peter-John crept up behind them to within twelve inches, then blasted the horn and swore at them as they leapt out of their raincoats and their terrified skins; before we swept imperiously past, our faces still fashionably deadpan, with Peter-John nonchalantly leaning one leather patched elbow of his hacking jacket on the window sill.

Thus, in twenty-five exciting minutes from Heaton Moor, we arrived in the jam packed street, opposite the covered market, outside Tompkin & Rider, where Peter-John braked to a sudden halt, double parked alongside a shopper's car, consigning the owner to a very long wait, leapt out, locked the van and marched wordlessly into a doorway, into one of the old low buildings surrounding the market, and up a narrow flight of stairs. I followed while our two friends went off to other destinations.

The offices were low roofed, long and narrow with ancient windows overlooking the street. As at the Rider's home, every useful surface, including the window bays, was covered with the new *Formica*, in dark oak patterns. In the office, his head brushing the ceiling, and having to manoeuvre his great girth sideways through the narrow doors, was Big Fred. He automatically put the kettle on the gas ring and lined up five large, deeply stained mugs, a half-used bottle of milk, a crumpled bag of sugar and a spoon secured to the table with string – and nodded amiably at us. No words were spoken but much understanding passed between us as Peter-John took papers, a small metal ruler and a building plan from a drawer, accepted the mug of dark-brown tea, with two sugars, which Fred pressed into his hands, and pored over the documents. Big Fred, as was his role, waited and didn't even attempt to read the obviously crucial management texts. He handed me a mug of tea. We all lit cigarettes, none of us offering our packs around – the rule being to smoke your own.

Eddie Rider browsed in from his room, smoking a cigarette and wearing a fabulously expensive straw coloured overcoat draped over his shoulders and an equally pricey dark suit with a silver-grey waistcoat. His tie was secured with an understated diamond pin. He was obviously going out and he was obviously in a hurry, but not so hurried to not have time for a mug of Manchester tea that Big Fred was, twitching nervously, mashing for him, and not before he'd passed the time of day with me.

"How tall are you?" he asked with a pleasant, boss's smile. I told him I was five-foot-ten and a half inches. The half-inch was of vital importance as it made me a quarter-inch taller, though he denied it to his dying day, than my older brother Richard.

"Now I'm only five feet six." Eddie told me, sleeking back his then still sandy, waved hair with a strong sunburnt hand, "...But I'll bet you a fiver..." five pounds was a lot of money "...that I'm taller than you – sitting down..." And he smiled up at me with a broad, bronzed, superstar sort of smile.

I knew that though Eddie was carefully not looking at Big Fred, who stooped to avoid collision with the ceiling, these remarks were more for the employee's benefit than mine. Peter-John looked up briefly and coldly at this time wasting pantomime. I must have looked a bit gormless as Eddie felt the need to explain.

"I'll bet you, young man, five pounds, that if we sit back to back, ...I'm taller than you..." and he snickered loudly like a happy horse, waiting for me to protest.

Though I was sure he was right, I politely obliged him and protested that such a thing could not possibly be. Eddie sneaked a look in Big Fred's direction and beamed at me triumphantly. I didn't have a fiver to take the bet but that fact was tacitly assumed and completely beside the point. As Eddie commandeered two precisely matched chairs and put them back to back, Terry Rider in labouring clothes and a cloth cap bounded in, saw the set-up, grinned wildly, grabbed a handful of notes from a petty-cash box while his father wasn't looking and dashed out again. Eddie bade me sit and to sit up straight, as tall as I could, before he sat down.

I couldn't of course see him and, sitting as still and upright as he required of me, it was difficult to turn round. Eddie though, quite rightly assumed I trusted his integrity in the matter; and, like a good Christian, that I would believe without seeing.

"…See…" said Eddie; though I patently couldn't see at all, "…I'm a good inch, maybe two, taller than you!"

I could feel his hand waving around somewhere just above my swept-back hair and I fully believed that he was flattening his own hair with that hand then, with absolute fairness, was moving it horizontally backwards, without deviation, across my head to make the comparison. Peter-John snorted contemptuously and found reason to march around our little competition stage, on serious business. His father was unperturbed by this disapproval.

"Well…" he said, extremely pleased with himself and generously waving aside the non-offer I was making to pay the bet, "…I have to get over to Williams and Glynn's bank in Old Trafford and quote for some new counters and safety glass they want…" He was now obviously in a real hurry. So he hurried out. Peter-John sniffed and Big Fred visibly relaxed.

Eddie's new car, a long black Humber Hawk, an automatic, with a radio, and which, inspired by American design, had squishy suspension that made its nose dip to the ground when braking at high-speed, as Peter-John had demonstrated to us at a valve bouncing one-hundred-and-two miles an hour on the Cheadle-By-Pass, was parked half on the pavement across the office doorway immediately below us. The market was as busy as ever, the streets blocked and, I could see for a fact, Eddie's car, built on a steel chassis, was irretrievably locked in, with market traders' cars, other big powerful cars, jammed up tight against his front and rear bumpers. We watched as he climbed into the Humber and started the engine. Big Fred, Peter-John and I knew that he could not manoeuvre out of there. Big Fred started to fret; he didn't want his boss to get upset.

Peter-John looked out at the problem with the reserved interest of a professional driver.

The Humber roared and jogged forward, pushing the car in front by two or three inches. We could see Eddie calmly flick the column mounted auto-gear change lever into reverse. The Humber roared again, more loudly, and half the street turned to watch. Eddie slammed the car backwards, clanging bumpers and shifting the car behind him an inch or two. Then he came forwards again, with even more revs

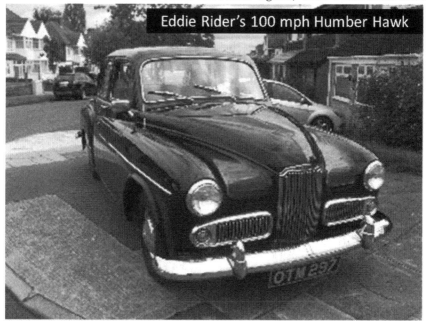
Eddie Rider's 100 mph Humber Hawk

than before, and smashed into the car in front, shoving it another three inches. Then back again, now with a loud bang that made the rest of the street jump round to see what was happening. The collision made another two inches of space and shoved the next car but-one into the lorry behind it. Eddie repeated the exercise, 'bang!' and 'bang!' and 'bang!'

Several people waved unconcerned 'hello's' to him as the Humber's bumpers were dinted and the other cars suffered visible damage.

Nobody seemed surprised or alarmed. Eddie Rider was a long-time resident here; nobody was going to pin a note on the damaged cars. After ten or so shunts, the gap for the Humber was long enough and Eddie put it in drive – and swept smoothly out into the street, oblivious of pedestrians and vehicles alike, which simply had to get out of his way – or die in their attempt to stand against him.

"Daft bugger" muttered Big Fred but in an admiring tone. This was the boss he gave his allegiance to, who had once again earned his respect.

Peter-John had finished with the papers. He put one or two bills of lading in a slim leather case which he tucked under his arm and asked Big Fred where the lorry was.

"I parked 'im in Market Street..." said Big Fred, and added with a veiled allusion to Eddie's driving "...where we can get out from..."

"...It's s'loaded. All ready to go."

"C'mon then," commanded Peter-John, starting to lead the way. But before we moved, there came an uproar in the street below that had us rushing back to the windows – imagining that one of the bashed cars' owners had turned up and was looking for someone to murder.

Across from us, under the covered market canopy, a bunch of people had gathered around three central players – then, the bunch, thinking better of it, had backed off a few yards from the three, forming a respectfully wide three-quarter circle around them.

Right in the centre was a woman. But this was no woman for virginal youths such as Peter-John and me to weave fond dreams around – nightmares perhaps, but not dreams. She represented the Prima-Materia of the Universe, the first Eve, the Mother of all matter, the foundation of the Earth. She was a large woman; easily as large as Big Fred. She wore the costume, unmistakably, of a fishwife. She spoke, or rather hollered, unmistakably, like a fishwife. She no doubt smelt, if one wandered into her perfumed ambit, unmistakably, like a fishwife.

Her sleeves were rolled back, revealing terrifyingly, impossibly broad lower arms that were attached to monstrous upper arms and hence to massive but shapeless shoulders. Her head, topped with insubstantial mousey hair tied up, incongruously, with an infant's red ribbon, was massive. Her face was a slab of lard, with a small mouth, which when closed was almost invisible and when open was like the maw of a

Sperm Whale. Her eyes were tiny compared to her face; dark, Gallic and piercingly fierce in their intensity. Her legs, mercifully wrapped in a long pink skirt and a stripped, waterproof apron, were elephantine; each would have adequately made the whole of my mere ten-and-a-half stone.

This apparition stood, monumentally still, with her arms outstretched, extended seemingly without effort on her part. One blubbery hand encircled the neck of a man; not a small man by any means but small and helpless compared to the creature who gripped him. The hand completely contained the man's strangulated neck, her fingers and thumb meeting at the nearside. The other arm, equally comfortably extended for as long as it took, ended in her massive fist. Within the fist were tightly gathered ample pleats from a second man's shirt, vest, tie, waistcoat, jacket and, causing certainly some inconvenience if not agonising pain for the man who still wore, or was attempting to wear, these garments, the fist also gathered in his braces and consequently hauled the crotch of his trousers two feet higher than his tailor had ever intended. We all wondered if the poor emasculated soul dressed to his left, or to his right – in normal circumstances.

"That's Big Nellie," explained Peter-John shortly, but even his quick voice betrayed a note of unconscious anxiety in the presence of this destroyer of worlds.

"She's …a bit bloody tough." said Big Fred, not bothering to hide his fear – and his admiration. "…There's nobody in Smithfield can take Big Nellie; not even her brothers."

We three stared transfixed at the trio outside.

"Don't know who the blokes are…" obliged Peter-John, stimulated into a rare volunteering of information.

It was clear that the two men had friends and supporters in the watching crowd. But the supporters had obviously decided to act in a purely advisory capacity, confining themselves to helpful comments.

Big Nellie – Destroyer of Worlds

"She can't hold you there all day..." one of the watching men encouraged the hapless prisoners.

Big Nellie slowly turned her head, like a hunting owl, and looked at him. He decided discretion was the better part of valour and shut up.

"She laid a bloke out last winter..." Big Fred told us, "...he wus a wrestler, you know, from Belle Vue; thought he was tough. She walloped him with just one arm. Just the one hit. He was in hospital for weeks. He never came back here..."

Big Fred sucked his toothless upper gum, being at the stage of waiting for a top denture on the National Health, and sighed heavily; whether from deep fright or suppressed love was difficult to decide. We each lit another cigarette as it was clear we would go nowhere until this drama was resolved.

"...OK Nellie..." soothed a big man in white rubberised overalls, shouldering his way into the circle.

"One of 'er brothers" supplied Big Fred.

"...Let's not do them any damage. After all..." he added reasonably, "...they've been good customers – them and their dad before them, for ... well for a long time."

Big Nellie was not quite convinced, she made no move, but to acute observers it may have seemed that she slackened her grip, a teeny-weeny bit. The strangled man's colour reduced from bright puce to pink and his eyes settled back into his head – a little.

Despite the stay of execution, neither of them yet dared to struggle.

A sound came from Big Nellie and all around was silence to allow her voice the airwaves and space it so royally deserved, "Cheeky bloody sods," she said sociably.

This was obviously a conciliatory statement as her brother came right up to her with some confidence and lightly held one of her ponderous wrists. "...I've a bloody good mind to just slap 'em around a bit, before we let them go..." she added evenly.

Both men tensed with renewed terror, completely powerless to defend themselves, but neither tried to speak.

"...No need Nellie..." said her brother, keeping his voice calm and offering her the nearest thing his face could make of a winning smile. "...They've learned their lesson, Nellie. They'll be good boys from now on... ...Won't you lads."

The 'good boys', who, when not suspended from Nellie's arms were successful and mature business men in their early forties, nodded with ingratiating vigour.

"...Well..." said Big Nellie, suddenly, horribly, becoming toe-curlingly coy, "...if they promise... I just might"

Nellie's brother looked at his two customers, probably themselves brothers in a fishmonger business, and said nothing, but they understood nonetheless and found their collective voice.

"We promise Nellie. We promise. Honest we do Nellie. No harm done Nellie, a bit of a joke really." They gasped in unison.

"You'd bloody better" she growled at them, her pacific mood waning fast, but she nevertheless let them both go.

Released, the neck man almost fell to the ground but two other men rushed forward and propped him up. The clothes man turned away and made brave attempts to tuck his crumpled shirt, through his twisted braces, back into his crumpled pants and to smooth out his crumpled waistcoat and badly creased suit as he stumbled quickly out of Nellie's immediate reach. The crowd, by common consent and in awe, politely parted to let Big Nellie through and waited for her to start on her majestic way back to the family office before they began to disperse.

Big Fred wiped beads of sweat from his forehead.

(In case you haven't heard of Kristin Rhodes, she's a competitor to be reckoned with and arguably one of the strongest women to ever participate in the sport. She's got a ton of raw strength, and over the past year, her training videos suggested a strong, healthy streak. Here's Rhodes on a farmer's-carry with 260 pounds in each hand – Barbend.com)

"Staf'ut go now," he said lapsing into broadest Lancashire.

Peter-John leapt into action, leading Big Fred and me down the stairs through the alleyways and out onto the main shopping street, Market Street, which sloped down from Piccadilly to Deansgate. Peter-John, as neat as ever in grey cavalry-twill slacks, a country-style jacket, a smart shirt and tie and his hair cut and groomed very like his father's, with his document case under his arm and a business like expression on his face, stepped out rapidly, clicking his shiny shoes onto the pavement with military precision. Big Fred, in a dark blue overall with bib and braces, checked shirt, a ragged tie and a favourite old cloth cap, ambled behind him with his big legs easily keeping pace. I had to skip and run a little to keep up as we weaved through window-shoppers, around parked cars, dodged behind vans and lorries and risked our lives leaping in front of the almost silent trolley buses that warned of their coming more by their ozone, electric smell and blue, crackling flashes rather than by engine noise. The Tompkin & Rider Bedford truck, loaded with bricks, was parked at the traffic lights on the corner by Lewis's main entrance and, as Big Fred had boasted, it was free of obstructions ahead. We scrambled into the cab, Big Fred now in charge, and the lorry lurched away, down the main street and turned right to detour out onto the road to Ancoats, as Big Fred wanted to call in at his home en route to the building site.

"Fred!" barked Peter-John, "...where're you going. Where are you taking us?"

Big Fred, not at all phased at being checked and challenged by this young management mosquito, calmly told us in a tone that allowed no discussion that he was going to swing by his house and pick up his lunch-box, which had not been ready when he left home at six o'clock this morning, while we were no doubt in bed, to go and get the bricks, now loaded in the lorry, which we were currently delivering.

With Big Fred's unhurried and expert driving we arrived without incident in the hilly streets of Ancoats; row after row of small terraced Victorian brick houses with polished windows, lace curtains and spotless soap-stoned steps, pierced every fourth house by an arched passage leading to the network of cobbled alleys which ran behind and connected the community of all these homes. Infants played out in the streets, despite a persistent bright drizzle of rain, and Big Fred manoeuvred the vehicle with patience, as Peter-John jiggled his knee and fretted in silence. We arrived and Big Fred clambered out and disappeared into one of the houses.

Peter-John and I lit cigarettes and opened the quarter-lights to flick out the ash.

Ancoats – Big Fred's homeland

"He was born here..." said Peter-John suddenly, with some proprietorial pride, "...Grew up here with his brother...   ...lived here all his life. And when he got married and his mum died, he and his wife stayed on. Right here."

"Oh" I said.

Big Fred came back clutching his lunch-box, a square Jacobs Cream Crackers tin, and climbed into the driver's seat.

Before the engine started Peter-John said "Fred!" but not quite as authoritatively as usual "…tell him about your brother…" and he nodded in my direction.

Big Fred looked at me carefully while he considered this request. He sucked at his gums and took a few moments to light a Woodbine. He weighed me up for another moment then decided he could tell me the family secret.

"Me brother…" he announced suspiciously, still scrutinising my face, "…Me younger brother, Charlie…" and he paused again, still not quite certain if I could be trusted with the information, "…Charlie, is a ballet dancer."

The information didn't fit. It demanded feats of imagination and a suspension of disbelief that were very, very difficult to conjure.

"Oh Aye – Our Charlie, he can dance alright" said Fred.

I looked at Big Fred; his great bulk; his huge hands and thickened fingers almost immobilised by hard labour and stained by building materials and tobacco; his half toothless mouth; his thinning hair splaying out from under his cap. I thought of the bits of ballet I'd seen on the television and on posters – Nijinsky floating through the air, his impossibly taut buttocks and shapely thighs sheathed in white tights.

I looked again at Big Fred and wondered about his age. I looked at the tiny terraced house, one of millions, and at the anonymous pavement. It just didn't work. But Big Fred was clearly deadly serious; and it was not a joking matter.

"Gosh – where did he – I mean, does he, dance?"

"Oh not round 'ere..." said Big Fred as if the very idea was not to be countenanced, "...down in London," he added with some relief, "...in a place called Covent Garden – it's a bit like our Smithfield up 'ere – you know, costermongers, fishmongers, butchers an' the like. Very big market it is. Bigger than Smithfield – much bigger...."

I thought he'd finished and I was trying to frame another question, but Big Fred had more to say.

"...and in the middle of it all; right by this bloody great market, they've built a theatre – a bloody huge theatre...   ...an' that's where Charlie dances...   ...I've bin there; me an' the wife...   ...We've seen 'im dancin'...   ...Our Charlie can dance alright..." he added ruminatively, his mind far, far from Ancoats and our load of bricks.

Then he suddenly turned on me – to catch any hint of mockery. "...We'd best get goin' " he said, starting up the lorry and shifting it into gear.

***

Chapter 28 - Party Time

TARDIS in Elms Road - Therefore - the successful construction of a single tesseract would give you eight times the volume in the same exterior space. Assuming such successful construction, building a new tesseract inside one of the component cubes would further increase the volume. How far this recursion could continue before internal navigation became a mental nightmare is anyone's guess. – Michael Daniel

As Peter-John dropped me on the corner of Mauldeth Road later that day, he reminded me of the party at the Riders on the coming Saturday. Just whose party it was didn't matter, as long as the age grouping was right. But it clearly wasn't Tony's as neither Peter-John nor I were allowed alongside his Cricket Club society gentlefolk. It wouldn't be Mary-Jo's as she was too young to produce and direct the resources for a party – and her two younger sisters could be completely discounted. It could be Terry's or Peter-John's. It certainly wouldn't be the parents; Eddie and his treasured, pretty and petite wife Eileen, throwing a party for the local youths, as their generous contributions stopped at not banning parties, of whatever size, in their home, of laying their kitchen and its contents open and available, and of diplomatically taking themselves away on party days, leaving early and returning late in the early hours of the next morning.

The Rider's home in Elm's Road, near Heaton Moor Park, was an optical illusion which could only have been contrived by a skilled and bold builder – like Eddie Rider. It was an Edwardian terraced house, albeit an end of terrace, which looked like a detached house. It occupied a sharply triangular corner plot, with a small garden at the front, and with the rear – where ninety-nine percent of visitors approached it – taken over by a yard and a double-garage attached to the house, which somehow, in a tiny space, provided parking for a fleet of vehicles. The always open back door let into a kitchen which Tompkin & Rider had enlarged, gutted and refitted with all their shop-fitting skills.

Immediately greeting all callers and the eight family members who lived there was tea making equipment of the latest design and largest size. It was customary for whoever arrived, at whatever time, to refill the almost certainly still hot kettle, fire up the automatic gas cooker, flush out the team-sized teapot, refill the sugar bowl and set it by, at the very least, half-a-dozen washed tea mugs, or however many more might be indicated by counting the crowd in the next room.

The next room was a sitting room which had also been shop-fitted and stretched to and beyond its physical boundaries. The Edwardian architects had visualised a space for, say, six suburban adults to meet and converse in reasonable, civilised, quiet comfort. After suitable treatment, the demolishing of superfluous walls, the addition of bow window bays finished in Formica, and radical rethinking of the traditional furnishings, the room resembled an airport lounge with individual seating – the comfortable, wide, cushioned, leatherette chairs that Eddie Rider preferred – for twenty-five. It also found room for a sixteen seat, Formica topped, dining table.

This room was more often than not half full of casual visitors, friends of, or at least known to one or another, of the Rider brood, smoking, drinking tea and swapping gossip, who Mr and Mrs Rider might join or, more often, passed through, exchanging banter and news, on their way to get changed or, dressed in their finest, - Mrs Rider in yet another new dress, looking half her age, slim, tiny, groomed and of whom it could not possibly be believed that she had given birth to six children - on their way out to eat a meal at the White House or the White Hart in Prestbury or to attend some other expensive venue.

The once modest end of terrace also accommodated, as well as the enlarged kitchen and commodious lounge, across its narrow hall, a small private sitting room where Peter-John liked to retire with his pals to play his Frank Sinatra records; and somehow, breaking all geometric and physical laws with impunity, laughing in the face of spatial reality, upstairs there was known to be a locked parental bedroom, with a wholly decadent and, to most reverent church goers, an unimaginable – "I mean why on Earth would you need one and what would you do in it?" - en-suite bathroom and toilet; for the exclusive use of Mr and Mrs Rider; who spent an unconscionable amount of time there. In addition to all this, the house found sleeping and private room for six grown and growing children.

The doors, day or night, were never locked and the lights were always on. It was a great house for parties.

Arthur Jowell, though local and well known, had somehow missed the previous dozens of parties at the Riders and the always open club like tea rooms. He had somehow overlooked the budding pale beauty of Mary-Jo and missed out on the stream of attractive girls who passed through the Riders. He was a busy young man, working hard and making money in any way he could, including selling shirts on Stockport Market. Richard and I had once tried to emulate Arthur's obvious success but even after queuing for a stall at four in the morning, in the damp winter cold, week after week, and investing in a range of shirts and cotton dresses, we found that selling was no easy thing.

Arthur was good at it. He too was large. Not nearly as large as Big Fred, and a mere sprat compared to Big Nellie but tall and filled out. He had straight blonde neatly cut hair, a fair chubby face and he always looked well-scrubbed, as if he had just had a bath or a shower. Arthur habitually wore a loose, smart white shirt, cuffs buttoned up and with a colourful tie at the starched collar. His manner was acquiescent – Arthur's customers were always right – he put his head to one side and talked with a slightly worried frown as if he was concerned for your point of view. But shining through the conciliatory mannerisms was an underlying watchfulness, the alertness of a good salesman, looking for the trigger, the little human weakness, which he might exploit in the nicest sense, and close a deal on a shirt – or a tie – or anything else he could offer. Arthur knew that the world consisted of the Quick and the Dead. He was Quick, he had grown-up.

But even the most dedicated careerist will from time to time lose their concentrated sense of direction, take a break and relax their guard. So it was that Arthur, the same age as Terry, two or three years older than Peter-John, accepted an invitation to the party, no doubt contributed to the barrel of beer purchased for the event and turned up that Saturday night at the Riders after stock taking and banking his sales.

Peter-John, I and our peer group were a bit out of our depth. Most of the guests were Terry's friends and so the girls were older than us and little interested in kid-brothers. But Mary-Jo joined in and she danced with us to the Elvis records, and one or two other girls of our age dropped by, lending a sexual potential to the evening, however unattainable, which kept us going. Among Terry's boy and girl friends there was much smooching, furtive fumbling and bedroom doors banging shut, which we could only wonder at and dismiss as drunken behaviour. As ever, at such parties, there were more males than females. At about midnight, Tony Rider came home with a couple of friends, slightly sozzled from another night at his Cricket Club, but still managing an aristocratic hauteur and effortless superiority which Terry mocked – which in his turn Tony the Elder dismissed as being beneath his dignity.

At two o'clock the ashtrays were not quite overflowing, the beer hadn't run out and the music still pounded out Rock and Jazz dances and intimate and romantic songs encouraging tighter and tighter embraces, when the parents, Eddie and Eileen returned. Every chair, corner, table edge and carpet, including the stairs, was occupied by young people at various stages of sexual hope, despair or scientific experimentation. Arthur, having lost the attentions of Mary-Jo who was in any case far too young for him, had been drowning his passion in larger than customary quantities of beer. He was part slumped, still pristine in his white shirt and smart tie but with some of the watchfulness faded from his eyes and perspiring freely, on the narrow, carpeted staircase.

Mr and Mrs Rider were not party-poopers. They acknowledged people they knew with waves, nods and bows and some few words as they stepped carefully through and sometimes over the throng on the way to their private, locked and secure bedroom suite. They needed nothing from the house and minded not at all that it was heaving with noise, fumes, beer and unrequited love. They would escape it all in their sacrosanct territory.

Eddie Rider was waylaid at the door of the lounge. Eileen took the key and went ahead of him as he chatted to one of Tony's friends who just might want the family shop redesigned and refitted. A few minutes later he followed his wife up the stairs. Ten minutes after that, Eddie came down again. He was wearing his smart trousers, fashionable braces and socks. But his jacket and shirt were missing so the braces snaked over a gleaming white string vest which covered his barrel chest. The party was in full swing and at full stretch.

Short as he was, Eddie was king in his own domain and made an imposing figure as he positioned himself at the head of the long lounge. He seemed to need no extra height as his gaze sought out and found one of his sons. He made motions with his hands and the son immediately knew to rush over and turn off the music. As it died, everyone stopped and became silent. All eyes found Eddie Rider. He waited until he was certain of everyone's undivided attention.

Then he raised both his arms in the air and spread them wide. "The Party…" he pronounced, his voice carrying commandingly through the house, without him having to shout, "…is over! Everyone must leave. Go Home!"

That was it. None argued or questioned the order. We all left within minutes and, as he suggested, went home.

The next day, as the regulars assembled without invitation or any time arrangement, to drink tea in the Rider's lounge, we learned from Terry what had happened. Terry was slumped happily in one of the easy chairs, unshaven, smoking and scratching his thinning hair. Mr and Mrs Rider had gone out to a Garden Party.

He jumped up and impersonated his dad.

"The Party…" yelled Terry, holding his arms up like Horatio at the Bridge, "…is OVER!" he giggled; bringing his arms down in a theatrical gesture and laughing some more.

"It was Arthur…" he told us gleefully.

"…Arthur Jowell. He was on the stairs. At the top of the stairs. A bit pissed 'cause he doesn't drink a lot. Not Arthur…"

"…and when they were going up to bed, Eddie was stopped by Bernard Cox, Tony's pal…"

We knew the Cox's as the richest respectable family around. I'd been to primary school with Winifred Cox and had quite a thing for her. Bernard Cox was a budding racing driver.

Terry pressed on.

"…anyway; Eileen went up with the key to the bedroom."

Nobody in those days referred to their parents by first name. It was faintly shocking. But then Terry was not 'Nobody'. And it made the story more narratable.

"And she had to step over Arthur as he was sprawled on the top stair with a glass in his hand…"

He paused to accept and light a cigarette.

"…So as Eileen puts the key in the bedroom door, Arthur lurches to his feet…   …Not to help her with the door though. He doesn't know who she is."

"And he leans over my mother – and says "I haven't seen you before Darling! - do want me to come in there with you?" He's propositioning Eddie's wife – in his own house."

And Terry went into shrieks and peals of laughter and had to drag on his cigarette before he could continue.

"Of course Eileen says nothing. She doesn't know what to say. Mother of six and being picked up at a party by a teenager - at her own bedroom door" and Terry again had to pause for breath from laughing – and draw on the cigarette for strength.

He wiped away a tear. "Then Eddie goes up – and she tells him what's happened."

Terry's mirth is boundless as he imagines the scene and the conversation. He can hardly carry on the story. His audience, all who had mother's, gave a mixed reaction to this shocking event.

But Terry's giggling was infectious; it was hard not to at least smile.

"...And even though he's part undressed – he issues forth – and..."

Terry is on the verge of collapse from laughing,

"...He does his John Wayne thing. In his string vest. Ha Ha Ha Ha Ha Ha .. Heh Heh. The Party .... The Party ... Heh Heh Ho ... Is OVER!"

Wisely, Arthur sobered up, returned to selling – and according to David Hall, made several millions of pounds.

***

Chapter 29 - Wrong footed by the Hun

Condoms have been made from a variety of materials; prior to the 19th century, chemically treated linen and animal tissue (intestine or bladder) are the best documented varieties. Rubber condoms gained popularity in the mid-19th century, and in the early 20th century major advances were made in manufacturing techniques – Wikipedia

4 Dec 1961: Birth control pill 'available to all' - Women who wish to have oral contraception will now be able to get it on the National Health Service. - The Health Minister, Enoch Powell, made an announcement in the House of Commons today but did not give any guidelines as to whom the pill should be given. - "It is not for me to indicate to doctors when they should decide for medical reasons to prescribe for their patients," he said. - However some GPs are in a dilemma over whether they can prescribe the Pill, as it is commonly known, for social as well as medical reasons. BBC News.

My school friend, Paul Godfrey, had a round baby and dimpled face, waved fair hair on a large head and big innocent blue eyes. He was as pleasant as he looked but his looks belied a fighting spirit passed to him, despite a year or more of his youth spent recuperating in a TB clinic, from his father.

Mr Godfrey, who hailed from London's East End, part Jewish through his father, was the sort of man you fervently hoped was not in the car behind that you had cut up, given the V sign to as you zoomed past and jammed your car triumphantly ahead of his, just before coming upon a two-mile stationary traffic jam; at which point he may decide to saunter up, lean down from quite a height and politely but firmly enquire just precisely what message you were attempting to communicate to him.

In civilian life he was a most respected manager in the Great Universal Stores Group – GUS, trouble shooting whatever problems arose in their numerous city centre furniture stores. In his previous incarnation – and this is why it would be wise to wave his car politely ahead of yours – he had been the British Army Light-Heavyweight Boxing Champion; he had been a regular soldier, rising to regimental sergeant major, who had fought in every major World War Two battle and, firing a large machine gun, he had led his troops when they stormed the French beaches on D-Day. And, this big, lean, toughened and seasoned fighter had taught his only son, Paul, how to take care of himself.

Paul, following in father's footsteps, was also invading France, in 1960, from his home in Fallowfield, with a platoon of energetic Brits.

At sixteen we had both left school, casting-off our royal-blue and red striped Catholic school blazers, simultaneously abandoning any pretence of sinless, celibate behaviour, however good for our immortal souls it may have been, and gone our separate ways. Paul to precociously manage GUS's main store on Market Street, Manchester, me as an apprentice at Bannister Walton Structural Steel Engineers in Trafford Park, through my first post-school winter, before switching to join my father's accountancy practice in a peculiarly narrow, white tiled building, like a high rise public lavatory, next to Manchester Cathedral and opposite the deep chasm which channelled the foul River Irwell, the border with Salford, which flowed fifty feet below street level.

The next summer rolled round and, with wages in our pockets and the post-war Depression lifting, young men planned their vacations. A key element in all such plans, in fact the element outweighing all others together, was the question of how, where, when and if there might be any engagement with - any tiny possibility, however small, of meeting with - the opposite sex.

Paul, visiting us in Heaton Moor, told us how his invasion of France had worked out.

He and five of his pals from the furnishings group, acquired a boat-like Ford Consul convertible, with a pram mechanism to raise and lower the soft top; two bench seats each adequate for three adults; no seat belts, of course, and therefore with a strong tendency for the driver, under inertial forces of gravity, to slide along the seat on tight corners, losing touch with the pedals and switches, a slide which he could counter by clinging onto the steering wheel and the steering-column-mounted gear stick, and hauling himself back into an upright position and, on most occasions, thus regain control of the speeding vehicle.

They brazened out the silent condemnation of the truculent customers in the barber's shop, in the dark cobbled alleyway off Market Street behind the GUS store, to buy a packet of six condoms, a six-pack of French Letters – one each - which they secreted in their wallets; drew their meagre foreign currency allowance as permitted under Exchange Controls by The Bank of England, packed their suitcases and camping gear, and thus equipped and with hope in their eyes, headed for France, the South and the dream of beautiful, seductive, accommodating and available, wholly amoral, Christine Keeler, Mandy Rice-Davis and, *Oo La la!* Bridget Bardot, look-a-likes.

Crossing the Channel and driving down to the French Riviera was quite an adventure in nineteen-sixty. There were no motorways, no auto-routes to the sun, no motorway services, no spares for British made cars, little tolerance for poorly spoken French language; and few cheap hotels on the Mediterranean. But these Manchester lads had map references for seaside camp-sites, with plumbed water and showers, shops, cooking facilities – and – most importantly, non-attributed urban legends of single girls, French single girls who had nothing better to do with their lives in France than to spurn all Frenchmen and wait in dedicated anticipation for real men, from Manchester, England, driving a fashion icon Ford Consul drop head coupe, and clutching a fistful of petrol coupons and ten to the pound Francs.

Of course, Paul and Co had never thought to ask, or even to consider, what any of the several million Frenchmen, who lived in France, with the legendary beautiful French girls, might think of the amorous ambitions of the invading English.

The three-day journey was fun. The camp site was comfortable and the summer was hot and fabulous. Other nationalities arrived to fill the sun drenched beaches, barbecue food and drink the occasional bottle of wine. There were no drug dealers, no crack or cocaine or heroin or uppers or downers or LSD or grass and there were a few, just enough to keep the adrenaline pumping and to stave off despair for twenty-four hours a day, apparently unattached girls; their nationality now a matter of no importance whatsoever. In fact, nobody's nationality was an issue in this peaceful post-war European Union - until the German's started playing water-polo.

The English were particularly obvious on the beach, not only for their terrible French, Stockport Baths trunks and thin worn towels, but for their pallid skins, ration-starved limbs and neglected physiques. Continental youths, more accustomed to sun, sin, sand and skiing, could not only speak each other's languages – and English – the smug bastards, but they also led a more open air life, giving them tanned skins and a physical self-awareness of shape, muscles and resort athletics. They raced onto the beach and played pansy games like volley-ball, and pat-a-cake with a tennis ball tethered to a wooden bat with elastic, and shuttlecock over a high net. Despite the English being the undisputed Sons of the Kings of the Waves and every British child being taught to swim, the Continentals could also swim – maybe not quite so furiously and bravely – they'd never survive half-an-hour in the North Sea, but with a lot more style. And – Paul and Co discovered, confirming all their British Island prejudices, even the men wore perfume.

The male perfume and a host of other small but obvious faults common among the Continentals, just managed to allow Paul and his friends to retain their self-respect and their sense of effortless superiority which was every Englishman's birthright – born as we were as citizens in the largest Empire the World Had Ever Seen – on which the Sun Never Set.

So Paul and his pals could lounge on the sand or strut about, within certain sight of the girls, despite their reddened skins and stringy muscles, with reasonable confidence.

But then the German's started playing water-polo.

The six or seven German youths were as easily identified as were the English. They were, inevitably, blonde. They had great haircuts – like film-stars. They were well muscled and tanned. Their towels and beachwear were top quality and leading in fashionable cut and colours. They spoke loudly in German, quipped with the girls in French and ever so politely switched to English to exchange pleasantries with Paul and the Manchester contingent – the smarmy bastards. They sunbathed; dousing themselves with expensive lotions priced way beyond English budgets, by strolling up and down the beach – even in that heat – with occasional dips, sudden manly plunges, into the azure blue water.

All this, the English holidaymakers could cope with, reassuring themselves throughout of the natural advantages of British-ness and never even once mentioning The War; at least not in public – Who Won the War, anyway?

But when the whole gang of blonde, blue eyed, sun kissed, Aryan Adonis's dived and cleaved in the blue, blue sea, passing a seriously heavy polo ball from athlete to athlete; leaping like dolphins from the spray to take a high catch, showing off their water streaming, carved abdomens, flinging a well-aimed ball with a bronzed arm and strong fingered hand – and when it was completely obvious that every female on the beach, of whatever age and status, was riveted by this brave and bold display – Paul and his pals decided it was time to assert themselves.

Subtly, not immediately so as to make it obvious, but with some diplomatic finesse and even some outright, outrageous flattery, which fooled the Germans not at all, the Mancunians worked it around to a challenge match. British against Germans. Islanders against Mainlanders. The British Empire against the (twice defeated) Reich. All Englishmen can swim – we excel at swimming; water is our second home. We fear not the depths of rivers, nor the tumult of wide oceans.

It was thus - with a few practice throws to get the feel of the ball, which the British boys performed deliberately poorly, to put the Germans off their guard - that two teams of six met in the sparkling water, all smiling and exchanging pleasantries and agreeing the rules – in English of course – with all eyes upon them. The lolling, beached Frenchmen made a pretence of being genuinely neutral, Paul thought, and the girls who were dotted about the beach adopted bored countenances with half-closed eyes, while keeping a very close watch on the competing young males.

...until the Germans started playing water polo.

The teams were evenly matched. Though the blonde, muscular Germans looked more of a team, the pale, mousey English were stronger than they appeared and they had that sense of fair-play, for which the British nation was world famous that encouraged cooperation and team work beyond personal glory. The goalmouths, edge on to the beach, were marked with four anchored, inflatable beach-balls; the shallow side-line was agreed to be at waist height and the deep water side was up to the neck. The Germans won the toss and elected to play the first half into the sun.

Paul was a rangy six-footer and, as a strong swimmer, he put himself out on the deep side, opposite a determined grim faced opponent who was particularly well built with broad shoulders and thick arms. The ball was tossed over their heads, a bad pass from the German centre to this taut faced winger. Paul lunged after it. The German plunged behind him. Paul swam hard, churning through the water in a fast, powerful crawl. The German swam past him as if jet propelled, snatched the ball without any break in rhythm and flung it hard towards the English goal. Paul puffed and swallowed too much sea water; his eyes narrowed.

The ball came again; a hopeless pass from the English fullback out to Paul. It zoomed over his head to land twenty yards from him and a good thirty yards from the German; Paul dived after it, churning through the clear Mediterranean at his fastest. The gimlet eyed German, looking neither left nor right, swept past him, slipping through the water like a seal, to scoop the ball back over his head in a high throw, straight to his Centre – who zapped it with a practised flick into the English goal.

One – Nil.

Paul's team-mates gave him a look, then looked away. Paul knew he had failed them.

The ball came again. This time the German was closer but Paul had got his ginger up and he smashed his way through the water, with arms swinging like demented paddle wheels and feet threshing like flags in a gale. But the German pulled easily away and got the ball – and took a long leisurely time to decide just where to pass it before Paul puffed up to make his challenge, reared heroically out of the water as the ball went over him, arms stretched, higher than any human swimmer has a right to leap from the deep, and fell back, down and down, to rise spluttering, part drowned and exhausted; to tread water. The German, some ten feet away, gave him a look of comradely concern and made inquiring thumbs-up signs until he was sure that Paul was okay and likely to live, before re-joining the game. A very sporting gesture.

"I'll get you, you Nazi bastard." Vowed Paul silently, through gritted teeth that he hoped gave the impression, to the watching girls, of a good natured, devil-may-care smile.

At five goals to three, they changed ends, the English now facing into the sun and the German's tossing the ball and the glittering diamonds which scattered from it, as high as possible into the sun, to blind and confuse them.

"There's a Hun in the Sun." muttered Paul grimly, again on the deep side and with the same lightning fast opponent to beat. The English fullback hurled the ball forward; Paul had his feet on the ocean bed and was able to leap into instant action, wrenching himself forwards into the blazing spray, aware of the German, at the opposite angle of a triangle, racing for the ball. They arrived simultaneously. This was a ball that Paul intended to have; at any price. As his arm broke upwards at the end of his powerful crawl stroke – and sure that the commotion and light hid his dishonour – his hand landed on the shoulder of the square faced German, and he levered himself, up and over the man; pressing him deep down under the sea – and flipped the ball across to his team-mate.

The German surfaced, coughing and choking, searching desperately for breath and thrashing around to stay buoyant. Paul trod water a few feet away, ready to help the lad – but the German recovered, saw Paul's thumbs-up query and innocently questioning raised eyebrows – and glowered at him.

They raced for another ball. Paul was definitely ahead. He was swimming superbly, a real racing sprint. No one could catch him. The German, blonde head cutting the surface like the prow of a speedboat, passed him and, as they both lunged for the same spot at the same time, he flipped a hard face-full of water at Paul, who sucked the salty spout into his yawning maw, and felt his shoulder batted with something hard, smooth edged but quite bruising, before the German scooped the ball in to his Centre, who flipped it across to the other wing.

"What the devil was that?" Paul shouted as he coughed out the water. But nobody could hear him above the noise of the game, the wind and the waves. His opponent was already far off, making for the English goal.

"It was a flipper!" Paul told himself. "A bloody flipper. – He's wearing flippers. ...Well flipping heck! That's cheating. ...No wonder he swims so fast. Bloody Hell! Would you believe it? Flippers..."

And Paul felt something turn cold and merciless inside him. The merest hint of the cold and merciless feelings his father had had when pounding up the beach, armed to the teeth, towards a German gun emplacement, on D-Day.

"No quarter" thought Paul in quiet and deadly mood.

From then on Paul, a pacifist until such treachery brought out his excellent boxing skills, trounced the winger. He shadowed him very closely. He elbowed him hard and meanly in the ear. He kneed the man in his guts as they closed for the ball. He stepped on his thigh and pressed him under the water and then greeted him as the blonde head surfaced, mouth agape and lungs needing fresh air, with a massive swoosh of sea, aimed straight into the Germanic gullet.

Paul, under water, accidentally of course, thumped the guy hard in the solar-plexus with one tight knuckle extended into a point ahead of the others, like a bony knife. The man doubled up in pain – completely winded.

The ball flew over to them as they jostled side by side, way out of depth. Paul knew better than to go for the ball. He couldn't outpace a man in flippers. So he went for the man. Bigger than the German, and with less water swallowed, in better trim than he was, Paul leaned on him; he pummelled him; he gouged him; he surreptitiously slapped him; he flooded his mouth with water; and he pressed him down by one shoulder to almost drown. All this Paul managed without it being apparent to the audience on the beach – though the other German players were beginning to cast very dark looks at him.

"Hey Paul!" called one of his mates "…Give it a break. We don't want another War" he added, nodding and winking in the direction of the increasingly irate – and well-muscled – blonde team.

Paul did a cartoon like whisper behind his hand to try to communicate that he, Paul, was still a nice bloke and a good sport, "…He's got flippers" he hissed, wagging his head at the soused and battered German. "Bloomin' Flippers." But his pal couldn't understand what was being said.

Paul kept up his contact-sport attacks and rapidly wore the German down. From five goals behind, the English started to catch up. Two pretty girls – without boyfriends in attendance, clapped and cheered with excitement as the English scored again. Paul, kept his man down; part drowning the cheat, part pinching and slapping him in passing – once even getting hold of his expensively styled hair under the surface and tugging it in good old rugger fashion, jerking the man's head back suddenly, so he sucked water straight up his nose.

The game ended in a draw. Honour was satisfied. The English, never having played the game before, equal with the Germans. "We beat them at their own game" they agreed as they stumbled exhausted from the water.

Paul and his tacitly avowed enemy, the German who cheated with swim aids, had furthest to go to the beach. Some yards apart they swam to the shallow water. Paul was more tired than he had imagined and concentrated on wading through the breakers as he slipped and slid against the undertow. He attained the dry sand and turned, and looked back in understated triumph as he saw his opponent still swimming in the shallows, obviously too exhausted to get to his feet.

Paul, breathing hard, watched the man absently; fully revenged and happy that he had helped his team to a good draw. "That'll show the bugger," he muttered tightly as the German staggered up in the shallows, waving away his friends who were offering to help. One of them was holding out a heavy staff which the winger grabbed and used to lever himself up and forwards.

"Making a bit of a meal of it." Paul told himself as he picked up a towel and rubbed his hair.

The German, indeed now clearly seen with his forward foot in shallow water, was, despite the visual confusion from choppy little waves, indubitably and unashamedly flapping a large, black rubberised flipper – which explained his extra-ordinary speed in the water.

He lurched to his left; clearly completely spent and exhausted. He took the staff with both hands and steadied himself. Still in a few feet of water, he waved, in German as it were, and his team mate sped down the beach with another large staff, which the winger grabbed and adjusted until he was partially supported by two staves, with the help of which he continued to haul himself up and out of the water.

"See..." called Paul to his pals, pointing to his vanquished foe, "...he's wearing bloomin' flippers. That's why I couldn't catch him."

His English friends nodded, cautiously.

The German, broad shouldered and lean bellied, young, blonde and tanned, struggled up with the aid of the staffs.

Paul's words froze in his mouth, which gaped open.

"He's really, really making a bloody meal of it..." thought Paul – uncertainly.

The German, who Paul had pummelled, hopped into a vertical stance and drew himself upright in just a few inches of water. With the staves, or to be more accurate – crutches - under his arms, he swung both legs onto the dry sand, accompanied, of course, by one flipper.

"He's only wearing one flipper..." observed one of the Manchester team.

The German youth, face set in handsome, heroic determination, made away from the water and up the beach – quite rapidly; considering.

"…That's because he's only got one leg…" added another Manchester lad.

"…Well; one-and-a-half legs…" said another, setting the record straight, "…it's only about a quarter missing – just an ankle and a foot gone – really…"

All the players, the sportsmen, looked at Paul the Pugilist. Manchester faces utterly neutral and non-judgemental; the German boys not quite as expressionless as the Mancunians but very still - and quizzical – making a sort of silent group exclamation of "Well?"

"Oh bloody hell. Oh bloody, bloody hell!" muttered Paul, burying his head in his towel.

***

Chapter 30 - Heaton Moor Rugby Club

6 Dec 1962: Choking fog spreads across Britain - A thick layer of fog which has covered London for the last three days is spreading all over the country. - Leeds has recorded its highest ever level of sulphur dioxide in the air and pneumonia cases in Glasgow have trebled. - A spokesman for London's Emergency Bed Service said 235 people had been admitted to hospital in the last 24 hours and issued a "red warning" to prepare for more patients as thick fog continues to affect public health. - So far 90 people have died since the crisis began and the fog is not expected to lift for another 24 hours.

David Hall at sixteen was tall, over six feet tall, slim, very neat, brushed polished and old fashioned and, as he told us, his Headmaster considered him to be intellectually challenged. His predestined fate was to be bashed, berated, bullied, beaten and belittled until – and unless – he achieved his father's ambition for him; to be selected for the Heaton Moor Rugby Football Club First Team. David bore this burden stoically, with good humour even, and never rebelled against it. But then few would rebel against the absolute certainty of Reginald Hall, David's large father and most pertinently, the President for life of the Club. It was also David's fate, his karma, to become a sales and marketing representative in the medical supplies industry – just like his father.

To reduce the dramatic tension already being built here to unbearable heights, readers will be pleased to learn that, despite the stories about to be related, which might indicate otherwise, that David fulfilled all these goals, married Chris (a girl; in fact a very attractive girl) who became a headmistress, earned a very good living in the medical supplies industry and, most pertinent to legends of Heaton Moor Rugby Club, he played Centre for the First Team, and later sired and raised with love and care, identical twin boys – six feet seven inches tall and big with it; not six-feet-seven at birth you understand but when they grew up. And nobody, but nobody – nobody in full possession of their senses – messed with the Hall Twins. And they never played rugger.

Richard, who was to excel as a winger at the club, didn't show the same level of respect to our Father, who competed with all his children, as David did to his dad. At St Bede's school Richard had been selected as a sprinter and invited to try for the County Team; a request that he turned down – for reasons our monosyllabic closed family never investigated. But he was famously fast on his feet. Father had been a racing and long distance competitive cyclist – and a swimmer – and was without doubt a sportsman. Returning from church, one Sunday morning, all of us in our Sunday Best and walking decorously home in quiet, spiritual contemplation, Father was jovially chivvying his six spruced up children along; "C'mon – step out! Left! Right! On the double. Martin! Take your hands out of your pockets and stand up straight. Don't walk as if you live in an igloo". To which encouragement little, sweet faced, blond Martin responded with a low truculent growl that oddly carried up and down the street "Bloody Grown-Ups" and he slumped even lower into his pockets and scuttled away.

It then occurred to Father that his eldest son was tacitly challenging his reputation as an athlete. He and Richard developed a conversation about how many seconds it took to run a hundred yards – and within minutes they were handing their coats and jackets to the bemused family – and close neighbours, and organising others to carefully pace out a straight one hundred yards – up the centre of Mauldeth Road – to the gates of Birch House. Cars and traffic were not expected and didn't in fact intrude.

"Oh – Don't be ridiculous Edwin" scolded Mother, from under her Sunday bonnet, as the course was marked by ten or twelve course referees – and it became clear from facial expressions that this was a serious matter of male pride and testosterone. She walked ahead, up to our gate, where I also stationed myself, to be at the Finishing Line.

Back near the Keegan's house, outside the gates of The Mayfield Nursing Home where Stephanie and Jeremy were born, Richard and Father lined up, in their best Sunday shoes, smart shirts, and Father still wearing his tie – as any gentleman would.

And They're Off!

The two athletes pounded towards me; side by side for the first ten yards; Richard slightly ahead at twenty yards; Richard well ahead at fifty yards; Father's face showing his blood pressure going off the charts, eyes wide and wild with despair; Richard effortlessly 50% ahead at seventy yards, without the faintest compunction for his failing, flailing parent's human dignity and with no concession to age or weight; and he flew, he floated, he skimmed home; as Father faltered and staggered and audibly gasped twenty or thirty yards behind. A young gentleman would have let the gap narrow, would have pulled his punches, imperceptibly slowed his pace and let this deluded middle-aged man draw level for the finish. But Richard wasn't a gentleman.

He was a pragmatic realist. And Father wouldn't have welcomed any obvious concessions or favours.

"Well" said Mother, as her husband literally staggered to our gate, on the verge of a major heart attack or worse, "I hope you feel as ridiculous as you look – you silly old fool".

Father, without the breath or spirit to answer, limped into the house – went to his bedroom, and wasn't seen for the rest of day. Richard, hardly breathing any harder than normal, walked off to the Rugby Club, without making any comment.

Dave Hall, as he was 'Dave' until he attained First Team status and insisted on being called 'David', had big feet, big hands, long arms and legs, a narrow body, an exceptionally small head and small, close-together blue eyes. He had his hair cut, even in the high days of Teddy Boy quiffs, grease and ducks'-arses, in a Perry Como style – very short, brushed close to his head, making the head look even smaller, and parted with razor sharp precision. Inevitably, to his endless irritation, a small spike of hair, of his fair to mousey hair, stubbornly stood up on the crown of this smallish head, a spike which he habitually patted down with a large unconscious hand.

His hair was so short, as Terry told it, that he was the only youth in Heaton Moor who brushed his hair with a flannel. At bedtime, Terry confided, David was so concerned with his appearance that the last thing he did before lights-out was to check himself over appreciatively, in his mirror, make his trademark, quick, stiff, half-wave half-salute at his own reflection and, as Terry mimicked it, cock his small bird like head on one side, give a tight smile at the perfection he observed and say "Goodnight David."

His clothes came from the same shop which dressed his father. David was a young-fogey. His very large shoes were brown brogues, even when his peer group experimented with blue suede brothel creepers with inch thick crepe soles and later with winkle-pickers. His jackets would have graced Kenneth Moore in the 1954 film Genevieve, and his trousers were cavalry-twill, pressed with military precision, using the old trick of soap inside the crease to hold it rigid. When married, returning home to two babies, boys who grew to be six feet seven inches tall, Terry insisted that Dave had bought a complete neck to ankle polythene romper suit, for himself, which he donned over his office clothes and wore until all threats of dribbling, leaking, snotting, food caking, puking and so on, were removed. David liked to be neat and clean.

His greatest quality was his love of mankind. David was a communicator and a visitor, usually an uninvited but not always unwelcome visitor, with the habit of attaching himself to one or two pals and then calling on them daily – twice daily – thrice daily, for news, conversation and companionship. Like the old storytellers and troubadours of old he wandered from habitation to habitation, always have a story to tell and had not the slightest reluctance to quiz his companions, nearly to death if necessary, about their lives, families, girlfriends, joys, sorrows and secrets. He was also an early riser, to the horror and consternation of his peer group, who like most teenagers could happily sweat it out without regard to society, conventions, their health or even their immortal souls, in their pitted beds until well after midday – if like sleeping dogs, they were let lie. But David would call, invade the family kitchen, make himself and them a mug of strong Manchester tea, with the standard two spoons of sugar, and blandly invade their privacy – launching into complex subjects as early as nine-thirty in the morning, flicking specks of their dandruff and bedroom squalor off his impeccable slacks and taking up his station, for the foreseeable future, on the end of their beds, apparently oblivious to their unshaven blurred faces, their absolute inability to respond coherently and their near-death states.

He had a very direct and practical manner and he was very polite to parents – who might be bemused to find this tall lad making himself at home, in their home, from early morning until – whatever time he chose to go. The strongest hints to get him to leave – even violent physical attacks – sloughed off him like the proverbial water off a duck's back and he would eventually go – in good humour – and then return, perhaps within the hour, to take up where he had left off. He liked being with people.

Even his Headmaster, exasperated to the point of attacking the boy, could not dint David's inner conviction that he was always welcome.

As David told us one summer evening - as we sipped Dandelion and Burdock or Vimto and played records on the jukebox at Lillian's Café, located on the other side, the wrong side, of Wellington Road - his very own Headmaster, in the week of David's otherwise triumphant and celebrated departure from Heaton Moor College, had called him into his study and berated him over his examination results and his general underachieving academic life. Starting with mature, controlled and polite deliberation, the Headmaster had, as his summary of David's attributes mounted, lost a little of his cool demeanour, risen to his feet and stationed himself at his familiar, cobra like striking distance and, as David so brilliantly parodied, delivered his final, fatal verdict, his last and Final Report; with his trade mark double finger slide down the right side of his nose, preceding a whip like action, causing the whole agitated, tutorial hand to strike out and down onto David's near shaven head, to give emphasis to key points and essentially to drive, indeed to hammer, or try to hammer, those points home.

He did the finger slide down his nose. "Boy!" snarled the by now besides himself senior tutor striking David's unflinching and unresponsive head sharply with his open palm,

"You are no good to your parents..."

David hee-hawed with mirth as he re-enacted the scene.

'Slap'

"You're no good to your school..."

David grinned, a small teeth clenching grin, and did all the actions – his arm swinging down on an imaginary solid schoolboy's head.

'Slap'

And the now completely out of control Headmaster was taken over by emotions raging at this immutable youth who had been in his charge and teaching system for eleven years without a shred of evidence, not the merest sign, that he had learned anything whatsoever about anything at all. His voice careened to heights of impotent hysteria:

"...and you're no bloody good to yourself. Good bloody riddance to you Boy!"

'Slap – Slap'

And David put his two very large hands over his tight little stomach, neatly enclosed in a well-tailored brown tweed jacket, and rocked forward in great, silent amusement, almost bending double and staying bent for some time before the need to breathe obliged him to come upright, draw in air, and then again descend to a ninety-degree angle, feet together, legs straight and his head shaking from side to side in utterly mute laughter at his own story.

But despite such scholastic drawbacks, and despite being no natural athlete, David left school, joined The Club and progressed painfully and steadily towards the First-Team.

Dave's dad, Reg Hall was forty or fifty something. He was large and red faced. He had a blustering, military bearing and a notable moustache. He was the President, possibly life president of Heaton Moor Rugby Club, rugby league of course. He spoke loudly and authoritatively. In fact, he not so much spoke as barked. He drank beer, seemingly constantly, without any noticeable effect on his concentration. He wore a strongly checked sports jacket with matching flat cap and, when watching a match, planted monumentally on the touch-line, Reg's rendering of "C'mon Moor" delivered sparingly in a decisively manly bass, held a degree of underlying threat that either galvanised or paralysed players at crucial moments, depending on their lifetime's experience of dealing with authority.

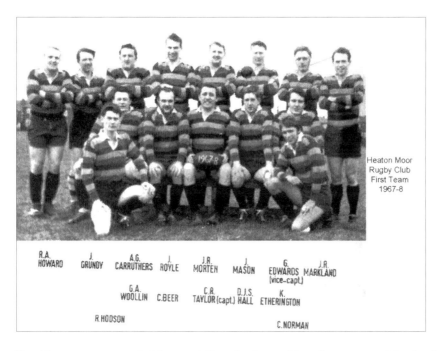

David was two years' older and four inches taller than me and he had been a friend of Richard from the age of eight. He called often at our home for his regular local news bulletins and tea. Annoyingly for me,

Richard had been to St. Bede's school, which was essentially a vulgar soccer playing establishment, and he had only taken up rugger, my game, at eighteen, to become an instant star of Heaton Moor's First-Team, as a fast as a whippet winger – who scored. He was a First-Team hero and, two and a half years older than me, exercised his right, one of many of the rights of the first born, not to acknowledge me at The Club. But Dave Hall did. He would nod in my direction, recognising me as a person who sometimes sat in their smoke wreathed poker, brag and pontoon games; games played for money, which Richard organised at our house, just long enough to lose all my spare cash, before being permitted to make yet another tray of tea for the card-school.

When I left school, I was sixteen and, though a very poor sportsman, I also had ambitions to be a star at the Rugby Club. For dramatic effect it will be left for some paragraphs for readers to learn what happened to that ambition.

Rugger is a "contact sport". Non-playing readers, needing a quick introduction, should understand that a game is played with fifteen players on each of two opposing teams. Ideally they should be "built like a brick shit-house" – and preferably be male. This was a rude reference to the shape, seven feet high and three-feet-six-inches wide, and an accolade to the solidity of outside lavatories, WC's, built in the backyards of Victorian terraced houses, with a goodly number still surviving into the late nineteen-fifties. Thirty such indestructible gentlemen plus a referee and two linesmen, on most winter Saturdays, stomped onto the Heaton Moor pitch. The captains shook hands and tossed a coin to decide who would kick-off. The kick-off team crowded forward to the half-way line and the defenders got well back near their own goal or "touch" line.

Reg Hall and other portly middle aged officers of the Club emerged, suitably garbed against the elements, carrying pint pots of bitter, which never seemed to empty, to walk the touchline and offer the experience of their years to the young pretenders on the pitch. A few hardy wives, pals and children lined the field as audience.

Ideally the sky was overcast, better still it should be raining, or, if not raining, then snowing and if not snowing, then it was good for the ground to be frozen into concrete hardness and the air temperature about five degrees below freezing. On cold days, some of the less rugged players were reminded by a ferociously cutting North-Easterly that the kit they were wearing consisted of one thin cotton shirt, gaudily coloured gold, black, white and burgundy, thin white cotton shorts –

short and tight on the thighs - a rarely washed cotton jock-strap protecting the testosterone pumping gonads - woolly socks to just below the knee concealing leather shin-guards and, of course, rugger boots, armed with, in 1958, aluminium studs – for stomping on people. A well-aimed North-Easterly could cut through these meagre garments in a fraction of a second and, not to put too fine a point on it, shrivel and freeze-dry a male's pride and its twin dependents to the size of a single walnut. If struck, Oh my God, if struck, when so shrivelled, vulnerable, tiny and blue, the pain was excruciating, as was a blow on any part of the body which was equally blue with cold.

Any contact on such days could be worse than fatal.

Mick Farmer - by Lee Chadwick

& Hawking at Heaton Moor Rugby Club

About 1957

Seriously damaged players with old scars and irreparable, broken noses, missing teeth and half ears – like the walking wounded after a battle, wore a plethora of safety straps. Some Moor players had leather wrist bands. Others had surgical bandages round their knees – or calves – or thighs. Scrum members often donned leather helmets with circles cut out to let air circulate in the vicinity of the brain and with ear-flaps fastened tight under the chin – to stop their ears being torn-off.

Thus adorned, these mammoths of the sporting world aligned themselves, each team in its own half of the field, for the kick-off. The ball was punted high and long; an "up-and-under" - long so as to fly into the opposition's territory and high to allow time before the ball falls to earth for the players to thunder up field, get under the ball, and catch it. That at least was the theory.

The reality was that all eyes swivelled heavenwards to track the ball, while thirty behemoths, built like brick shit-houses and weighing much the same, rang down to their engine rooms to set their thighs, calves, ankles and hips in rapid thundering motion, designed to carry them at considerable speed – about eighteen miles an hour – towards the place where their brains, invigorated by the cold air circulating past their heads, calculated the leathern egg would descend. The objective being for a player to catch the ball, run towards the touch-line, the opponents' touch-line, not their own, avoid being "tackled" – that is hurled to the ground and jumped on by one or more opponent, cross the line and "touch-down" with the ball as near the goal posts as possible – and thus score a "try" – which does not mean "trying" - as it had already succeeded, beyond trying, but refers to the three, or tri, points awarded to the heroic player's team; simple really.

But it was not so simple in practice. With the ball still high in the air, sometimes lost against the bright sun or scudding clouds, and with a combined impact speed of thirty-six miles an hour, two players, between them weighing thirty-stones or four-hundred-and-ten pounds, two hundred kilos, urged on by Reg Hall's, "C'mon Moor" both gazing skywards and lifting their arms to catch the ball – could do themselves considerable harm when they met; skull cracking on skull, knee smashing on knee and ribs bending against ribs. In car crash tests – a thirty-six miles an hour collision smashes the car's engine back about five feet, driving it through sheet metal and crushing whatever gets in its way.

Now multiply that impact by fifteen times.

And wonder, as you let your imagination loose, wonder if the architects of this great game had thought it through. Had they intended these consequences – or had they intended that the players, like their sensible American cousins, should be armoured from head to toe and as immune from injury and harm as a big girl's blouse?

Now for the scrum down; many readers don't understand the scrum.

In the ensuing melee – inevitably – the ball is dropped. As a hand reaches out for it, a metal studded boot will, as likely as not, stamp accidentally down on the groping hand – drawing blood. Tempers flare. More players try to snatch up the ball. More hands are stomped on. Another hero plunges down to collect the prize only for an anonymous groping hand to grab the hero by the hair and swing him violently sideways. Tempers ignite. Death is threatened – but, the referee steps in, recognises chaos when he sees it and whistles loudly. All the players obediently stop. A scrum-down is announced. Order is restored.

"Built like a brick shithouse."
7 ft tall, 2.5 ft wide & solid

Many homes had outside lavatories.

Six burly giants unite – or five giants and a smaller "hooker"; No! not that kind of hooker, but a man, a player, who, supported by the two prop-forwards, can hook a loose ball with his legs – we'll get back to that.

The two prop-forwards link arms with the hooker between them so the hooker can swing between the two props. That makes a front row, "The Front Row Forwards" of three. Behind comes the second row of two men, the real engines of push, who also link arms, bend double, and stick their heads between the front-row thighs, wrap their other hands around the outer thighs and squeeze them all together. This now makes five men. The Front Row, still upright, tends at this stage to lean back against the weight and energy of the "Second Row" who are like large dogs on leashes, always straining forwards. The Second Row splays about with the vigorous pushing. This is cured by the sixth scrum member, the largest of all, who comes up behind the Second Row, bends double and sticks his head between the second row forwards, winds his arms round their outer thighs and pulls. He is the "middle-of-the-back" and is sometimes referred to as the "lock" forward.

Both sides have built their scrums which are now brought together by the referee, like elephants to a mating ritual, with care; and the two front rows lock their heads and necks. It is done. It is ready.

During this construction period the "scrum-half" of the team awarded the privilege, has the leathern egg and fusses around outside the scrum as the building of it proceeds. The other team's Scrum-Half is consigned to the back row of the scrum where he fusses about, keeping a view through the legs of the scrum, of the "tunnel".

Spatially intelligent readers, following this text, will have pictured by now that the two scrums when locked in opposition, form between them, a veritable tunnel. And we are at last getting to the point of the whole complex exercise. Into the tunnel, providing no player is cheating by obstructing the tunnel unfairly, the egg is thrown. As it enters the tunnel, the hookers seek to hook the ball with their feet, back into their own scrum, back beyond the legs of the Front Row, and beyond the legs of the Second Row, where the Middle of the Back can deliver it to his Scrum-Half, usually a smallish and quick player, who is then allowed to fish the ball out by hand – and pass it out to the "Backs" who are strung in a line across the pitch – and who then race forward with the ball to score.

However, a scrum rarely delivers up the ball so cleanly and easily. The Forwards are required to push. So as the ball is hooked backwards and starts to make its way to the waiting hands of the Scrum-Half, the opposite Forwards heave and push the scrum backwards with the effect that they walk over the ball as it were and cause it to now emerge from the back of their scrum – to their Scrum-Half who will snatch it up and out to their Backs. BUT, the original team will see this ploy and they will also push and strike in with their feet in an attempt to recover the ball, egg shaped, so it is laid egg like, from the back of their scrum. Meanwhile, inside this heaving mass of humanity, weighing in all about two-thousand-five-hundred pounds, more than a ton of flesh, the individuals do what they can to discomfort opponents and diminish their power to push or kick the ball. What a way to spend your Saturday mornings. And it gets worse.

Wholly illegally, a gentleman will stick a finger up another's nostril and twist, or poke an unguarded eye, or bite an unprotected ear while the two hookers, their task of hooking now done, swing on the strong shoulders of their props and viciously kick whatever bits of the opponents they can reach. If these tactics don't baffle and confuse then there is always a strong chance on a warm day that an olfactory sensitive player may swoon, overcome by the perfumes within the tunnel. Eventually the ball emerges and one team or the other runs-off with it. The scrum disentangles and all players chase after the ball.

It was to such a battle-field that Reg Hall, like the Biblical Abraham who was asked by God to sacrifice his son Isaac, chose to dedicate his only son David – or let him die in the attempt.

And I shared much the same ambition for myself as Reg did for David.

It was on the back of the reputation of my sporting if academically mediocre schooling at St Ambrose College that when I left school at sixteen I joined Heaton Moor Rugby Club and was there rapidly demoted down team after team until I reached my appropriate level on the eighth reserves, with an ill assorted bunch of the elderly, unfit, wounded, halt, lame, blind and feeble minded who, for reasons we never discussed, all felt it a duty to go to The Club, up the cinder surfaced Green Lane, on Saturdays in season, in the winter, and play up, play up and play the game.

As well as being slow, for a rugger player, and oddly unsighted in one eye, over my years at school, where I had played at Prop-Forward for six years, I had also shrunk. Well, I had not exactly become shorter but relatively speaking, compared to my age group, while the majority had accelerated in height and girth, I grew slowly and thinly due to persistent undetected duodenal ulcers - miraculously cured in my mid-thirties. But, in the Year of Our Lord 1959 as I donned the Heaton Moor Rugby Club colours – and learned to correctly intone the touch-line utterance "C'mon Moor" in as deep a bass as I could muster - I was simply skeletal and undoubtedly the only short, stick-like rugby prop forward in the whole League.

But I was a player and I had the shirt. And, alongside my team mates on the 8th Reserve, some of whom arrived at the pitch on zimmer-frames or were held together by an assortment of strange prosthetics and surgical appliances, I was a reasonably fit, if slight, prop forward. My remarkably bony shoulder protuberances and my low centre of gravity actually worked in our team's favour, as I had a certain stamina and stubbornness, enabling me, however much pressed by the opposing scrum, to just manage to remain, while decidedly bent and very close to the floor, just marginally in legal play and still functioning a few millimetres off the grass, like a frontward crouching limbo dancer.

This wiry crouch forced the other team's scrum to collapse down to my level on one side, my side, a situation which they omitted to train for, while for my team it was a standard and familiar geometry, causing the whole heaving scrum to either wheel rapidly and dizzyingly round me as a sort of bony fulcrum screwed immovably into the earth, or for the opposition to suddenly scrunch down on my side with all the weight of their largest players pushing up and through which, like a prize judo throw, suddenly pitched them over, turtle-like, in a unit, still bound together in their tight - non-homosexual - embrace, and go head over heels.

Thus, as at school, while I could not run, pass, catch, kick or see well, I remained on the team. And I turned up. I was reliable. Like a good Alcoholics Anonymous member, I turned up.

It was in the Heaton Moor –v- Wigan Town 1961 match where I was obliged, for the sake of the sport, to eat coal, and my First-Team ambitions suffered a set-back.

Coal, a shiny black flaking carbonate stone, you may be old enough to recall, was, prior to Prime Minister Margaret Thatcher, dug from the ground by the now extinct species Homo-Arthur-Scargillius and burnt in power stations, factories and every home in the land; emitting fierce gassy flames and masses of black choking smoke. The Clean Air Act, brought in around 1956 to tackle smog, which reliably killed off the old and infirm every winter and thus kept National Health Service costs down, banned coal from most towns and cities – but the ban did not extend to rugger pitches.

The week before our Wigan game, the 8th Reserves selectors had realised that a small, thin prop-forward, even one as experienced as I, was not always to the team's advantage. My brother Richard, who I resembled in size and features, was a celebrated First-Team winger. They, the Demi-Gods of Heaton Moor Rugby Football Club, decided almost fatally, to try me on the wing. I was to be a fast sprinting, quick thinking, cunning, catch the pass on the run, surprising winger. I, like my First Team brother, would win them the match.

It was a grey, drizzly, not cold, not warm, ill-defined sort of a Saturday, a good day for a funeral, when we were transported from Green Lane, Heaton Moor, on an ancient (8th Reserves style) cream painted charabanc, to a club house on a small green plateau in the middle of Wigan, slightly higher than the majority of coal spoil heaps and the back-to-back houses which surrounded it. Gaunt metal lattice towers supporting huge wheels and mine shaft lifts, the winding gear, reared up menacingly around the grounds. We changed in a cramped room on wooden benches alongside the Wigan team.

"Built like a brick-shithouse" Observation on rugby forwards' anatomy – Anon

They were coal miners – and perhaps ought to have been playing Rugby Union, not Rugby League, which is more the refined preserve of accountants, solicitors, salesmen and shop-keepers. They had all the muscularity of men hardened by daily shovelling coal, hoisting massive drills and jack-hammers and beating each other in the face with their bare fists – just for the fun of it. They unquestionably voted or supported Labour and we Heaton Moor'ons equally unthinkingly voted Conservative. It was but a short leap of logic to assume, with good reason, that they resented our middle-class aspirations and our assumed management status.

A scrum-down in the game of gentlemen.

I stumbled against the Wigan player next to me who was putting on his socks and balancing on one leg. It was like falling onto a concrete wall. He did not budge and may not even have noticed the collision. I surreptitiously compared my clerical, pen wielding arm to his size-twelve-shovel digging arm. His arm seemed longer than mine, maybe that was a trick of the light, but it was definitely wider; and it was knotted and brown where mine was smooth, not to say flaccid, white muscle. His was like a gnarled willow tree, clambering sinuously down from his enormous shoulder in intertwining rippling ropes of muscle and tendons that flexed, animal like, with each movement. His elbow was at least twice the width of mine with deep definition of interconnecting tissue that anchored his lower arm to his upper arm and carried the underlying pneumatic flexible JCB pipes with a lifting power of several tons. His forearms were like Popeye the Sailorman's, wider than his bulging biceps and terminating in hands that could, and no doubt did, crush rocks. I speculated on whether one of his hands could encircle my neck – and concluded that indeed it could. My hands were excellent for accurately pressing little keys on a desktop adding machine; in a year, I had calculated by measuring the key pressure, I toned my body by pressing as much as two tons. He probably shifted ten tons of rock a day. He finished adjusting his socks and straightened up. He was at least four and maybe five inches taller than me. He donned a leather helmet that was stained with dark ominous patches – with blood perhaps - his or someone else's? I didn't have the temerity to examine his legs in case he misconstrued my motives and killed me on the spot, but as he walked away the floorboards buckled under each step and then groaned back into place. He was one of the smaller Wigan players. I hadn't had the chance to check if his teeth were filed down to points. He hadn't smiled at me.

The pitch, when we emerged bravely from the dressing room into the thin rain, was well drained and strangely sparse of grass and weeds. On closer examination it was obviously, obvious to an observant and intelligent office clerk who might shortly be forming an intimate relationship with the surface, a piece of land reclaimed from a spoil tip, levelled and planted with grass seed in the middle and clusters of blackened thorn bushes at the corners, thorn which was hanging on for dear life with a truculent determination to survive. The good news was that it wasn't muddy. Our mothers couldn't abide us getting our freshly laundered shirts and white shorts soused in mud. The bad news was that the lack of mud was due, not to low rainfall, but to a fundamental lack of soil. The surface was ground stone and, amongst the stone, lumps of black shiny coal. It echoed hollowly as we trotted over it with our aluminium studs, not yielding at all. The surface was as hostile as a Wigan cheese-grater – but it was well drained.

Miscasting of our players aside – I mean it didn't help that I, a seasoned, if small, prop forward, was for the first time in my life cast as an allegedly star, scoring, sprinting winger – we had to admit they were the better team. They were bigger, stronger, faster, more accurate, merciless, psychopathic killers who knew how to play as a team. The score against us mounted like a milometer on a fast car. Out on the wing I had little to do as we rarely won possession of the ball and even when we did, and it was passed triumphantly along the line of Backs to one of our Centres, the momentary triumph would be overwhelmed by the heavy pounding of feet, metal striking stone, like jungle drums, as the Wigan players bore down on one of our hapless, puffing, terrified team-mates – and, if he was lucky – they simply plucked the ball out of his hands before continuing their charge, across our touch-line, for yet another three points. The score was something embarrassingly gargantuan to NIL when, due to a brief, overconfident loss of concentration by Wigan, we got hold of the ball. We could at that point have waved a white flag and surrendered but foolishly we responded instinctively, like Pavlov's dogs, to our years of intensive training and our Backs raced, or hobbled manfully, forward with the ball.

I'm not a sprinter, whatever the Heaton Moor selectors may have assumed, but even after eighty minutes I was almost fresh to the game, held in secret reserve as it were, and I was able to keep up with my fellow Backs and keep position out on the left wing. Oddly, the Wigan Team seemed to me to be gathering, threateningly, like storm clouds on my side of the pitch, crowding towards the left side touch-line along which I might race, free as a bird, if I ever had the ball, to score the only try for us in the entire match. They were not only tough and disciplined players but they also displayed strategic thinking of a surprisingly high order – as it was not at all obvious to me that the prized egg might ever reach me, the play to that point having provided a mass of empirical evidence that it would not – but they somehow seemed to anticipate that it would, and they were assembling a defensive wall of bone and muscle that only I, with a turn of speed, agility, selling dummy passes by the dozen and with dazzlingly bewildering footwork, might dance through, like a will-o-the-wisp, to their eternal consternation – and score. Hurrah!

It wasn't quite like that.

Our Backs were corralled by their Backs into a smaller and smaller quadrant. We drummed over the stony surface, faultlessly flinging the ball from genius player to genius player, without a hitch; but getting ever closer to a fence – no - to a wall - of Wigan miners who seemed to have taken it as a personal insult, a slur to their manhood and a foul curse on their sainted mothers' graves that we had any possession of the ball at all. Into the valley of death plunged the Heaton Moorons. About six feet from the maniacal phalanx of coal-miners, my friend and colleague, my team-mate, may he die a horrible lingering death, my Centre, passed me the ball. Shockingly, even though it came from my right, where I was all unknowingly completely short-sighted with a focal length of about three feet, where I usually lost contact with the ball and thus dropped it, I foolishly caught the ball. I was the last in the line. Either I scored or it would end in an untidy scrimmage – and we would lose possession yet again.

I set my jaw. I gripped the ball. I accelerated – not with smoke coming off my heels but I did accelerate. I jinxed. I weaved. I had seen this done by wingers in hundreds of matches. I dodged. I made as if to pass – and dummied. But not only did these miners have Herculean bodies, they also had Einstein-ean intellects. They, astonishingly, even up against a first class, office honed brain such as mine, anticipated my every move. They heroically hurled themselves against my charging torso, giving no thought to their own safety. Within a second I was buried beneath twelve, seventeen stone, Wigan miners, all grasping for the ball which I had fallen on, upside down. It took a dozen of them to pin me down. The other three Wigan men stood off a few feet, in case I lurched to my feet hoisting the whole dozen – and carried them and the ball over the touch line. The pile set. And, at the base of the pile I lay, twisted and mangled beyond recognition, and imagined that I would suffocate and die on that foreign field far from home.

After an eternity and infinity of knees and elbows and skulls and fingers and honest sweat and foul body odours, the referee and the two linesmen managed to unravel the top Wigan man, and then the next and the next, until at last the two immediately above me could stir and started to lift themselves. The ball had disappeared and I wasn't at that moment overly concerned with its whereabouts. I found, as daylight trickled down to me, that I had been turned yet again, lying on my face with the rest of me elevated at forty-five degrees and, due to the great weight above, my lower teeth had engaged with the cheese grater surface, where they stuck, forcing my mouth open – which was filled with an honest lump of Lancashire coal, slowly splintering against my back molars.

Though nothing was broken, at that moment, rising Phoenix like from the ashes – or at least from the coal dust - I had an insight. I was not the right material for rugger. And at the end of the Wigan game, I resigned my commission, and never played again.

What had I given up, that David went on to conquer and claim as his Kingdom on Earth?

A Rugby First Team Wife
Look but don't touch.

Leaving school at sixteen and eventually becoming a Heaton Moor player, had given me privileged access to the hot communal plunge pools shared by all the teams, even the 8th Reserves, which in turn meant that when dried off, dressed in civvies, flaunting a Battle of Britain pilot's style silk cravat, and no longer muddy, only soiled with team shared earth and curdled mixed body fluids, years before deodorants became de-rigueur, I could saunter out of the dressing rooms alongside First Team and other Olympian players and take my rightful place at the club house bar, only slightly inconvenienced by being at shoulder height and half the average dimensions of the other men, hearing tales of near death experiences and scores that might have been – "if only" – with the best of them.

The bar-room, a large wooden shed that could hold a hundred or so meaty rugger types, was also frequented by a few of the bolder girlfriends and young wives of team members, who flaunted in a middle-class sort of way, their priceless assets, on a ten to one basis – ten males for every female – but exclusively reserved for the pleasure of their two-hundred-and-twenty pound escorts. It would have been suicidal – for me at least – to ogle any of these players' molls, squeezed Jayne Mansfield and Diana Dors like into tight upholstered sweaters, with waist cutting wide belts. Such obvious interest would be more dangerous than snatching a peeled, ready to eat banana from the fist of King Kong as he lifted it lovingly to his anticipatory lips; it would definitely be ill-advised; very ill-advised. But I could secretly admire.

All this I gave up when I quit the 8th Reserves, leaving the field open to David Hall to triumphantly snatch the glittering First Team prizes.

***

Chapter 31 - Cleveland Road

"The flying coffin" – *Streetwise description of the Jaguar XK 140.*

The XK120 was replaced by a car that looked and felt very much the same - but when you have a winning formula, why change it? The XK140 was offered in three forms - coupe, roadster and drophead coupe. The coupe was larger and heavier than the XK120, but had more power to counteract those extra kilos. Some would say that this changed the character of the XK line, moving it from out-and-out sports car, to a more relaxed long distance cruiser. The Coupe was fitted with small rear seats and the C-type's rack and pinion steering, which for the first time, was offered with - gasp - optional power-assisted steering. Despite all that, the XK140 is a fine car to drive, and if anything, a better classic car than the XK120 – Honest John.com

I wasn't any more talented at making music than I was at ballroom dancing, but Tats had invited me to his house in Cleveland Road to join him and three girls to play recently released Lonnie Donegan skiffle records and I might be permitted to strum along on Tat's old guitar, as he had bought himself a new enviable electric guitar; which he could really play. Guitars were expensive items in those days. So, prepared to have a go – on the half beat of course, on a quiet summer's evening I ambled along Mauldeth Road, around the corner and high wall of Doctor Curtis's house, crossed the empty highway to the Cleveland Road turning and paused – as I heard engines revving at high speed coming up from Burnage.

Speeding around the wide bend by the Cox's new mansion, came two racing vehicles, neck and neck – straddling the road, relying on their Guardian Angels and the lack of traffic at that time of the evening to stay alive. I instantly recognised, on the safer inside position, Willy Mason's bright red Jaguar, and, dangerously on the wrong side of the road, the Tompkin & Rider small pick-up van, a white Standard 10, driven by Terry Rider. They hurtled at me and I leapt into a gateway as both vehicles, as if on tracks, still side by side, screeched to their left off Mauldeth Road into Cleveland Road. The pick-up van missed me by inches. Another miraculous escape – that Mother would have ascribed to my Guardian Angel; perhaps she was right.

Willy just had the edge and nudged in front. To stop Terry overtaking, he slewed his beautiful car from side to side across the narrow street. Terry immediately flung his van – Bang! – up onto the pavement.

Having narrowly spared my life, Terry, grinning like a fiend, gunned his red and white van between the lamp-posts and the neat suburban gateways, knowing with the utter certainty of One of The Masters of the Universe that no-one would foolishly step out of their home onto the pavement, to die under his racing wheels. As he sped along the pavement, his eyes shining with glee, high on nothing other than his own adrenaline and rewarding floods of dopamine coursing through what his Xaverian school teachers had ultimately refused to recognise as a human brain, he screamed and yelled with laughter, flashing neat clenched teeth at his two passengers - both sucking furiously on cigarettes – crammed, paralysed and terrified beside him in the small cockpit.

Alongside, on the street, glancing up from his open top car at his rival on the pavement, raced Willy Mason at the wheel of his father's brand new, lethally unsafe even in the best of hands, red Jaguar XK 140. Willy was sporting cream and leather driving gloves, matching the upholstery, and a smouldering Black Russian Sobranie cigarette clamped in the very centre of his thin blue lips, pointing rifle-like at the right angled bend just two hundred yards ahead of them. Willy's were not, as his father's insurers might attest …the best of hands.

Cleveland Road had not been used as a race-track for three years since 1956 when the Mallalieu family had moved from semi-detached Number 2, to a superior new detached house at a better address opposite the golf-links, a few hundred yards and three quiet streets away. Pauline's father, Derry Mallalieu, was a small, buttoned up Yorkshire engineer, with a dry sense of humour, a moustache, an ever smouldering pipe and an uncanny understanding of machines. He had no understanding, relationship or empathy with his daughter, but had a deep spiritual link with old cars. Before they became fashionable and valuable antiques, after the war, Ex-Ghurkha Captain Engineer Durham Frank Mallalieu, or Derry, bought a Type 35 Bugatti, in pieces in a box, re-assembled the legendary 140 mph French car – and raced it at weekends.

The rest of the week, he spent every evening repairing and rebuilding it in the small garage at Number 2; which of course involved numerous short test runs, nightly, on the street; blasting the neighbours into life and waking their babies. Nothing was said directly to Derry, but when he moved and took his high revving, exhaust booming, hill climbing blue chariot to a new location, the polite Cleveland Road neighbours breathed a collective sigh of relief.

Durham Frank Mallalieu "Derry" in his Type 35 Bugatti at Prescott – Oct 1955

Terry's van and Willy's Jaguar, one on the pavement the other on the road, posed an infinitely greater threat to the residents than the cosseted Bugatti ever had.

The white, Standard 10, open backed pick-up was five-feet-and-one-and-a-half inches wide at its widest point – the front wings. The lamp posts - erected just a year ago by the Stockport Public Works Department to replace pre-war, cast-iron, yellow-glow gas-lights, with these neon blue-glow, concrete electric beacons – stood at the pavement's edge, back from the residents' walls and gates by just five-feet-one-and-three-quarters of an inch; on average. The paving slabs beneath the wheels were uneven.

It was by the grace of that quarter of an inch differential, as if the Town Council or God or Providence had anticipated and designed it for the very purpose, that Terry had been able to dodge round Willy's high speed blocking tactics as they neck-and-neck hand-braked turned off Mauldeth Road into Cleveland Road. To Willy's immense surprise, Terry not only drew level – but started to overtake the infinitely faster and superior sports car, which had the added advantage of being driven in a legally designated traffic lane.

The pick-up pitched and rocked on the pavement surface as another concrete lamp-post threatened on their right and the oak gateposts of Mr and Mrs Robert's neat semi-detached home intruded from the left. Terry snatched in his nonchalant elbow, a split second before it was smashed against the lamp-post, and yelled with excitement as his companions clamped their hands to their eyes, blotting out their own imminent executions, and the rocking, rolling, snorting, clanging vehicle hurtled through the gap, polishing its paintwork on either side – as all the while Terry hurled friendly abuse, hand gestures and challenges through its open windows at Willy.

Willy Mason's (his Dad's) XK140 bright-red Jaguar

"The Flying Coffin"

Terry Rider's Standard 10 Builders' Pick-Up

Without shovels

Photo by Maz Wooley

But, Willy could keep his cool. The ash on his Black Sobranie had grown a smidgen longer but, showing its aristocratic Russian quality, did not droop. Willy narrowed his small, weak blue eyes to peer at the corner ahead by the new houses, noted the lamp-post, the acute angle, gates, walls and the back end of a lovingly polished Ford Popular protruding slightly onto the pavement – narrowed his eyes further into slits of cunning intelligence, measuring the yards, feet and inches and, at his left hand side, being aware of the swaying, revving and pitching of the vulgar little builder's van and its chortling, gesticulating driver – and he murmured to himself "Don't get mad – get even!" and with controlled slow pressure he stepped on the accelerator of his, or to be more accurate his father's, superlative red Jaguar with his hand-made, pale brown, leather brogues – and with an exhaust roar born of vast spending power applied to rare copper alloys, Willy leapt yards into the lead.

I watched open mouthed as the perilous race developed and the booming exhausts powered away from me, up the short street of once safe and peaceful semi-detached homes. Willy, in the hugely fast Jaguar, would obviously win. He had to.

As he triumphed, as the winner's laurels were in his grasp, and as Terry and Co kangarooed along the pavement to almost inevitably suffer an untimely and tragic end, as their bucking Standard Ten plunged into the un-navigable corner – Willy had to look. He had to see it happen. He wanted to watch as the metal crumpled against the concrete; as the garden wall smashed the offside headlights before it tumbled block by block onto the bonnet; as the three occupants, decades before seat belts, continued to travel forwards at the same crazy speed while their vehicle stopped, very suddenly, dead still, and the three shot out through the windscreen into the modern, designer front garden of Mr Jefferies, the new, young, local dentist who was raking it in from rapid and ruthless deployment on child and adult alike of the Australian Trench method. He had become rich by drilling out the inner core of every molar in sight with his new-fangled electric drill, while his competitors relied on slow and painful foot powered drills, and filling the excavated trenches with lethal heavy metal amalgam, for which the National Health Service obligingly, unquestioningly and monthly paid him two shillings and sixpence per tooth; teeth that he had permanently neutralised and destroyed.

But, triumph was an ephemeral, virtual dream as Willy in his deepest inner self had known from the outset – before this ill-advised race had barely begun. "All is vanity" he might have mused had his smaller than average brain in his oddly narrow head sitting atop possibly the thinnest, if best dressed, teenage torso in Heaton Moor, been capable of framing, or even of repeating parrot fashion, such a philosophical concept; which was highly doubtful. The very idea that Willy, multiple wrecker of Rolls-Royces, Cadillacs and all that was most flashy in shiny cars, had the slightest hope of out-driving Terry Rider was risible; or, to translate that uncommon word for Willy's benefit, laughable. Too late did Willy realise that he should not have looked back to crow; he should have continued looking ahead; looking at the corner which, I could see as I ran up the pavement, his red Jaguar also had to negotiate – albeit with far more road space than Terry had, but still a sharp and narrow turn for the killer XK 140.

I doubted that either of them could make the turn.

The new Jaguar, boasting all the sophisticated technologies developed by the British Motor Industry in the ten years since the War, which, to reduce a car's possible life span excluded any rust-proofing; had rapidly proved itself to be the charismatic, mechanical assassin of a large percentage of the privileged few who could afford to buy one. On analysis by the keenest and most critical motor sport intelligences in existence – teenage boys – it was already classed as an I-beam with a monstrous engine, nicknamed "The Flying Coffin", which in theory could go very, very fast in a straight line – though often it pitched sideways for no good reason – but could not be steered or stopped when required.

Any such teenager could have explained to Willy that an "I-Beam" had no Biblical connotations to do with human eyes and, after taking some minutes and wholly failing to explain the words "Biblical" and "connotations", would have continued to say that it referred to rolled, cold steel beams of whatever length with a cross section shaped like the capital letter "I". Basically, the car was an iron girder with wheels.

But Willy, at this racing second, knew nothing of his car's street credibility, or lack of it, and, as we said, had made the basic mistake, at a crucial moment, of peering triumphantly back at Terry's predicament instead of concentrating on his own immediate future.

Mr Jefferies, nemesis of the Tooth Fairy, dentine driller and molar extractor extraordinaire, had invested his ill-gotten gains in a brand new detached home built at the end and on that vexed ninety-degree corner of, the row of pre-War 1930's semi-detached homes, which occupied half of Cleveland Road. The dentist had also bought a new car, which at this late hour was polished and parked on the new flagstones in his front garden, gleaming under the almost midnight sun, and …unbeknown to Willy, or Terry, who only rarely visited Cleveland Road and even more rarely used it as a race-track, …Mr Jefferies had also bought, with no expense spared, an enviable, sleek and most modern, cream coloured ocean going speedboat – a beautiful craft currently mounted on a grand trailer – for which there was no room beside the new car in the front garden; so it was parked, or should that be 'berthed'; displayed for all to envy, on the street, just around the angle of the bend.

The booming exhausts, screeching tyres, shouted imprecations and the great sound of the massive collision and tearing metal as Willy made intimate contact with the speedboat and its carriage, reached a glorious crescendo, and had me running up the street in excitement and trepidation; as he singularly failed to double de-clutch, change down, use opposite lock, brake and steer all at the same time – as he had to do to stand any chance of controlling the red beast and save the boat from destruction. The boat, to his surprise had suddenly loomed into view – a double surprise, firstly that there was anything blocking his chosen path at all and secondly – that the blockage was a large white boat, some seventy-five miles from the nearest sea-coast.

The red car smashed into and penetrated the craft with such a noise that it overpowered Tat's, Lonnie Donegan inspired, skiffle guitar chords that he was playing, without my half-beat accompaniment, to his Audrey Hepburn look-a-like girlfriend, Pauline Mallalieu, and her two inseparable companions, Jennifer and Margaret, in the front room of Tat's newly built number 34. The collision also shocked the Stockport meat-pie manufacturing heirs, Tommy Titterton and his younger brother, John, at number 17, and brought them running out of their house; saving Titterton the Younger from being dispatched to bed at nine-thirty where he would resentfully have lain awake in the sunlight listening to the sounds of activity outdoors. And the noise rousted out the tall, blond, handsome, pleasant but largely silent, Laurie Roberts, from his garage at number 29 where he'd been puzzling, mutely, over the mysteries of carburation in an old Austin Ten he was restoring.

We teenagers, representative of the hundreds of Heaton Moor, War Bulge teenagers, swiftly gathered round the wreck, still smoking and groaning as it settled. A few adults slowly approached, eyes staring in shock and wonderment as Mr Jefferies, disturbed from surreptitiously listening to the Goon Show, emerged haltingly, step by painful step from his front porch and moved as if in a bad dream towards his magnificent, now fatally injured, white craft.
****

About a mile away, as the crow flies on a south-south-west bearing, Stephen Court, slumped in his favourite, old, too small for him, upholstered chair in the windowless little room behind his mother's shoe shop on Heaton Moor Road, subliminally heard – or felt the vibes in his car-loving soul – as the beautiful, if deadly, Jaguar plunged into the heart of the boat, bringing about their mutual destruction; and his dark eyes glanced in suspicion, sideways from under his heavy brow, astonishingly, if he were to be observed, looking precisely in the direction of the crash.

Had his mood not been so dark and had he been in Cleveland Road, Stephen would have made a gruff, brief, clever comment and uttered a deep bass, throaty short laugh at the foolishness of bad drivers, and at the over-indulged, reckless Willy Mason in particular, and at the fate of all humankind. But his mood was dark and no light, no repartee, alleviated his brooding mind this night, for earlier in the day something disturbing had happened.

Stephen could read feet, or more precisely he could interpret shoes and the feet within the shoes and, by extrapolation, intuitively understand the rest of the person who was attached to the feet, and, this late afternoon, serving in the shop after school, he had encountered feet, in and out of their shoes, which had chilled his intuition to its very core.

"Mother", he had husked, sotto voce, as the unwitting customer innocently and all unawares left the shop with his new shoes boxed and wrapped in brown paper and white string, "...there is something queer about that man."

His mother, short, white haired, indomitable and rotund, shaped not unlike the late Queen Victoria in her last decade, exuded plain common sense, brains and practicality. After all, hadn't she single-handedly raised her now big-boned son and apprenticed him in the commercial ways and means of shoe manufacturers, wholesalers, sales representatives, faithful customers, children's growth spurts and toe wiggling room, repairs in leather and rubber and the black arts of double-entry bookkeeping? Yes she had. Without a husband or father ever mentioned and with a stone wall erected which barred all and any questions about the mysterious missing male, Mrs Court had kept the tiny shop going since the War and raised Stephen to be, ...well it had to be admitted, ...a bit of a young-fogey with his sensible dark grey suit draped over his large frame, sober tie, his wartime, Hitler haircut complete with collapsing fringe, and, of course, his heavy leather black brogue shoes – the shoes of a gentleman. She had brought him up as a fine young man; if a little old fashioned.

But practical and no-nonsense as she indubitably was, it was she, Mother, who had also inculcated the esoteric art of foot-prophecy into her boy. So now she took his statement seriously.

"What is he up to?" she asked confidently.

"I don't know – yet. But I'll think about it."

And it was this thinking that he was now immersed in, as the red Jaguar penetrated the white speedboat – and something died in Mr Jefferies' usually joyous, positive, if pecuniary little heart and communicated itself to the brooding shoe-shop manager.

By "queer" Stephen meant nothing with sexual overtones, though his contemporaries and he used the word, if they felt unkind, to jeer about a noticeably prancing, mincing male with a feminine voice and limp wrists, of which Manchester had a couple of notorious, self-publicised examples; but he meant it in the context of "strange" or "peculiar" or, as his mother had without question, evidence, trial, judge or jury concluded, of someone who was "up to something".

The truly great threat, which in this introspective mood Stephen could not help but devote many hours to reconsidering, was of course, as warned of in the Bible, the good book, the source of all knowledge, - we repeat – the threat was of course, The Yellow Peril. Even in the absence of a single Chinese restaurant in the whole of Stockport – or indeed anywhere in Manchester as far as he knew, and without a single sighting of a Chinaman other than western actors playing the arch-villain, Fu-Man-Chu in B movies at the Savoy Cinema, Master Stephen Court was completely certain, beyond all reasonable doubt that the prophecy was true and that the Yellow Peril would indeed engulf the Earth – and all civilisation.

But that, he nodded grimly to himself, was for later. He could foresee the time when every High Street in Britain – and perhaps throughout the world – would bristle with Chinese Emporia, and cafes and Dim-Sum breakfast bars, and drug dens, and opium parlours – and the crowded thoroughfares would be overrun with godless Orientals. And it would happen, oh it would certainly happen! – But that was for later.

Just now – and more pertinent to the thirty-odd year old, inoffensive seeming, white Englishman whose shoes had triggered Stephen's teenage instincts and made the hairs on the back of his neck stand in rigid defence – was the real and present danger of …Communism. The man; the man who needed shoes; the man who walked in a crab like fashion but so subtly that only a foot expert like Stephen could notice it; the man who came into their shop as cool as a cucumber, pretending normality; that man could be – and if the renewed prickling on his scalp was anything to go by – which it almost certainly was; that man could be a Red-under-the-Bed.

Stephen paused as his inner thought processes brought him to a conclusive understanding and knowledge with a shudder of fear. Reds were everywhere. Yes, he could be a Communist …or, perhaps, Stephen toyed for just a few seconds with the idea before dismissing it abruptly – Was he an Alien? No! even though the building of the new Astronomical Radio Telescope at Jodrell Bank, south of Alderley Edge, had attracted many, many UFO's which were reported in the local newspapers in ever increasing numbers – Stephen knew that he would know, and would know that he would know, if he were ever in the presence of an alien foot – or feet; however well disguised. No! The suspiciously-footed customer wasn't an alien.

But a Communist?

Yes! That could be it.
*****

As Stephen sat back in a far more relaxed yet still sombre mood, to contemplate the infiltration of Britain's institutions and Trade Unions by communists and their fellow-traveller sympathisers, and to list in his head all the Trade Unions which had Chapters in Stockport and Manchester – which was most of the powerful and influential Unions – to see if his new shoe buyer might fit into one or more of the niches Stephen's questing mind could imagine; a little less than a mile away in Shaw Road, behind another shop window – this one blanked out to be used as an office – a fervent non-unionist; an independent printer who resisted all communist attempts to force him into unionising his rugged one-man business – or to be forced out of the business completely – slept, despite the light evening, in preparation to starting work the next morning at 5.30am, as was his custom. He snored and slept – uncannily and frighteningly - with one eye alert and wide open.

This fiercely independent soul, with his alternating Cyclopean eye – always, to the great consternation of his family, either having both eyes open or – while asleep keeping one eye open for a time – and then the other, was the father of Goulash, our tall, willowy friend, with ginger hair, deeply nicotine stained fingers and an engaging way with words. His real name was David O'Hanlon and thus his one-eyed-at-a-time father was Mr O'Hanlon who had learned his eye-that-never-sleeps ability on active duty in the desert battles of the War. Mr O'Hanlon had been a Desert Rat serving under 'Monty', Field Marshall Montgomery, and fighting against our noble enemy, Rommel, whose chivalrous courage had won the respect of all good Britons.

Mr O'Hanlon returned after demob, learned how to set thousands of inch long lead soldiers of type into inky metal trays the size of pages – backwards in mirror writing – and to tamp them down with lead wedges and special packing, to set these in presses, which he operated by hand before switching to electricity in the late 1950's, to run off samples which he proof-read, corrected any errors, and then set up his machines with masses of black ink for multiple print runs. And he made a passable living in Heaton Moor. Colour was, of course, a whole different ball game. And while he could run to two or even three colour prints – he always tried to talk customers into the technically simpler black and white.

And the peacefully sleeping, one-eye-alert, ex-Desert Rat had taught his son, these printing skills at a young age. Goulash could set a page of type in half the time his father took. And his father was proud to have provided for his family and apprenticed and trained his heir, and thus he slept the sleep of the just; and, as attested to by his one unblinking eye, he slept the sleep of the deeply paranoid.

He would not have slept so soundly had he known that the madly racing Terry Rider, whose home was just a few hundred yards away on Elms Road, had earlier that evening driven up Shaw Road and obliged Goulash with a lift in the cab of the little Tompkin & Rider pick-up van, then crammed in another equally tall slender boy, Michael Howard from Priestnall Road, just a few minutes before he drove across Heaton Moor and encountered – for it was an utterly compelling encounter – the flamboyant driver of a flaming red chariot; the legendarily wealthy, Willy Mason; who Terry and his helpless passengers – not that they complained – simply had to challenge to a race – which as we know, but Mr O'Hanlon had no inkling of, ended in an almighty crash – for at least one and perhaps for both of the racing vehicles.

As one of the highly polished spoke-wheels from the Jaguar jigged off the crumpled, settling iron chassis to which it had been attached and rolled steadily away south-eastwards, along the new extension of Cleveland Road towards the farm that by footpaths linked this settlement with the lower end of Shaw Road, and as the incredulous residents gathered silently round the wreck, Mr O'Hanlon twitched in his bed above his printing shop and responded to the need to close his glaring right eye – and to open his freshly alert left eye; as he felt danger coming from that side. And, to a universal observer who had all the facts and knew the local geography, this peering left eye did indeed stare, just as Stephen Court had unconsciously turned to stare, – through walls and trees and posts - directly at the place where the vehicles had so violently, just a few seconds ago, collided and interpenetrated.
*****

Terry, who we may have just witnessed being fatally involved in a dreadful accident – or who we may find to have miraculously escaped, to be reborn Phoenix-like to add yet another fable to the fantastic Tales of Heaton Moor - had some months earlier come home after completing a year-and-a-half with a dishonourable discharge (for losing his tank) of two years of National Service. Terry was, by a freak of his date of birth, among the last to be Called Up to be mandatorily trained to fight for their King and Country – and he narrowly missed being lucky enough to spend some of those eighteen months actually fighting, killing and being killed in the Korean War.

As soon as he had unpacked his kit-bag at Number One Elms Road, Terry cadged some money from the First-Born, his aristocratically attired brother, Tony – which was no easy task – and, running a wet hand through his rapidly thinning hair and throwing on a stupidly expensive hand finished shirt, Terry, on foot, made straight for Lillian's Cafe.

Across the junction of Wellington Road and Heaton Moor Road, in a row of small shops variously offering meat, fashion and whale-boned undergarments for stout middle-aged ladies, bicycles, second-hand-cars, green-grocery, toy-trains and hardware, the legendary Lillian had carved out her four hundred square feet empire in what had been a haberdashers; removed the coloured cellophane, shelves, pigeon holes for wools and cottons, and removed the backing from the window, painted everything white, installed a Formica and glass counter on one wall, put a Dandelion & Burdoch plaque in the window, stuck a Vimto drink poster on the glass of the door next to an exotic American Pepsi-Cola roundel, arranged nine circular yellow Formica tables with four ex-NAAFI chairs at each, invested in nine large shiny black ashtrays advertising whisky, bought nine salt & pepper cruets, being holiday souvenirs from Llandudno and, the piéce-de-resistance – guaranteed to bring her the customers she wanted – Lillian installed a curved, illuminated, chrome and glass, 50 records capacity Juke-Box.

Lillian was indeterminably aged, in her thirties or even forties. She was calm and self-possessed, not large but not small either and she had a presence which brooked no nonsense. It was reasonable to imagine that she had had some contact with American service men during the War, which had awoken her to the emerging possibilities of American youth culture – and imbued her with the experience of dealing with groups of youngsters – and of suspending the critical attitudes about British Youth, which the vast majority of her peer group rigidly and firmly held.

Her authoritative, non-intrusive character – and the Juke-Box – drew the crowds and Lillian's was always full.

Terry had walked or slumped in, smoking of course, to welcoming cries as befitted a home-coming warrior, adulations which were cut short as the crowd was listening to and rolling around laughing at a story that an oddly stiff, tall young man, David Hall, – every bit as much of a young-fogey as Stephen Court but cast in a more vigorous and sporting style - was telling; a tale related elsewhere in this book.
****

The vibes from Cleveland Road, broadcast at wavelengths that most teenagers and a few eccentric adults could receive, spread from the impact by the dentist's house. They penetrated the walls of houses and shops, pubs and clubs causing some to shiver as they passed. "Ooo! Someone's just walked over me grave" shuddered Mrs Cowlishore; our redoubtable char-lady, office-tea-lady and unsung psychic, as the vibes passed through the tiny kitchen of her back-to-back terrace, behind the Greengrocers on Heaton Moor Road.

The vibes found Graham Fish racing down Long Hill from Buxton, as he and his powerful motorbike both screamed down towards Stockport, faster than a speeding bullet. Graham later told me and a goggle eyed crowd, of this flight down through the Peak District – and his encounter with an Austin Cambridge.

Graham on his speed trial of the five snaking miles down Long Hill to Disley village, had identified and was now reacting to, an insult which was unforgivable. Graham owed it to himself to avenge the insult. And he was, as the vibes found him on the mountainside, intent on a response.

He had set his line up for the fifth 'S' shaped hairpin out of Buxton, which coincided with the crown of a small awkward hill in the road, and was throttling back and changing down from a modest eighty-miles-an-hour to swing through the chicane at a safe forty or so, sweeping the surface with his leather-clad knees, politely ignored two creeping saloon cars, the lead one a Wolsey; the tailing one a smart new Austin Cambridge, occupied by a middle-aged and utterly respectable couple.

Graham Fish later died in a motor cycle race.

The male, driving of course, with one casual elbow on the window-sill, a cigarette in his fingers, was buttoned up in a three-piece charcoal-grey suit and the latest partially starched white collar, with an old-school or ex-military tie. She, holding on with her left hand to the passenger panic handle – not of course that her husband's excellent driving provoked any fear in her loyal and well supported bosom, girded against any risk of arousing his or any other male's flaming passions by a tweed coat up to the Lewis's silk scarf tied gaily at her throat, tightly closed over what might have been a solidly inflated Royal Lifeboat Association life-vest but was in fact her ample breast – with the whole ensemble topped off by a blue-felt hat banded in a Matta Hari scarlet, locking in her dangerously seductive auburn permanent waves – also safely concealed, Muslim like, from male view.

The long Austin, barely run-in, negotiated at a safe fifteen miles an hour, the same 'S' bend with the quick hillock as did Graham. This was unexceptional to the Screaming Fish and would barely have drawn any more of a glance than he might have spared a wandering sheep or collapsed hill walker; just one of thousands of sudden obstacles on his Isle of Man TT training run down Long Hill towards Heaton Moor.

But, as Graham expertly slipped down the oiled gears and minutely set up the line of his beautifully polished five-hundred CC Norton into the admittedly, even for Graham, difficult bends and in a split second had instinctively configured not only how to snake through the contours, deal with the loose roadside grit, narrow his eyes to counter the blinding glare of the late setting-sun as he breasted the hill and weave past the two dawdling homeward bound sightseeing cars; this driver, oblivious to any retribution he might attract, deliberately, had jinxed the swaying saloon into Graham's path and ruined what was otherwise a particularly perfect line.

This in itself could have been a mistake – and Graham was at heart a gentle soul who forgave the mistakes of clumsy and inept users of the Queen's Highway and he would have generously adjusted his speed, his gearing, his angle of attack, his entire strategy, even lost vital seconds on the stopwatch – had not the man looked back at Graham in his wing mirror – and smirked.

It was the smirk that drew Graham's full attention and triggered his sense of revengeful humour.

As the Austin's tyres squealed, even at that very low speed, on the rubber-shined asphalt, and as the man focused fiercely on navigating his canal-barge like car between dusty grass verge and a precipitous drop to his left and the steel studded, tyre wrecking cats-eyes holders right, he picked up a nerve wracking high pitched sound which made him check if steam was being forced from the car's new radiator.

He slowed even more and leaned forward to grasp the steering column mounted gear change. As he did so the noise became overwhelming and a shadow fell across him from his right, where no shadow should be. He darted a quick glance sideways – and met Graham's crazed, not entirely unfriendly, grin beaming down at him – uttering his Goon Show scream. He yelped in fear and tried to yaw sideways – but fortunately as the Austin was too slow to react – he didn't.

Graham had the appearance, not so much of a vengeful Goth, riding down fleeing peasants, but, in his wind expanded leather flying jacket, with his oiled Elvis Presley big hair and with his naturally large, wide mouthed but somewhat shortened face – wearing that awesome grimace – Graham appeared to the man – and to his wife, who was by now also screaming, but at a puny level which crept into her husband's nervous system like a surgeon's saw grating on an amputee's thigh bone – he looked like a monstrous toad astride his bike, probably poisonous, and definitely suicidal; as the two vehicles, sedate sedan and growling Norton, side by side with the motorbike in the oncoming traffic lane, drove along the twisting public highway; the driver's eyes staring, stalk and bug like.

Graham leaned the Norton even closer, blipped the throttle and drew level with the front wing; where, still grinning he calmly leaned down and tore off the car's right hand wing mirror, plucked it without visible effort from the British Leyland tin body leaving a ragged hole; the very mirror that the man had smirked in. Graham flourished the mirror in the air; turning in his saddle to smile his ever more lunatic smile at the terrified couple.

Then, suddenly, he dropped back and disappeared.

Lumbering 1958 Austin Cambridge. Its mirrors vibrated with the engine. Body rusted in 5 years.

In deep shock, the driver, seeing a straight stretch ahead and with no sign of the Norton mounted, leather clad, car-wrecking toad, pulled away – as fast as the wobbling Austin Cambridge could gain speed – which wasn't very fast at all. He checked the two remaining mirrors, one inside vibrating fast as Austin interior mirrors were, oddly, designed to do, the other, a fine chromium-plated example of British engineering, bolted onto the left wing and also vibrating in time with the engine.

But, a Manx TT ready racing bike, with five hundred cubic centimetres of cylinders and tuned by a perfectionist like Graham, needs little distance to catch up a heavy saloon car, as it strains for the next corner. The Norton effortlessly fled across the gap between them and, before the Austin squealed at low speed into the next corner, the lunatic was again upon them.

He swayed to their right, onto the wrong side of the road, then onto their left, tracking up the dry grassy verge inches from the long steep fall into the Goyt Reservoir. In another instant the giant Norton was alongside the left wing mirror, which Graham grabbed and tore it from its mountings.

The lady squealed and the man went deathly pale and almost forgot to control his car as Graham swerved from side to side in front of them, produced the other mirror from his leather jacket, waved both with a backward arm, then, at sixty miles an hour, with another straight stretch, clambered up and stood on the foot rests, and he tossed the pair over the narrow verge, to fall, and fall and fall down to the deep, threatening, slate grey waters below.

Then he vanished, in a puff of smoke. Never to be seen again; as neither had thought to note his number plate.

By the time the Austin lumbered through Whalley Bridge, ten miles from Stockport, Graham had come to rest many miles further on, in Heaton Moor Road, and the sun was going down for the night. As he cut the engine by William & Glynn's Bank, employed the stand and reached for a cigarette, Graham felt compelled to turn his face towards the late setting sun which coincidentally exactly took his gaze along a line that intersected the Jaguar riven speedboat, a mile away in Cleveland Road. And he screwed up his eyes, nose and mouth in an expression that was part smile, part lament and part puzzlement.

On the fateful, bright evening of The Cleveland Road Race, another driver, but a most careful and responsible driver, Paul, my school friend, from Fallowfield, was returning a borrowed, large Ford Consul convertible, gratefully polished and impeccably swept, and still boasting exotic GB plates for use on "The Continent", to the father of his and my long standing school friend Roger Clarke, in Queen's Drive; a mere arrow' flight due south of Cleveland Road.

As the vibes raced out from the crash site, just as Paul parked the Ford, he suddenly shivered, as he swivelled to face the exact direction of the collision. As the youngest ever manager, at seventeen, of the largest GUS furniture store, on Market Street, Manchester, Paul's precocious and concerned sense of responsibility unconsciously responded to the utterly irresponsible madness of the two racers, and so he shuddered.

In contrast to the general transport wreckage in Cleveland Road, the wholly reliable Paul ...and Roger, had driven to the South of France and back, in the borrowed car, and Paul was now returning it in better condition than he'd received it three weeks earlier. Though the travelling had been incident free – Paul had almost triggered another European war during a friendly water-polo game.
****

Within the split second of Willy slicing into Mr Jeffries' new boat, carelessly parked round the right-angled bend by his new house, Terry stamped on the brakes of his clattering, pavement mounted van, a few feet from Mr Jeffries' low, smart garden wall, protecting his new car, and, as the gods mercifully judged that the poor man had suffered enough, Terry miraculously flicked the van through the inadequate gap, round the final inconveniently sited lamp-post; bounced off the pavement onto the street, headed straight for the rear end of Willy's XK 140, buried in the white boat and silver trailer, snatched-up the handbrake very hard from under Goulash's right buttock and slewed the van sideways; screeching to a stop three inches from the mashed and mangled Jaguar.

Then Terry grinned and before his two crammed, shocked but unharmed passengers could think, he gunned the engine and made a fast exit. He and his father's trade vehicle were more than a mile away before Mr Jeffries, neighbours, youths and overly inquisitive policemen arrived to ogle at the wreckage – from which Willy, true to form, as ever, emerged unscathed, with the ash still on his Russian Sobranie cigarette and a carnation in his buttonhole. His legendarily rich father would pay the damages and hire lawyers to keep his son out of prison, free to drive on the public highways.

All the distant observers: Mr O'Hanlon, Stephen Court, Mrs Cowlishore, Graham Fish, Paul Godfrey, and even the couple in the slightly disfigured but repairable Austin Cambridge still manoeuvring down Long Hill; unconsciously relaxed and breathed sighs of relief as the Cleveland Road Race ended without loss of life – or even injury.

***

Chapter 32 - Monte Carlo Rally

Beeching the nation's most stupid and wasteful man. *1963: Railways to be slashed by a quarter - Large parts of the British railway system are uneconomic and under-used, a far-reaching report has declared. - The report, from the chairman of the British Transport Commission, Dr Richard Beeching, says only half the network's routes carry enough traffic to cover the cost of operating them.- British Rail is currently running at a loss of £140m a year, and Dr Beeching has made it his job to "make the railways pay". – "It will in some areas reduce public transport to a lower level than in the horse age" - Lord Stonham, National Council on Inland Transport*

As he rid himself of the obligation of ferrying his wife and six children, driving fast became Father's overriding passion and in nineteen-sixty-two when I was nineteen and he was forty-eight or so, Triumph fitted his two-seater TR4A with engine number one and made him leader of their rally team for the Liège-Rome-Liège Rally. Later that year he also privately entered the car, red, low and lethally quick, in the Monte-Carlo Rally that then still ran on public roads, mostly through ice and snow, from Edinburgh or London and other European capitals, across France, into the French Alps, through the cols and over the peaks, and down after three days and nights of frantic driving, without sleep, to the warmth of Monte Carlo. Of course this event required preparation and practice. The car was equipped with six additional spotlights plus

an adjustable spotlight on the roof for examining snow covered French signposts. The engine was tuned to perfection and a new copper straight-through exhaust added, to give it tone. Racks were welded on to help carry the four spare wire wheels fitted with spiked ice tyres.

This was Father's 5th or 6th entry as a private competitor and he spurned the modern, dependent, corporate idea of a support team in a van carrying all the spares they might need.

Perhaps in late latent revenge for the locked Llandudno lavatory, or more charitably, maybe stirred by a distant feeling for what other father's seemed to do with their sons, or perhaps he needed me as navigator to get the weight right, Father invited me one rare snowy evening to accompany him on a practice run. He had to use every snow and ice hour that came, to test and hone his driving skills.

We burbled menacingly out from *Balnacraig*, the large white house in Wilmslow that followed Birch House as our home, onto the deserted roads towards Alderley Edge as snow fell heavily and silently in the darkness. In the passenger seat I was confronted by technical instruments screwed roughly onto the fascia and an additional horn button – all aids to the navigator. The large red horn was to relieve the navigator's mounting tensions and terrors as the car hurtled into blind corners on sheet ice, on public roads, often with a thousand foot drop at the side. Airplane cockpit type harnesses pinned us into our seats. We turned towards Prestbury and growled through the deepening snow as all the Manchester millionaires withdrew into their mansions and turned up the heating – this was no night to be out and about. The road took us through Macclesfield and up into the narrow stony lanes of the Pennines. As we passed the last terraced cottages Father opened the throttle and fed full power into the new snow tyres, that span and spat grit and stones viciously as the rear of the car snaked and slithered and the exhaust boomed its challenge to all comers.

Father's TR4, flipped near Monte-Carlo. His only rally-car accident. Triumph rebuilt the car.

I pitied the would-be navigator who would sit in this madly bucking seat for three days, inside the protective steel cage welded under the roof, all the way to Monte Carlo, head buried in maps and shouting warnings of what twists and dangers the road ahead presented. We shot up the narrow main road towards Whalley Bridge, slipping and sliding into hairpin bends at sixty miles an hour to skid through them sideways, wheels on opposite-lock, relying on the power of the engine to the rear wheels to thrust the car forward in the right direction at the correct split second, and to avoid cannoning into the murderous black rocks flanking the road. Exciting stuff on the main road but far too easy for Father. At the Highwayman Inn, lighted but closed-up and deserted, we turned off into narrow lanes, past the stone inscribed with the mystery of the death of a faithless husband, and scrambled and scraped at dizzying speed through the lanes towards the forbidding and mournful Goyt Valley and its vast, deep black reservoir, as the snow fell ever faster. Now the spotlights came into their own. On a good straight the TR4A could rocket up to seventy or eighty miles an hour making it important to be able to see at least a little way ahead. Brakes were of course completely useless at those speeds; the driver had to rely on rapid gear down-shifts and screaming deceleration to reduce to speeds where we stood the slightest chance of chewing the car through the next unsympathetic bend. The eight lights streamed ahead of us into the snow laden air, forging a fabulous white, glowing, dreamlike tunnel through the black night; a tunnel that we fell down, faster and ever faster. Father, hands in his lap, spun the steering wheel from below at an impossible rate, passing it through his dancing fingers. *'Never, never, never cross your hands when you are driving'*. He advised his absent audience and whoever happened to be in the car at the time.

Not all of that part of the Pennines is uninhabited. There are remote hamlets, lonely farms and gaunt isolated houses with immovable rusted gates set into unwelcoming stone, blackened by the industrial revolution. The taciturn and hill toughened locals mostly have the wisdom to lock their doors and stay off the roads in snowstorms. But sometimes, just sometimes, they have to venture forth. Thus it was, as we thundered down to Wild Boar Clough, through a snow tunnel on one of the rare straight stretches, at eighty miles an hour, with eight headlights searing through the snow tunnel, with the narrow lane reduced to less than a single track by new snow banked down from the walls, banked over the rocks and spread blanket like on the verges, that the local district nurse, out on an errand of mercy, nervously steered her black Morris Minor 1000 through a right angled bend in the snowy night and came face-to-face with us at the bottom of our straight run. Our six spotlights and the two headlights were all full on. As we plummeted towards her, every minute feature of herself and her car's interior was blindingly illuminated. She was driving, sensibly, at about five miles an hour, we were plummeting down at her at eighty miles an hour and behind her was an unforgiving, craggy rock-face that marked the tight bend that she had, a moment ago and a lifetime away, so carefully negotiated, little suspecting that within a split second she would be in the limelight and facing total annihilation.

I knew that our time had come and was able to reflect briefly on my short life and its adventurous end. I could hear Stephen Court, my long headed, fatherless, young-fogey friend who owned the shoe-shop on Heaton Moor Road and who warned us constantly of the apocalyptic Yellow Peril that would soon invade the district and who greatly admired Father's driving, breathing in his hushed slow baritone, *'Magnificent'* as they untangled the tortured red metal and chrome lights from the Triumph embedded in the staid black metal of the Morris, and tried to reconstruct the deconstructed people. I dispassionately noted the hairs on the mole on the District Nurse's completely startled face, the minor red veins in her popping blue eyes and the wording on her jaunty little hat. The phrase *'Rabbit in the headlights'* came easily to mind. She in her turn could see nothing. She was blinded by the light and transfixed by panic. Instinctively, and some might say, intelligently, the District Nurse stopped her car in the middle of the snowbound lane.

Father, hands flying from steering wheel to light switches to gear stick, feet tap-dancing back and forth to effect a double de-clutch, feather the brakes and modulate the accelerator, muttered "Bloody Fool." at the hapless nurse, flipped the red missile, TR4A, engine number one, up the snow bank on our left, on my side of the track, at a forty-five degree angle, where the ground miraculously held firm, around the paralysed Morris Minor and its briefly illuminated woman driver and down again into the roadway with just enough time and space, about forty yards, to get the hurtling vehicle into a sideways drift at ever reducing velocity, into the right-angle of the bend, from where we screamed out again in second gear, full power to the bucking and slithering back wheels, to regain the speed the bloody fool of a nurse, now plunged back into total darkness and undoubtedly composing a UFO report, had lost us by freezing-up in the middle of the track at such a crucial moment.

Edwin Hodson's 1962 TR4 – restored by David Stanley in 2015.

"You're in luck lads-the Bench are all rally-drivers who don't approve of the 70 m.p.h. maximum." Dec 30th '65

Father refused to try people exceeding the new 70 mph limit. He predicted it would cause motorway pile-ups.

On a racecourse, such as at Oulton Park, her obstruction could have cost a split-second - and the winner's laurels.
"If only..." Father might say,
"...if only people would learn to drive properly before they took to the Queen's highways, the world would be a better, happier and a safer place."

Some years later, as a Justice of the Peace on the Bench, to Mother's eternal embarrassment, Father enjoyed a moment of infamy. He was interviewed on TV by the fearsome, merciless intellectual Bernard Levin, and was caricatured in the Daily Express by the famous cartoonist Giles, for refusing to try motorists who exceeded the new seventy-miles-an-hour speed limit; on the logical grounds that if everyone drove at that same low speed, they would lose concentration, drive in convoys and it would cause Motorway pile-ups, killing God only knows how many district nurses in the ensuing chaos. And who, apart from Bernard Levin, in the light of subsequent events, could assert that he was wrong? - a prophet in his own time and country. And we, the loyal family even including Mother, after full consideration, concluded that Bernard Levin had at last met his match.

***

The Cat & Fiddle

My first car, which I bought for a few pounds, was an old and tired Ford Popular. Its engine was so small and weak that I had to use reverse gear, the lowest gear, to get up steep hills. But it gave me the freedom of the roads, even if it was confined to the flat lands of Stockport.

Then came a heavily built, rusting, grumbling Singer, with the gear stick on the steering column – which could be revved up noisily to give me an impression of speed.

Next I bought a Renault Dauphin, from Jeffrey Osborne who later owned car dealerships; the Dauphin was so rusty, under a thick coat of paint, that it split in half and stretched a few inches – disconnecting the engine from the gear-train. Jeff gave me my money back.

As office manager at Edwin Hodson Sons and Co. part of my pay-package was a new, neat little red and white Triumph Herald, which doubled as Mother's car – though she couldn't drive and only learned a few years later. Her worst learner moment was setting off at traffic lights – in reverse; colliding with a very surprised motorist. She did eventually pass her driving test and got her first ever bank account that same year.

But between Pauline's return from New Zealand and her emigrating to Connecticut, Father taught her to drive – and pass her test – in the Triumph.

Driven fast, for example on our unofficial time trials on the notorious Cat & Fiddle road across the Pennines, the Triumph tended to bounce into the air on bumpy surfaces and tuck its wheels under itself, due to novel suspension; which was unsettling. On one such bounce, at full pelt, as the car hit the ground, on a sharp bend, the body twisted, the passenger door burst open and my passenger, Paul Godfrey, was thrown out towards a nasty, hard dry-stone wall and some alarmed sheep. He was saved, and punched back in to the car unharmed, as the door hit some low rocks; we did not of course have safety belts – in those days. Paul didn't join our time trials again. Steve Court, our shoe-shop friend, who was a keen amateur rally-car enthusiast, oddly bought a VW Beetle to race around in. Its fast revving, breathless air-cooled engine was in the back; so to compensate, Steve loaded sand-bags into the front – which did seem to make the car stick to the road. And his VW did often beat my Triumph over the Cat & Fiddle from Macclesfield to Buxton.

The tiny cockpit of the Triumph Coupe was not at all convenient for in-car romance in dark lay-bys, where passionately experimenting couples could – and did get wedged, in the dark, trapped and immobilised between harsh racing-seats, the tiny sloping rear window and the unavoidable, rudely and intimately intrusive, gear stick and hand-brake. Love and lust were, by necessity, replaced by frantic sessions of contortionism and escapology.

I swapped the Coupe for a Triumph Herald Van, needed as a family luggage carrier, to follow Father's fast saloon to a holiday near Rome – when I had two nearly fatal road accidents, on the fiendish, twisting La Spezia road, trying to keep up with one of the UK's faster rally-drivers. Later I swapped that for a Mini-Van - vans being 1/3rd cheaper than cars - and in which couples could recline in some dignity and comfort. Some desperate, frustrated youths carried airbeds in their cars; which had to be concealed from inquisitive parents and required more brass-neck and stronger lungs than mine, to inflate – under a harvest moon, without losing the romantic moment.

My Gold Renault-Dauphin-Gordini
Fast & Quirky.

The car I loved most was my gold Renault Dauphin Gordini; rare, fast and quirky. In secret, for my wedding-day, Father swapped it for a new Fiat 500, which struggled to get up to 50 mph, downhill, with a following wind, and I often had to push-start. Thus, with this generous gift, he disempowered me; at the start of our honeymoon. One down, only five more kids to compete with.

The underpowered Fiat 500 Noddy-Car That Father swapped for my Gordini. For our honeymoon journey.

Chapter 33 - Astral Travel

Essential Guide - Astral projection is something that can be learned. - While the amount of effort to reach a lucid out-of-body experience can change from person to person, a bit of theory and selecting the right approach can make a world of difference. - This article is divided in 3 sections: the process, tips to help you get started and an overall look at the benefits that the OBE entails. - THE PROCESS - Out of Body Experience for Beginners in 3 Steps - When trying to explain how to astral project for beginners, I usually summarize the process in three steps:
1) you need to take off
2) you need to manage to stay lucid while out
3) you need to recall the experience once you go back to the physical body
UKiac.org

1960

Richard Hodson
Of
Mauldeth Road

Sylvia Williams
Of
Priestnall Road

Richard, aged just twenty, had married Sylvia, the girl almost next door, leaving me for the first time in my life, in 1960, with my own bedroom at Birch House. I was seeing both blonde Susan, a jazz band singer, and dark-eyed Anne at the time – for a short time before striking up a long friendship with Susan; Susan because she was not only attractive and clever but I was also very, very fond of her; and I dated Anne, a beautiful professional design artist, who I found very,

very sexy. These more often than not frustrated and unfulfilled opportunities for pre-nuptial intercourse didn't wholly calm my irrepressible libido and I might return home and indulge in the Mortal Sin of Onan, (n.b. we have established that that's not with animals), at least doubling if not trebling the threat to my immortal Catholic soul.

Mortal sins are acts that are so heinous, so horrific in the eyes of God that you can actually kill off your immortal soul by doing them. Doesn't seem logical I know; and it seems to be a contradiction in terms, but Catholics believe that Immortal Souls can be nuked by Mortal Sins. As you would expect in a religion dominated by zealous celibates, sex heads the list of these killer sins, of course, just a little ahead of eating meat on Fridays and denying that the Earth is at the centre of the universe.

I had come home late from Susan's house in an unusually untrammelled frame of mind and I finished off one of a series of esoteric Tibetan books, written by T Lobsang Rampa, before going to sleep.

This book, The Third Eye, explained in great detail how one could perform a relaxing meditation, so profound, that the life-force, the soul or essence could rise out of the body and travel …anywhere. I decided to give it a go.

It was a warm night, even in Manchester, so the large sash bedroom window was open, as were the curtains. I decided to take the risk of losing my entire life-force, as in astral-travel there is always a risk of severing the spiritual umbilical cord and wandering the universe as a lost ghost for eternity.

It was some years later that I discovered that T Lobsang Rampa was or had been in fact a Liverpudlian bus driver, which is not a banned occupation for high ranking Tibetan monks, but, had I known it at the time, I may have assumed that he wasn't Tibetan at all, which might have reduced my confidence in his instructions; which involved me putting my life on the line so as to speak – on his say so – extending my lifeline to infinity and beyond. Fortunately, that night I trusted his careful authorship, authority and intent.

The book had given a blow by blow, step by step account and I lay flat as instructed and relaxed my body, muscle by muscle, as instructed, and then started on the process of emptying my mind, as instructed. With my supra-relaxed body feeling as if it was sinking through the bed, I imagined the blackboard at school – an empty blackboard. Every time a stray thought meandered across the blackboard, I rubbed it out, leaving the blackboard entirely black. All of a sudden – or suddenly – as my English teacher preferred it written - I felt the psychic jolt that preceded my soul leaving the body. Any nervous jump at this point and the whole exercise would be ruined. But I was steadfast and courageous and was rewarded by my soul, my life force, drifting up to the ceiling above the bed from where, as instructed, I turned and viewed the prone body lying in deepest relaxation below. *So far so good.*

This was my first ever and only out-of-body experience, but those of you who are old hands at astral-travel will know that once freed from the earthly flesh, the soul, or astral-body, can travel anywhere in the universe and transcend any time frame. The Universe was my oyster. I could soar into the clouds. I could flow to Mars and Saturn and Venus. I could traverse the vast distances to other galaxies in seconds.

So, I decided I would go to Susan's.

She lived just two or three miles away as the crow or the astral-body flies. I manoeuvred myself out of the window with ease and with very great pleasure at being able to fly. I drifted up the house until I could see the detail of the roof. I set a course and bobbed lazily across Heaton Mersey, over Heaton Moor, marvelling at the detail and new sights I saw from that height and then gently down to Susan's semi. It was late and the house was closed up and asleep. The book had given no instructions about such situations, it assumed communion with other astral-travellers but none were about, so I had to improvise. I drifted to Susan's bedroom window, knocked politely, in a soft immaterial fashion and thoughtfully said...
"Don't be frightened it's only me."

…before realising that if she did open the curtains and saw me floating there it could be truly terrifying – as Susan knew nothing of the T. Lobsang Rampa book.

So I drifted down to the glazed front door and knocked softly on the frosted glass. Within moments I saw Susan come to the top of the stairs in her nightdress. She peered uncertainly down at the door, with the street light shining in – and through me – then she turned and fled back to her room. This was not as easy as I had thought. I returned home in an instant, to think things through. Still floating, I decided I was being too cautious. I could go anywhere, anyplace, anytime and here I was bothering Susan. I was also still in love with Pauline who had gone to live in America years before. I made ready for an Atlantic crossing, but at that moment the Universe intervened and I fell into a deep and refreshing sleep.

Next day it was easy to assume the night's happenings had been the work of an over-active imagination. I said nothing. And that evening I called at about seven o'clock at Susan's. Her mother came to the door in her inevitable twin-set and pearls, looking worried.
"I'm afraid Susan isn't very well – and she's asleep." she told me.
"She heard somebody outside the house last night; somebody who said 'Its only me, don't be frightened' and then she heard them at the front door – so she went onto the landing to look, but though she heard somebody tapping on the glass, she couldn't see anyone. She got very spooked and sat up all night on her bed wrapped in a blanket. I'm sure she'll be fine tomorrow."
I kept my counsel and went about my business.
This is a true story.

But astral-travelling was not a miraculous and life changing event, according to my therapist and according to me.

The first miracle that saved me from Mother and the family was, despite the life threatening early betrayal, falling in love with Pauline.

Pauline Mallalieu aged 15.
Portrait by Graham Chadwick
Summer 1958

Pauline was and is slender and very neat. I was thin but still thought of myself as a robust rugby prop-forward, the ulcers being an unreal or temporary part of my make-up, and I was of untidy habit. But Pauline was born thin, just three months after I had been born, in the War while her father was away fighting with the Ghurkhas, and she never put on weight. She also looked uncannily like Audrey Hepburn.

As I reported earlier in this book, my good friend Peter Tattersall, Tats, who in adult life achieved national fame by composing and recording at his Stockport Strawberry Studios, *'Grandma We Love You'* with the Saint Winifred's School Choir, was going out with Pauline. We were all fifteen. Tats foolishly went on holiday and asked me, in the uncertainties of local teenage life, to keep an eye out for Pauline. I nobly did that and invited her to a party we had at Birch House and walked her home afterwards.

This was the evening when I fell in love and I heard music and saw rainbows; of which I was sensibly suspicious. So I said and did nothing. I made no move, drank my tea politely and went home.

Richard must have been away as I then sat up for hours in the bedroom writing to Pauline. I was very smitten and hopelessly in love.

Tats returned and rapidly moved on to another girlfriend and after a few months Pauline and I started courting, spending every possible minute with each other. I turned sixteen and left school the next summer and, in the absence of any better advice, Pauline and I went hand in hand together to the Labour Exchange in Stockport to start my job hunt. The Labour Exchange sent me for interviews in Trafford Park, Salford, then the largest industrial estate in Europe, where residents enjoyed a life expectancy of thirty-eight; where I became an apprentice structural engineer and started work. Tragedy was however looming. Pauline's father had left for America and Pauline's mother was alone. Her father, Pauline's grandfather, the indomitable trouble-up-at-th'mill Harold Bailey, decided they should sell their house and go and live with Pauline's Aunt and Uncle in Auckland, New Zealand. As they left to go by ship to the utterly inaccessible other side of the world, I wept for several days and nights, wandering the highways and byways where I could be alone to grieve; to the silent consternation of the chain-smoking engineers in Trafford Park when I turned up for work looking swollen faced and distinctly odd.

So after a few short weeks of the purest love, even by Catholic standards, Pauline sailed out of my life, forever it seemed. But I wrote; first to every port of call on their voyage, then daily to her in New Zealand – and she replied daily. So love, the Royal Mail and my compositions defeated all and Pauline and her mother came home after six months, again by boat. Pauline was courted by any number of exotic young men on the ship, was proposed to by the ship's bursar, a Roman, and came back utterly changed, grown up, a world traveller.

As a gesture of universal justice, as I had taken her from Tats, she ditched me for my closest friend, Peter-John, and after just a few months in England, went with her mother to join her father in the equally inaccessible America, hotly pursued by the loyal Peter-John. I was betrayed and desolate. I spent the next few-months, when not at work, having taken a temporary job in Father's office, in the empty attics of Birch House.

In a big house and a big family, it is easy to slip away after Tea, at seven-thirty and let everyone assume that you've gone out to join the scene, on the streets or at friends' homes or in the burgeoning fashionable coffee-bars – Yes, even in Stockport. This was the revival, after a decade of post War depression, of teenage power and we pretty well did what we wanted.

I didn't go out – for a time. I crept up to the still empty attics and spent many months, every night, well into the dark hours, in the long back attic, approached through two doors that could be locked. It had a window that looked sixty feet down an uninterrupted brick wall to a concrete apron below. I was silent and without feeling, almost catatonic, but it is a testimony to life or to cowardice that however often I contemplated the jump – I couldn't do it. The intelligence of the body is usually very reliable. When the intellect is telling you life is hopeless, when your emotions are saying, give up, that it is all over, let the body take over and its deeper, older, faster intelligence will see you right.

Eventually, I went out again, driven by teenage testosterone that could even suppress my acute social-phobia, and I joined the party.

Heaton Moor was overflowing with teenagers and every weekend some innocent, unsuspecting parents were foolish enough to take a break by the sea or a similar retreat, leaving their homes open to the abuse that only a gang of cider drinking, rock and rolling, Elvis inspired, sexually experimenting, overpaid teenagers, with their vinyl disks and multi-stacked electric record players, could heap upon those solid Victorian and Edwardian villas. Most homes survived the onslaught but many a post-mortem was held involving skilled and unrelenting cross-examinations, becoming particularly heated over unmentionable stains found on brightly coloured Candlewick bedspreads; coitus-interruptus still being the most common form of prevention for Protestants and Catholics alike, in a nation where contraceptives were bought at huge cost only by premeditated lechers in dirty raincoats, from seedy barber's shops.

One fabled party giver was of course, Willy Mason, who we've met before, writing off expensive cars, smashing into speed boats and being cheated by card-sharps; whose family occupied the very large half-timbered Edwardian house on the corner of Mauldeth Road and Priestnall Road, catty-cornerwise to Fylde Lodge School.

Willy was indeed amazingly rich and astonishingly thin – but his style completely contradicted the fashionable wisdom of Wallace Simpson that "you can never be too rich or too thin – darling". Willy was too thin – or too tall, or both. But he was cool.

Before his father's activities in acquiring and disposing of bankrupt bakeries made it possible for them to quit Heaton Moor and Manchester and to move to a private estate in Wales, Willy had some great open-house parties that all the teenagers in the district and from far beyond were drawn to, like moths and butterflies around a bright, noisy flame.

At the weekly parties, I met lovely Susan and Anne and other girlfriends. And, a year or two later, I found T Lobsang Rampa and his Astral Travel instructions.

Shortly after my aborted astral-travel trip across the Atlantic and several years since I had heard from Pauline or of her – Peter-John lasting just a few months in America and having returned empty handed years earlier – Pauline suddenly turned up in Manchester and phoned me. Now I don't ask you to even start to contemplate that I had somehow made astral-contact that night when I thought I had fallen into a deep sleep, but here she was, a fashion model of sorts in New York, still looking like Audrey Hepburn but with an American well fed bloom to her, now formally engaged to a wealthy Yale graduate and about to get married.

She took a vow of poverty, ditched the Yale man, went back to America to pack her things and came home to join me on twelve pounds a week in Heaton Moor, where she quickly won back her natural slenderness on a low protein northern diet. There are few lifestyles on the planet that compare favourably with living in a damp bed-sit in Heaton Moor; not if you properly analyse all the factors. And that, according to David Holt my Jungian therapist in Oxford, was the first rescue event in my life. I think the next major magical influences in my life came from my Jewish friends.

***

Chapter 34 - Drink & Be Merry

Fans of booze and/or history may know a few things about gin's past. One being that the gin craze raged in London between 1720 and 1751, during which time adults would drink an average of half a pint of gin a day. The gin consumption of the average child wasn't far off this either. Internet item.

1950's Heaton Moor Photographs by Lee Chadwick

Lee Chadwick, and his younger sister Barylin, lived on the other side of Heaton Moor Park from the Rider's ever-open house. The Chadwicks were an intellectual, left wing family, albeit who went into business as publicans and restaurateurs, who could read and write - surrounded by self-made, self-employed, unconscious, unthinking right wing business families, who thought and wrote as little as possible – and who naturally voted for The Conservatives.

I was seventeen going on eighteen when in 1960 the twenty-one-year-old rascal, Terry Rider, dated young Barylin, who was only fifteen or so, and introduced her to our crowd – who mostly lived to the west of Heaton Moor Park. The Chadwicks lived on the east side, as did many of their friends. Terry infamously "borrowed" money from Barilyn, who imagined she loved the man, and when after some months she pressed him to pay it back, he squirmed and wriggled and eventually said "I've spent it all, you daft bird!" which ended their unevenly aged and unbalanced relationship. Terry never did pay up.

But in the process, I met Barilyn and older brother Lee, and was invited to A Party at his home. A party was usually fuelled by large bottles of Bulmer's Cider which was, for apple juice, surprisingly alcoholic. As we became more sophisticated the cider became dryer and stronger; at about seventeen, most teenagers migrated to beer, locally brewed bitter that we bought in small barrels.

But Lee's party was an unforgettable night in my life because in the first half-hour another guest gave me a tumbler half-full of gin – a clear perfumed liquid I had never before encountered – and encouraged me to down it in one; which I bravely did. Within minutes I collapsed, conveniently behind a long sofa next to a wall, and thus concealed, lay flat on my back paralysed, unable to move or speak, but able to see and hear quite clearly. After about three hours, normal service was resumed; I rose like Lazarus from the dead and joined the party – meeting Angela Crook and Sandra Dodgeson – who later joined us on a blind-date. I didn't touch gin again for about thirty years.

Noel – aged 17 by Lee Chadwick

Perhaps to compensate me for that alcohol-near-death experience at his home – Lee, an accomplished photographer, took and gave me a set of portraits – with my Elvis-homage rakishly swept back hair – pictures that I sent in a letter to Pauline, who had returned from six-months banishment in New Zealand, briefly lived again in Heaton Moor, dumped me for Peter-John and abruptly emigrated to Connecticut – to join her parents. Peter-John had pursued her to the USA but could not compete with her new, rich, Long Island, sophisticated Ivy League friends and returned a few months later.

This left the question of Pauline's and my Romeo and Juliet unresolved affair. But even Lee's great artifice and skills couldn't make a silk purse out of a spotty angst ridden teenager – and on her receiving my portraits, our correspondence ceased, for several years.

Chapter 35 - Cona Coffee Bar

1963: Profumo resigns over sex scandal - Secretary of State for War, John Profumo, has resigned from government, admitting he lied to Parliament about his relationship with a call girl. - Prime Minister Harold Macmillan accepted the resignation calling it a "great tragedy". - Profumo, 48, made a personal statement to the House of Commons on 22 March in which he admitted being misleading about his relationship with 21-year-old call girl Christine Keeler.

In 1961 I was eighteen and was the precocious, unqualified office manager of my father's accountancy practice, which we had relocated to York Street just off Piccadilly. Richard joined the firm that year and we shared a room; me working long hard hours for £12 a week, Richard gambling all and every day on horse races, being banned from two city centre bookmakers for winning too often, and later in the commodity markets, especially in Cocoa beans – winning and losing a year's salary in a few minutes, by phone; which was most distracting for me and the other humble, humdrum wage earning staff.

It was the year of The Profumo Affair, a sex and spy scandal which gripped the imagination of all real males – and most females also. The two girls who had been paid to attend sex-parties with John Profumo

MP, Defence Secretary, at stately homes in the shires and in London, Christine Keeler and Mandy Rice-Davies, were photo fodder for all British newspapers for months; arousing fantasies of all sorts of exciting and libidinous goings-on. The saga involved Russian Naval Attaches (spies), London fashionable glitterati, government-fixed judges and court cases – and ultimately the suicide of Stephen Ward, the establishment's patsy – who in 1963 after years of rigged court cases took the fall for the whole rotten, but endlessly stimulating, mess.

Though memory is now dim, I know that I fancied one of the many girls who flitted and fluttered around the wealthy, tall, dark and handsome Barry in the Cona Coffee Bar, set in a cellar off Albert Square in central Manchester, that we both frequented at lunch times as a brief escape from our respective fathers' small businesses in the city centre; Barry's dad was in textiles, mine was an accountant. He and I were the same age. There the similarities ended.

One of the less obvious qualities of all the Jewish friends I have is that they are all, without exception, among the ten percent of the nation who can count accurately. It is a scientifically true factoid that 90% of people blank out, as I did at my Eleven-Plus exam, when faced with a page of numbers. This may account, as we are here accounting, for the legendary success in business of Jewish families. It is a distinct advantage to be able to read, to write and, marvel heaped upon marvel, to be able to count.

Maybe it was my recently hard-won skill in and appreciation of counting, painfully gained in my father's accountancy practice that attracted me to Barry, a Jewish lad, who almost certainly had been born with a natural talent for arithmetic. But, far, far more likely than a shared ability to count, the chaotic attractor was most likely to have been, yet again, sex. Not that I fancied Barry; not that Barry was not fanciable; I'm sure he was – to most women. But I have remained stubbornly heterosexual all my brief life. Next lifetime I may try the same gender stuff.

Barry was, and remains, tall, fashionable, sophisticated, well educated, dark, wealthy, handsome and a born presenter. Barry was a limelighter, perfectly at home in any spotlight, with any audience, at any time. I was his opposite in every conceivable way being short, fair, homely and mute. He also boasted a floor length black scarf and owned a fabulously theatrical, yet discreet, consumptive cough, that, if you hadn't watched him subsequently add on many decades in robust health, as I have, you might have unwittingly joined the many sympathetic females who swooningly imagined that he was handsomely, tragically and compellingly expiring, with all the dignity and grace of an operatic hero. Honest girls – he wasn't; he really wasn't.

But for some inexplicable reason we talked and we clicked. Soon an astonishing coincidence emerged that I can only ascribe to the astral-travel I had experienced thanks to T Lobsang Rampa – or perhaps more prosaically, to stick to the arithmetical theme of this chapter, to the "Only Two-Handshakes From-The President" statistical syndrome.

Barry's most admired and radical childhood friend, Tony, was engaged to a beautiful girl, Hazel, who hailed from Offerton, Stockport. I had once had a girlfriend in Offerton, but that wasn't the coincidence – not by a long way. Hazel was a fashion model. Like prize fighting was for black-men trapped in the ghettos, so in the Fifties becoming a fashion model was a route out of obscurity for under-educated trapped females – whose only alternative was to become a "housewife" and to take to breeding in the suburbs.

Hazel, at that time, was in America. Who, you might ask, out of the two hundred and fifty million people living in America, was Hazel staying with that week, the week I first talked with Barry? She was staying with my long ago vanished, first and only love, Pauline.

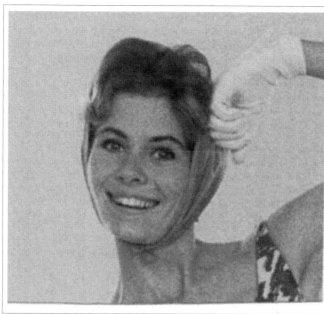

Pauline. Working as a fashion model, aged 17 in 1960

Pauline and Hazel had never met in England and had their first encounter in Connecticut just about the time that Barry and I met in Manchester, England. Jung could have penned another three massive volumes about the synchronicity of these amazing events, had he but been alive. Einstein would have dismissed it as an inevitable coincidence that I had highlighted from among the other fifty-million incredible coincidences that occurred on the same day and that occur every day of the year – and that slip by unnoticed; and he would affirm his belief, against the sage analysis of T.Lobsang Rampa that there can be no action at a distance. But what weight can we award to Einstein's conclusions, compared to the demonstrable wisdom of a Buddhist, Liverpudlian bus driver.

And so, on the strength of this coincidence, we talked some more and became firm friends. Mother, who held strong opinions on everything, was not anti-Semitic as many of the primitive Manchester people from her background were. On the contrary she excoriated The Church and the Infallible Pope at great risk to her own immortal soul for not helping, and as we slowly learned, for deliberately endangering European Jews during the Holocaust. I had grown up, as we all had, with the terrible shadow of that slaughter of the innocents darkening our developing minds. Through my embarrassed, red, glowing, perspiring hazes, I had several times raised the issue in religious studies, putting a pointed question and a double-bind for the Catholic

God's ethics, without any satisfactory answer, other than the stock phrase, inevitably delivered in a broad Irish accent "Ah! 'Tis a holy mystery of Faith;" … and you'd better believe it. A few million Jews here or there didn't seem to matter much with the Catholic clergy or laity. Forming my judgements of the Church leaders, I added their psychopathic attitudes about the Holocaust to their odd belief that the Sun orbits the Earth, and the scales of judgement and credibility dipped yet further away from Catholic congregational insanity to favour individual balance. Father had many Jewish clients and as usual had no opinions. So, I had no prejudices to overcome as Barry and I met more often and exchanged news. What intrigued me more and more as I got to know this street-wise city networker, was the odd fact; odd in the same way I had found our neighbours, Dr and Dr Sykes, rather odd, that Barry's parents obviously and demonstrably liked him.

"What's not to like" Barry would have shrugged expressively, dismissively, fashionably and with all due modesty.

What I meant is that his parents and his extended family, liked him as a person. They wished him well. They were Barry's well-wishers. My family experience was exactly the opposite. If any member did something "good", if we achieved something – anything, or especially wanted to do or have or make or win something, the event or ambition was derided, obstructed or totally annihilated by being ignored. We six children, or at least the first four, were reared in a distinctly hostile environment. Compared to the Jewish children I came to know, we were roundly, fully and utterly disliked by our parents. It must be an English thing – hostility to one's own children. Add in the Viking heritage where weedy babies were ducked in freezing mountain streams to kill or cure; then add the Catholic contribution of never touching anyone – particularly your own children so as not to disturb dormant paedophiliac tendencies that lurk in every holy celibate fibre of our beings; and add the Catholic fact that all children are born damned by Original Sin and are therefore inherently evil, and the result is very strange. The result is distinctly hostile and is bloody confusing for the average psyche, best dealt with, as happened to an Oxford neighbour of ours when he was just five years old, by despatching the suspect children off to boarding school (with their wilful tempting looks - as one of the UK's controversial judges so well judged - as he dismissed charges against a gang of vicious paedophiles who had obviously been seduced by a small child against their wills and best intentions).

"Goodbye little chap. Here's your suitcase. Mr Grimly Slasher, your headmaster will meet you off the train. If you need anything, write to us – it only takes four weeks for a letter. Don't blub boy; and we'll see you when you are eighteen."

At which stage and age they are groomed for high office and power in the British Establishment to pass on to the general population the abuse they've endured and have come to accept as normal.

The undefeated, suicidal crack troops and bodyguards of Scandinavian nobles, the Berserkers, were trained in a similar way; being selected only from the best candidates, then trained hard and flogged cruelly and regularly on the one hand but awarded the highest of privileges and power on the other; to make very special, totally self-deluding, violent utter loonies – a training method adapted and adopted by British ruling class parents as the foundation of our Great Empire.

So, over many years, through Barry I came to know that sane, intelligent families liked their own children and wanted them to succeed.

Barry introduced me to John Hamwee, a little more than half Barry's height, who bobbed rapidly down into the Cona Coffee Bar one lunch time, on his way to or from Oxford, looking more like Woody Allen than Woody Allen, seeking an advance copy of *Mellow Yellow,* a record that I, non-shopper and non-traveller that I was, airily brought back from New York just a few weeks later, as if I crossed The Pond to buy new record releases every other day. John's life has threaded and intertwined with ours in significant and helpful ways forever after.

"Goin' down the alley wiv' the school…"

Barry's father, Wilf, was the driving force behind charities set up to resuscitate Manchester's dilapidated and failing theatres. I was the family's guest at a concert staring the genius David Oistrakh, brilliantly playing Beethoven's violin concerto, with The Halle Orchestra. It was the first concert I had ever attended and it blew open my mind. It also at last illuminated for me a previously incomprehensible sentence – in my family's mute tradition, yet another never discussed, misunderstood, unquestioned utterance – this one by our fifteen-year old office boy, who, like Father had been inadequately educated in Gorton, who told us "We went down the alley wiv' the school; at the Free Trade Hall". The alley was of course The Halle Orchestra. I first "went down the alley wiv Barry's family."

Barry took us to London. Pauline, unable to resist my Giacometti style body, (she only married me for my body) my wholly unwelcome and accidental anti-capital status, my twelve pounds a week income and the heroically borne indigestion pain that crossed my gaunt face every few hours, rejected America and flew on a Comet BOAC airliner into Ringway Airport, walked across the tarmac, and decided to marry me. So "I" became "we" and as we saw so much of Barry, the "we" became "three" and sometimes "four" when Barry brought one or another of his exotic girlfriends, such as the gorgeous Mirelle from Paris, to Pauline's ill-equipped and unheated flat in Heaton Moor.

It happened that Father that month was in the Monte-Carlo Rally and that this year the UK entrants were to start from London, from Chelsea Barracks. Barry, of course, knew London intimately. In fact, I believed it to be more than likely that London could not exist without Barry's patronage. I had, despite rumours to the contrary, been to London – to the Earl's Court Motor Show actually, twice in fact, and so had Pauline. But we certainly could not boast of the familiarity and to owning the keys to the City that Barry could, with good reason, claim for himself.

Inevitably, Barry had a-la-mode friends in a basement, sorry, Garden, flat in central London. These were the pre-dawn days of beards, beads, flares, flower-power, singing *"I'm just sitting watching flowers in the rain",* Beatles and the coming of Bob Dylan. And Barry could and often did, without warning, utter short gruffly melodious snatches of the most collectible and memorable lines of new music, delivered in perfect synchronisation with the merest yet exquisitely unpractised flicks, bends, gestures and philosophical scowls from arm, knee, foot, neck, shoulders and face as appropriate that would only be possible and might only carry the depths of message and meaning that they did carry, when performed by a six-foot-three, eleven stone, black garbed fashion icon, such as Barry. In fact, "such as" is not permitted here – it had to be Barry or no one. None other would do.

We arrived late at night and crept into the hallowed semi-basement apartment without meeting our hosts and slept on damp mattresses on the floor.
Late, late the next morning after breakfasting on black coffee and a strange mixture of seeds, grains and raisins called muesli that impressed me not at all but we were far too unfashionable to allow ourselves to comment, we were informed that the hosts, Dave and Angie, were awake and ready to receive us. Barry looked serious. What had he done, what mortal blow to his image might we represent. Dave

and Angie were serious, professionally fashionable people. He glowered down at us from his full dark six-feet-three inches.

"Now don't..." he warned us heavily, leaving no room at all for quips or smart retorts,

"...Don't go in there looking all wide eyed and provincial."

Dave and Angie were, years before John Lennon and Yoko Ono ever thought of it, receiving guests in bed. They were artists and actors and intellectuals. They were embryonic hippies. Dave had a Viva Zapata moustache. The bed was a careful construction of rugs, cushions and carpets from around the globe. They were smoking – what I had no idea but it grew in plant pots on the kitchen window sill. They were almost covered by their night attire, just loose enough for us to see that they needed no formal or even day clothes to meet honoured guests. They, of course, never wore beads. They loved the whole world in a clever kind of a way.

A new era of freedom, light and enlightenment had dawned. The Sixties' revolution had begun – and one day the enlightenment would even reach as far north as Manchester. Hope had arrived.

***

Chapter 36 - And they all lived happily ever after

Afterword

Did Noel live happily ever after? Throughout all the ups and inevitable downs of a long life and marriage, he has enjoyed, admired and loved two clever and beautiful daughters, who married two admirable men, giving him three wonderful grandchildren. He has initiated and run businesses, been instrumental in enabling people to work from home and much more, he has had a busy and productive life.

When Marjory Barlow banished Noel from her dance class and told him that he "danced on the half beat," she was expressing her frustration with a determinedly un-compliant fourteen year old, who would not match her steps on the ballroom floor. She had identified an characteristic of her pupil; to be his own man and dance to his own tune. Although at times self defeating, it was this inner strength and self belief that enabled Noel to survive an unsettling and confusing childhood better than any of his siblings.

Noel's inner world was, and continues to be, an imaginative and magical place, a powerful and compelling ally against a world that can seem frightening and untrustworthy. He deals with mortgages, holidays and bills and embraces the practical world of science and technology, but it is his drive for understanding, which is the compelling pulse in his internal world, that he truly trusts.

However, it is when the inner and outer life come together, when science and technology meet imagination, when the half beats combine into one full glorious beat; that something truly creative can happen.

—and what of "the love of his life" – me?

Well, you should see us dancing together - quite definitely on the full beat.

Pauline Hodson – Oxford 2017

Appendix 1- Stanley Mathews

Blackpool FC - The **1955–56** season was significant for many reasons; firstly, two of the club's greatest servants, **captain** Harry Johnston and Stan Mortensen, both departed to face new challenges. Johnston became manager of **Reading**, while *Morty* went to **Hull City**. Their places were filled by Roy Gratrix and Jackie Mudie, who switched to centre-forward, allowing Dave Durie to take over the inside-left position.

The highest-ever attendance of 38,098 at Bloomfield Road was recorded this season, when **Wolverhampton Wanderers** visited on 17 September 1955.

On 29 October 1955, in a 6–2 home defeat by Preston North End, George Farm became one of the few goalkeepers to score a goal. He injured a shoulder and replaced Jackie Mudie at centre-forward, where he proceeded to open the scoring with his head.

At the season's conclusion, Blackpool had attained their highest-ever League finish. They were runners-up to Manchester United, finishing eleven points behind *the Red Devils* and ahead of third-placed Wolves on goal average.

Stanley Mathews : he spent 14 years with **Blackpool**, 1947-61 where, after being on the losing side in the **1948** and **1951FA Cup** finals, he helped Blackpool to win the cup with a formidable personal performance in the "**Matthews Final**" of 1953

By Source: Football And All That An Irreverent History, Norman Giller, ISBN 0340835885, Fair use, https://en.wikipedia.org/w/index.php?curid=2826458

Appendix 2 – Osborne Bentley School of Dance

[2]Osborne Bentley School of Dance
From: Allan Coxson [mailto:acoxson@bigpond.net.au]
Sent: 15 July 2015 05:26
To: noel@noelhodson.com
Subject: Osborne-Bentley School of Dancing

Hi Noel

Surfing the net for something entirely different I came across your Heaton Moor blog and in particular your experiences at the Osborne-Bentley School of Dancing. I was trundled off there at the tender age of eleven or twelve so Marjorie Hilton-Barlow could try and make a young gentleman out of me, returning home on the no 92 bus to Great Moor with my ears still ringing from her strident 'Slow, Slow, Quick, Quick, Slow – no not like that'.

'Both Osborne and Bentley seemed lost and forgotten in the mists of time' Just so that the name doesn't fade totally into obscurity – a brief history:

*The school was founded by two school friends, Molly Osborne and 'Midge'
Bentley in the mid 1920's. They taught a range of dance from Free Form (based
on classical Greek) through to ballet. They sold the school to Marjorie Hilton-
Barlow in mid-1939 when both Molly and Midge got married.*
*Molly married Arthur Coxson of Frederick Coxson & Sons Ltd of Tiviot Dale
and then Portwood, Midge married George Payne, if I remember rightly a
Solicitor.*
*After the war, producing two sons (myself and my brother) and still living in
Great Moor, as we grew up and wended our way through school and scouts
Molly became in high demand as an adviser, choreographer and instructor to
the local schools, scout groups, amateur theatrical groups etc whose productions
required some dance routines. Molly also went on to become a leading light in
the 'Women's League of Health and Beauty' (known by my father and his mates
as the Women's League of Wealth and Duty) and represented Stockport at the
annual rallies in the Royal Albert Hall on several occasions. Molly finally hung
up her dancing shoes for the last time in 1999, a couple of months short of her
90th birthday. What happened to Midge I don't know as I lost touch with them.*

*The school achieved some fame when Joan Bakewell admitted In a radio
interview that she had her first sexual experiences at the parties Marjorie ran
(as did most of us I suspect) or at the back of the no 92 on her way to Hazel
Grove..*

*I gave up my lessons in 1962 to pursue a career at sea, but dropped in
occasionally when on leave to see how it was going, and finally left Stockport in
1970 to get married. I believe the school lasted until the 1980s when it was
knocked down to realign the Longshut Lane / Buxton Road junction and to
develop a car yard. My brother tried to salvage the sign and a piece of the dance
floor from the demolition men but failed.*
    Hope this is of interest

    Kind Regards, Allan

    *Allan Coxson, PO Box 173, Healesville, Victoria 3777, Australia
    Tel: +61 (0) 3 5962 5473*

---

[1] Osborne Bentley

Atom Bombs

Mother's awful fears, through the nine months she carried me, and each of my siblings,
were unconsciously passed on to her babies in the womb and through our infancy and
childhood. They echoed the general ever-present fear of everyone in Britain; fears of the
terrible slaughter and of the threat of invasion by Nazis in the Second World War and
afterwards, the fear of obliteration as the Cold War and the threat of Nuclear
Annihilation gripped our hearts and minds and flooded our cinema newsreels and our
newspapers.

As school children we practised diving for protection if and when the nuclear-bomb sirens sounded – by putting stout paper bags over our heads to stop the nuclear flash burning out our eyes, and sitting in a stoutly framed doorway, to stop the building's fifty tons of masonry falling on us and crushing us to death. If the A-Bomb or H-Bomb didn't get us, the Communist Hordes from the Evil Empire of the Eastern Bloc behind The Iron Curtain would sweep onto our small island and send us all to Siberia or the Salt Mines, to be worked to death in the name of Lenin's Socialist Revolution. These very real, omnipresent terrors started in 1945, when Uncle Joe Stalin, later credited with murdering 60 million souls, President Roosevelt, Winston Churchill and Charles de Gaulle carved up Europe - and the Iron Curtain fell across the continent, cutting Berlin in half. The universal terror reached its crescendo in 1961 when Russian ships carried nuclear weapons to Cuba and President Kennedy faced Nikita Khrushchev – each with their index finger on The Nuclear Button. Thank God we had the Post-War-Depression, Ration Books, The National War Debt, Gangs wielding cut-throat razors, The Goon Show, Hancock's Half-Hour and, according to our parents, the rise of the anti-Christ in the writhing loins of Elvis Presley; to take our minds off The Bomb.

Made in the USA
Columbia, SC
04 May 2017